Merilee S. Grindle

Jobs for the Boys

Patronage and the State in Comparative Perspective

HARVARD UNIVERSITY PRESS

Cambridge, Massachusetts, and London, England   2012

Library of Congress Cataloging-in-Publication Data

Grindle, Merilee Serrill.
Jobs for the boys : patronage and the state in comparative perspective /
Merilee S. Grindle.
     p. cm.
  Includes bibliographical references and index.
  ISBN 978-0-674-06570-3 (alk. paper)
  1. Civil service—Case studies.   2. Public officers—Selection and appointment—
Case studies.   3. Patronage, Political—Case studies.   4. Civil service reform—
Case studies.   I. Title.
  JF1651.G75 2012
  324.2'04—dc23   2011043156

To Steven, Alexandra, Stefanie, and Peter

Contents

Preface

Methods of appointments to public office seem a dull focus for a book about the politics of change. Yet how public servants are recruited, how their careers unfold, and how they think about their jobs are central to the historical evolution of countries around the globe and to the conflicts that punctuate and shape that evolution. Kings and parliaments, politicians and their parties, reformers and moralists, democrats and authoritarians have, throughout history, struggled to control how public office was acquired and used. Their conflicts shaped institutions of governance in widely divergent circumstances and help explain the differences among them. Far from dull, these struggles are intriguing; they are also consequential for states.

This book is about these struggles. It considers how patronage, as a mechanism for staffing the public service, was important in the histories of a variety of countries but also how these systems were challenged and, at times, replaced by those who sought to institutionalize Weberian civil service systems. Research and reflection about these issues address a number of themes that have been of interest to me in prior work—patronage and its uses in government, the role of institutions in shaping the way political decisions are made and the content of those decisions, and the processes that account for institutional creation or innovation.

Long ago, I studied how a finely constructed patronage system in Mexico was an essential factor in promoting policy change and accomplishing some of the modern activities of government, even while it buoyed an unjust political system and encouraged corrupt behavior (see Grindle 1977). Over the years, I have seen how patronage systems in other Latin American countries are critically important in electoral dynamics, policy change initiatives, regime stability and failure, organizational trajectories, and concerns about corruption and mismanagement. In writing this book, I have had the opportunity to study a series of initiatives to replace such institutions with merit-based civil service systems. Manichean rhetoric often accompanies these efforts at reform, making them seem essential and even inevitable, yet patronage systems resist change with remarkable consistency.

I have tried to understand such struggles against the background of countries that were—eventually—successful in altering the institutions that manage recruitment to the public sector. In doing so, similarities across countries in terms of how change happens became as evident as the differences among them in how legacies of the past colored what was possible in introducing reform. This work suggests some ideas about why institutional change often does not happen, why and when it sometimes does, and how winners and losers grapple over the shape of change long after major policy decisions have been made.

Jobs for the Boys considers the ubiquity and flexibility of patronage systems in the public service of a significant number of countries, explores the historical process through which they have been replaced by merit-based civil service systems, and attests to ongoing struggles over how the public service is organized and managed. It takes a historical and process-oriented perspective on how systems work and how they change. It makes a claim for the primacy of politics in the construction, deconstruction, and reconstruction of systems of appointment to public office.

Thus, in contrast to what is often discussed in technical and administrative language—the language of job descriptions, pay scales, criteria for promotion, conditions for dismissal and retirement, rights to pensions and benefits, mechanisms of control and delegation, budget constraints—I focus attention on larger themes of the persistence, change, and consequences of institutions of governance and on the struggles between advocates of change and those who seek to undermine reform initiatives. My purpose is to explore what we can learn from history and how that knowledge might help in understanding contemporary efforts to alter institutional parameters in government.

I have had a great deal of help in this enterprise, although errors found in this work are, of course, my own. I am very grateful for research assistance provided by Jason Jackson, Elisabeth Megally, German Sturzenneger, and José Zapata while they were students at Harvard and MIT. Katherine Guevarra and Karen Armstrong-Menard ably assisted in the production and review process. Patricia Villarreal worked computer magic with figures and graphs.

In exploring reform initiatives in Mexico, Argentina, and Chile, I am deeply in debt to the many people who helped to lead me through what had happened and why. Among them, I am particularly grateful to José Luis Méndez, David Arellano Gault, María del Carmen Pardo, Gustavo Merino, Mauricio Merino, Darío Treviño, and Salvador Vega in Mexico; Alfredo Rehren, Rosanna Costa, Salvador Valdés, Mario Waissbluth, and Claudio Orrego in Chile; and Oscar Oszlak, Eduardo Salas, Jorge Giles, Andrés Rodríguez, Fernando Straface, Dora Olansky, Juan Manuel Abal, Mercedes Iacoviello, Christian Asinelli, Hugo Carranza, and Carlos Acuña in Argentina. Along with many others, they provided me with some fifty hours of interviews and discussions that informed much of the analysis of recent reform initiatives in their countries. Their time and insights were critical to writing about the process of change.

Throughout the process of research and writing this book, I have benefited from insightful ideas of Judith Tendler, Mary Hilderbrand, Matt Andrews, and Kenneth Winston. My debts to the literatures I have consulted—from biographies to institutional histories, from explorations of theory and concepts to stories that derive insights from practice, from studies that detail individual cases to those that attempt to draw conclusions across several—are immense. I also found the critiques of several anonymous reviewers to be extremely helpful in reconsidering the book's overall argument and its structure. Michael Aronson of Harvard University Press has been a consistent supporter of its publication.

The Harvard Kennedy School was an extremely appropriate environment in which to develop this book, sheltering as it does faculty and students who are deeply committed to the idea of public service and the conditions that underlie good governance. While director of the David Rockefeller Center for Latin American Studies at Harvard for several years, I have had multiple, and often unexpected, opportunities to meet with and discuss the topic of public sector reform with scholars from across the region. I am fortunate indeed in the colleagues and environments I have encountered.

Throughout a long career, Steven, Alexandra, and Stefanie have been amazingly supportive and tolerant of my projects, and now this family circle has been enlarged to include an equally accommodating Peter. They have my deepest love and appreciation.

Acronyms

ADP   Sistema de Alta Dirección Pública, High Level Public Management System in Chile

ATE   Asociación de Trabajadores del Estado, State Workers' Association in Argentina

CEP   Comisión de Estudios Públicos, Policy Studies Commission in Chile

CIDE   Centro de Investiación y Docencia Económicas, Center for Economic Research and Teaching in Mexico

DASP   Departamento Administrativo do Serviço Público, Administrative Department of the Public Service in Brazil

ENA   École Nacionale d'Administration in France

FLACSO   Facultad Latinoamericano de Ciencias Sociales, Latin American Social Sciences Faculty

IDB   Inter-American Development Bank

ITAM   Instituto Tecnológico Autónomo de México, Autonomous Technological Institute of Mexico

MARE   Ministério da Administração Federal e Reforma do Estado, Ministry of Federal Administration and Reform of the State in Brazil

MOP   Ministerio de Obras Públicas y Transporte, Ministry of Public Works and Transport in Chile

OECD   Organization for Economic Cooperation and Development

PAN   Partido Acción Nacional, National Action Party in Mexico

PBS   Public Broadcasting System in the United States

PRD   Partido de la Revolución Democrática, Democratic Revolution Party in Mexico

PRI   Partido de la Revolución Institutional, Party of the Institutional Revolution in Mexico

PT   Workers' Party in Brazil

SECODAM   Secretaría de Contraloría y Desarrollo Administrativo, Ministry of Auditing and Administrative Development in Mexico

SECOGEF   Secretaría de la Contraloría General de la Federación, Federal Auditor General Ministry in Mexico

SINAPA   Sistema Nacional de la Profesión Administrativa, National Professional Administrative System in Argentina

SPC   Servicio Profesional de Carerra, Professional Career Service in Mexico

UCR   Unión Cívica Radical, Radical Civic Union Party in Argentina

UDI   Unión Democrática Independiente, Independent Democratic Union Party in Chile

UNAM   Universidad Nacional Autónoma de México, National Autonomous University of Mexico

UPCN   Unión del Personal Civil de la Nación, National Civil Service Personnel Union in Argentina

JOBS FOR THE BOYS

Weber's Ghost

Party government isn't organized for efficiency, nor to serve the people. It is organized to provide jobs for the boys.

Syracuse Herald, October 23, 1913:8

The story is well known. In 1883, the United States Congress passed the Pendleton Civil Service Act, establishing a merit-based public service system in the federal government. Borrowing from a previous British reform, the act established a Civil Service Commission whose job it was to wrest the public service from the control of party bosses. This commission was widely supported by a reformist movement, composed largely of middle-class professionals who railed against the pervasive practice of filling public jobs with the party faithful. These reformers had struggled long and persistently to see a civil service established in law. Now, with the passage of the Pendleton Act, "patronage-mongering methods of administration" were to be relegated to the corrupt and partisan past; a new era of professional government was at hand.[1]

Except, of course, that it wasn't. Indeed, the story less often told is that of the first half-century of the civil service in the United States, when its future was far from assured. The old patronage system yielded to the reformers slowly, and only in a context of a government that was increasing in size, thus minimizing zero-sum conflicts between the politicians and the advocates of change. In fact, it was only in the mid-1920s that the civil service incorporated as much as 75 percent of the federal public service, a figure that reached 80 percent in the early 1930s.[2] Yet, in that decade of economic depression, the newly institutionalized system faced further challenges as political leaders sought to bring fresh

1

directions to government by appointing administrators outside the rules of the civil service; incorporation into the "new" system fell to 60 percent of those employed. Thus, long after reformers had declared their victory over the forces of patronage and spoils, control over recruitment into government office was still being contested and negotiated with the politicians who claimed jobs for the boys.[3] In the United States, the career civil service was politically constructed—and not easily. Indeed, for long periods, it was the focus of efforts to deconstruct and reconstruct it in ways more advantageous to anti-reformers.

This experience is not unique—many countries that now have well-institutionalized civil service systems experienced significant and lengthy contention over the nature and control of recruitment into public service. Conflict characterized the introduction of reform, as those who benefited from extensive patronage opportunities struggled against those extolling the virtues of a merit-based civil service. And the struggle continued long after reformed systems were introduced. Although sometimes marked by the approval of major pieces of legislation, change from one system to another was protracted, with successive numbers of positions being incorporated into the new system, often over decades. The institutionalization of new rules for public employment was, for long periods of time, fragile, incomplete, and contested.

Characteristically across a wide range of experiences in different countries, new ideas about how the public sector was to be staffed found political traction at particular moments—a political or economic crisis, a regime change, an electoral draw among parties, a scandal. These moments provided reformers with opportunities to advance their projects, most commonly based on designs worked out by small teams of experts who often looked abroad for inspiration. And consistently across numerous countries, the introduction of a civil service system was resisted and often subverted through the persistence and ingenuity of the politicians and office seekers who had more personal and political aims in mind for the public service.

Today, the same kind of struggle over public sector employment is being played out in a number of countries in the developing world, despite the strongest intentions of a new generation of reformers. While pressures are mounting around the globe to replace the remaining patronage-based public administrations with career civil services, the older systems are resisting the loss of jobs for the boys. As in the earlier cases of now industrialized countries, more recent experiences in which patronage has long been embedded in political structures indicate that contention characterizes the promotion and introduction of reform, and that consensus around new systems is far from clear while reforms are being implemented. The consolidation of new institutions, then, is fraught with opportunities for altering, undermining, or curtailing them.

Even while each of the historical and more contemporary cases is a story unto itself, together they point clearly to the conclusion that career civil services were and are politically constructed, forged from conflicts and compromises among those who have very different views on how appointments to public sector jobs should be made and who should control them. These struggles point to important commonalities: historically, patronage systems have been both ubiquitous and multifunctional; when challenged by reform initiatives, such systems were effectively altered by reformers and their projects only during unique moments of opportunity; the construction of civil service systems was significantly challenged again and again by deconstruction and reconstruction; and new systems developed pathologies that had to be addressed by new generations of reformers. At the same time, the conflicts and potential for reform were constrained by institutional legacies of the past, particularly as those related to how political decisions were made, how social structures of class and education were defined, and the presence or absence of competitive political parties.

In a nutshell, this is a book about why patronage systems have been so ubiquitous in history, how and when moments for reform have emerged, and why an understanding of that moment tells only half the story. Through an analysis of ten historical and contemporary cases, it is centrally concerned with the motivations of political actors, the multiple uses they find for jobs for the boys, the strategies adopted by reformers in trying to replace traditional and well-institutionalized systems of public employment, and the consequences of post-reform contention over the nature and scope of change. Yet it places these concerns within unique contexts that shape and constrain the choices of reformers and the dynamics of the process of change.

It has become commonplace among social scientists to acknowledge that "history matters." In the following chapters, I hope to add to discussions of how and when it matters and why the process of change is critically important for understanding outcomes. I hope to contribute to an appreciation of why much-maligned jobs for the boys have proved useful for a variety of purposes, not all of them deserving of dubious reputation. At the same time, I hope to suggest that struggles over public sector jobs are also conflicts over the distinct virtues of flexibility and stability. And I hope to raise questions about why the claims of history are taken seriously in understanding public sector reform for some countries (notably those that have achieved important levels of wealth and development) and disregarded for others (notably those that are instructed to reform in numerous and specific ways if they expect to become wealthy and developed). The process of public sector recruitment, then, is about much more than employment.

Four Themes: Persistence, Change, Challenge, and Consequence

Jobs for the Boys presents a comparative exploration of four themes surrounding institutions of patronage and career systems in the public service.[4] First, it considers the political history of patronage systems in the governance of a number of countries and demonstrates why they endured and how they served a variety of purposes—ones that differed across time and place. Second, it surveys the political construction of career civil service systems in a range of countries for insights about how change occurs over time. Third, it explores the politics of post-reform efforts to challenge the consolidation of civil service systems and describes the institutional consequences of such initiatives. Fourth, it assesses the implications of the consolidation of civil service systems for subsequent struggles to introduce greater flexibility in initiatives to improve the performance of government.

The book pursues these four themes by considering two sets of countries. First, it considers the historical experience of public sector reform in six now developed countries—the United States, Germany (Prussia), Great Britain, France, Japan, and Spain. In the nineteenth and early twentieth centuries, these countries, each of which had a deeply embedded system of appointment to the public sector through patronage, introduced and consolidated career civil service systems. Exploration of their experiences provides opportunities to observe distinct patterns in the persistence of embedded practice, efforts to introduce change, ongoing skirmishing about the content and scope of new institutions, and subsequent efforts to replace much-vaunted stability with greater responsiveness.

Then the book turns to the more contemporary experiences of conflicts over civil service reforms in four Latin American countries—Brazil, Mexico, Chile, and Argentina. While Brazil has a long twentieth-century history of contention over mechanisms to staff the public service, the other countries are sites for more-recent struggles. Each provides an opportunity to witness, in near history, the interaction of reformers and their opponents in contexts that are rich with detail and in which the actors involved in promoting and opposing change could be consulted about the conflicts they faced and the strategies they selected for managing them. While the first set of countries, now developed, are emblematic of scholarly efforts to understand the dynamics and consequences of historical experiences, these developing countries are much less frequently understood in the context of their own experiences, and they are much more subject to demands that they adopt reforms as if history didn't matter. Their stories should help right this scholarly imbalance.

In consequence of these two sets of cases, the book is organized into two parts. Chapters 1, 2, and 3 (Part One) focus on the persistence and reform of patronage systems in the now developed countries, and indicate the problems of governance left unsolved by these changes. Thus, these three chapters provide a survey of early modern practice in several countries of Western Europe and Japan, focus more specifically on the eighteenth and nineteenth centuries, and then consider the conflicts over public sector employment that surrounded efforts to consolidate civil service systems in the same countries and the United States. Part One, then, highlights the ubiquity of patronage, conditions surrounding reform initiatives, and the actors who sought change and those who resisted it in a variety of different ways. It shows how these factors eventually molded new rules and how they would be applied in practice.

Part Two, comprising Chapters 4 through 7, delves into the history of patronage and reform in Latin American countries that have made serious efforts to introduce civil service systems, focusing primarily on the twentieth and twenty-first centuries. It draws lessons from Part One and considers their relevance for four countries in the region. Again, the focus is on the process of introducing and contesting institutional change in ways that reveal how history matters. Brazil, Argentina, Mexico, and Chile provide distinct cases that confirm clear patterns about how and when reform initiatives are likely to emerge and the ongoing challenges they face.

The conclusion suggests a series of generalizations about the agents of reform, the projects they promote, the moments in which these projects find political legitimacy, and the contentious aftermath of those moments. At the same time, it indicates a set of contextual factors that can account for some of the differences across cases. Then it turns to the difficult issue of the relationship between public sector reform and good governance. While in theory these two outcomes are expected to coincide, the case studies in *Jobs for the Boys* suggest that such expectations need to be carefully reconsidered. Patronage systems are quite flexible; civil service systems are remarkably stable. For public sector reformers in today's developed countries, greater flexibility is valued as an antidote to what reformers struggled to achieve in earlier centuries. Their concerns signal the limitations on what public sector reformers in developing countries might anticipate.

Persistence

Patronage systems have proved extraordinarily resistant to the demands of reformers in a wide variety of settings. They have also proved adaptable to changing circumstances, their flexibility appropriate for a variety of ends. Some have been transformed from the domination of kings to the control of parliaments, from the executive to the legislature, from the government to the party, sometimes even from the party to the union or the party to the military junta. Moreover, they have frequently demonstrated the ability to accomplish a multitude of complex bureaucratic tasks related to state building and governance. One purpose of this book is to consider the durability of patronage systems in the face of reformist zeal. Indeed, the very persistence of such systems—and their adaptability to the demands of modern state administration—is a topic of analytic importance. Why have such systems been so pervasive, and why do they resist change so consistently?

Interestingly, evidence presented in subsequent chapters suggests that contenders for power have at times sought to use patronage to create and maintain both administrative capacity and loyalty. As such, patronage was important in the consolidation of royal power, the creation of modern states, and the construction of competence in government. Yet, clearly, patronage is also found contributing to long histories of incompetence and malfeasance in office, along with the systematic abuse of power. In explaining such variance, my evidence indicates that the ends and means of patronage systems were affected by legacies of prior allocations of power, the agendas of those who controlled the distribution of patronage, and the ability of those wrestling for control of this mechanism of power to prevail over other contenders.

In the following chapters, I use case studies to explore the ubiquity and flexibility of patronage as a mechanism of power and the conflicts that have surrounded its use. The practice of patronage no doubt is older than history itself, but for my purposes, its story can begin with the consolidation of monarchies and modern states and then the changing political dynamics in the nineteenth and early twentieth centuries. Historical cases of France, Prussia, Japan, Great Britain, Spain, and the United States provide insights into the ways in which the use of patronage power contributed to these processes, while more contemporary examples from Latin America suggest the wide and important presence of the benefits that politicians continue to find in its use. Indeed, discussions of macropolitical achievements such as the building of national states, the centralization of executive authority, the consolidation of revolution, the rise and fall of empire, or the development of mass-based political parties cannot be fully comprehended without acknowledging how recruitment to public office played a role in determining outcomes.

In Chapter 1, evidence indicates that in Japan, France, and Britain, patronage was closely associated with governance by elites of class and education, even while it offered some chance for upward mobility for those who found cracks in the glass ceiling of highly restricted educational systems. Initial efforts to create a unified state in Prussia were managed through appointments to positions of authority in disconnected regions in order to establish that state as an important military power. In Spain, a delicate balance between central and regional power managed through patronage helped maintain some semblance of political stability across monarchical and republican eras, although fiscal exigencies and ongoing political conflicts undercut the ability of those dispensing patronage to use it consistently to advantage. In the United

States, long prior to the Jacksonians, the founding fathers used patronage to fill government positions with those characterized by social class and education; the Jacksonians raised the idea of patronage to a democratic ideal for the common man. Patronage flourished during the heydays of urban development, when party machines were able to provide thousands of public sector jobs and contracts to the working class, often of immigrant origin. These experiences underline the persistence and flexibility of this form of recruitment into government service and its place in the historical record.

Chapter 5, in Part Two of the book, assesses widespread evidence of patronage in Latin America. It demonstrates that patterns observed from the sixteenth to the twentieth centuries in Europe, Japan, and the United States find parallels in the experience of this region of the world. Jobs for the boys were used to consolidate political power and to contest it. Across authoritarian and democratic regimes; across conservative, liberal, and revolutionary governments; across unitary and federalist systems; across no party, one-party, and multiparty systems—patronage systems proved durable and adaptive in Latin America. As a standard procedure for staffing the public sector in the region, patronage accomplished some modern functions of government in very traditional ways. Discourses of reform highlight themes of partisanship, incompetence, and corruption; comparative history suggests more nuance is needed in order to understand resistance to trading this system for a stable civil service regime.

Change

However ubiquitous, it is still the case that many patronage systems were eventually replaced by more-professional public administrations along the lines of a formal civil service. Indeed, part of the attraction of civil service systems for their advocates is that they seem to have been triumphant historically, having bested patronage systems in all advanced industrialized countries and not a few developing ones. Where they have not triumphed, they are held up as the logical and desirable—even inevitable—successor to patronage-based public services. Given the durability and adaptability of patronage systems, how were they displaced by career civil service systems?

In response to this question, a second purpose of this book is to explore the history of reform initiatives across a number of countries and to generate insights from the conflict and negotiation that attended movement from the domination of one form of public sector recruitment to the introduction of another. In most cases, a protracted period of coexistence characterized the transformation of a patronage to a civil service bureaucracy. If we ask, then, "How is private and party interest minimized or removed from the offices and administration of government?" the answer for many countries was "slowly and gradually."

In six cases considered in Chapter 2, Weberian bureaucracies were constructed in the nineteenth and twentieth centuries. In each case, political entrepreneurs championed change, worked with small teams of like-minded reformers in crafting projects for achieving their reform objectives, and used discrete political moments strategically to advance these projects. The ways change was introduced varied and reflected political structures and decision-making processes in each country. In some cases, top-down initiatives were spearheaded by authoritarian leaders; in others, elite accommodation was a dominant mode of transition; and in still others, competition among political parties vying for electoral support was important. With the important exception of the United States, however, conflict and negotiation over changes in the public service were carried out far from public view, among political, administrative, and party elites.

Further, Chapter 2 considers the difficult question of why the characteristics of these new systems varied. In each case, legacies of the past are important. Authoritarians concentrated considerable power in introducing public sector change, but they also had to grapple with the claims of traditional elites for preferment to public office, and consequently emphasized the importance of traditional loyalties, which were themselves only transformed over time. Other cases demonstrated an ongoing process of evolution that recognized established claims of class as evidenced through educational systems. Often, dual systems lived side by side for long periods of time in order to accommodate old and new. In the context of a mass democracy, a flexible system with low barriers to entry was constructed out of long public controversy in the United States. Clearly, reformers understood that they were dealing within constraints set by prior practice and the expectations of important groups.

Nevertheless, reformers also had some room for maneuver in that each of their initiatives was pushed significantly forward during unusual moments of crisis or challenge to ruling elites or parties. In their initiatives, they worked closely with experts and borrowed ideas from other countries. Thus, Japanese reformers studied issues of public sector recruitment, stability, and appropriate expertise, traveled abroad to assess other countries' experiences, and borrowed liberally from Germany. American progressives were familiar with the staffing of the public sector in European and Asian countries and found inspiration in the British reform initiative, but adapted it to their understanding of the U.S. context. Spain was compelled to take the French model seriously in the Napoleonic period, but also found ways to invent adaptations to an embedded domestic system of clientelism.

In Part Two, reformist efforts in four Latin American countries add to evidence about the importance of elite projects and opportunistic action at politically important moments to move a process of reform forward. In the 1930s, Brazil embarked on a major civil service reform initiative; Argentina sought a similar path in the 1990s; and in the 2000s, both Mexico and Chile introduced initiatives to follow suit. These more recent reform initiatives, considered in Chapter 6, reiterate the importance of political negotiation in the construction of new systems and the importance of marrying a political project with an opportune political moment in order to promote change. Indeed, in the early twenty-first century, Latin America provides a contemporary palette of opportunities to consider why and how changes in the public service happen and how struggles for reform define expectations about the performance of new institutions. These cases also reflect institutions for making political decisions, embedded social structures, and the characteristics of political party systems.

Building on these historical and more contemporary cases, I seek to present public sector reform as a process that is historically grounded and politically contested. These cases point to the importance of knowing "how things happen" in political life, reflecting legacies of the past but also the interventions of strategic actors to create something new. There are commonalities in the stories, and although each case is unique, taken together they suggest how public sector reform can be viewed as a comparative discussion of "politics in time."[5]

Indeed, it is through analysis of the process of political construction that it is possible to see how institutional outcomes are affected by legacies of prior practice, the capacity to mobilize influence and power, and the strategic choices of political actors engaged in conflict and negotiation in specific formal and informal institutional contexts. Some outcomes may be preferred to others—as the current literature on good governance amply illustrates—but the process of getting from what is considered an undesirable here to a more perfect there is not often enough explored, particularly in the case of developing countries, where analysts are less likely to appreciate the constraints of historical experience.

Challenge

The construction of civil service systems is by no means secured with the passage of a law or the introduction of a new institution. Indeed, implementation of new rules of the game for staffing the public service is fraught with challenges. Post-reform circumstances, in the sense of what follows official approval of change, can even witness more political fireworks and conflict than the initial acceptance of reform. During the years, even decades, after a reform has been adopted, civil services face constant challenges to their continued existence and to their form and operation. The construction of public sector reform, then, is regularly followed by efforts to deconstruct and reconstruct what has been created, and opponents of the new rules of the game consistently adopt similar strategies for undermining them. Again, these challenges and resultant changes can only be understood through an assessment of the process of policy reform, a process that continues long after reformers have decreed their victory over the forces of patronage.

Chapter 3 presents cases of *après* reform in the six countries considered in Part One. These cases indicate that new civil service systems are vulnerable to efforts to destroy them, to conflicts over who will control them, to disagreements about the characteristics of those who should be recruited into them, and to serious questions about the loyalty of the systems to regimes and administrations. Chapter 7, dealing with the four contemporary Latin American experiences, confirms that these are critically important conflicts in the post-reform period. This chapter also suggests that anti-reformers have a wide range of strategies they can employ for altering, undermining, or curtailing the reach of public sector reform. Indeed, the content, scope, and success of public service reform is actually determined *after* it has been officially announced.

Conflicts surrounding the implementation of reform initiatives also indicate moments in which politicians who wish to preserve or reintroduce jobs for the boys are able to make significant advances in doing so. For example, when governments must meet important external threats, such as during wartime, personal appointment as a form of recruitment into service is likely to expand. Similarly, when regimes or administrations are engaged in introducing major policy changes, political leaders are likely to revert to patronage to fill many new and old positions with "their people," that is, with those who share their commitment to new kinds of public policies and strategies for national development.

Comparing the implementation of civil service systems in six historical cases with that of the Latin American cases, it is clear that in the former, career services were eventually consolidated and became the norm for recruitment, advancement, and retirement from government employment. The futures of the career systems in the Latin American cases are much less clear. This may simply be the result of their relative youth. At the same time, these more recent reforms provide evidence of considerable fragility in the face of challenges to them and the significant possibility that new systems will be pushed to the margins of political relevance or reengineered in ways that undercut their purpose. This is a useful reminder that the triumph of civil service reform in the now developed countries was often preceded by numerous episodes of failure, and it is thus possible that declarations of victory in Latin America are premature. Recent experiences are not necessarily unique in terms of the history of patronage and patterns of transition; what is notable, however, is that most Latin American countries have not yet decisively replaced the older system with a career civil service.

Consequence

Post-reform politics also raises the question of the consequences of introducing a career civil service system. That, is, what is the relationship between civil service systems and good governance? Civil service advocates argue for a clear and direct relationship. Indeed, where such systems have been consolidated, they have created more neutral, more stable, and less politicized public administrations; they allowed for further development of bureaucratic autonomy.

But have they also necessarily produced efficient, effective, or responsive governance? The answer, according to many contemporary public sector critics, is no.[6] These critics have elaborated on characteristic weaknesses of civil service systems—their tendency to aloofness, their obsession with process rather than outcome, their resistance to change and capacity to sabotage change initiatives, their insularity, their tendency to become hyper-segmented, their facelessness and lack of accountability, their transformation into interest groups focused on security and conditions of employment. Even Max Weber, the intellectual father of the historical imperative of modern professional bureaucracies, was not unaware of the alienation implicit in their impersonality, nor of their inherent authoritarian and secretive tendency.[7]

It is interesting, however, that such critics focus their attention on the consequences of consolidated civil service systems in developed countries; reformers focused on developing countries continue to extol the imperative to install career-based civil services. For the former, assessments of many negative consequences of the institutionalization of a civil service system, along with often invidious comparisons to private sector organizations, have suggested that expectations about the performance consequences of career services should be moderated. Indeed, disappointment with these systems has helped stimulate a movement toward management by results and indicator-driven contracts between public sector managers and their "principals," concepts at the heart of the new public management. For example, in New Zealand in particular, but also in Australia, Britain, and the Scandinavian countries, the Weberian notion of modern bureaucracy was significantly turned on its head in the 1980s and 1990s through the introduction of reforms associated with this new approach.[8]

For developing countries, however, the Weberian model survives virtually unscathed. The literature on good governance regularly insists that developing countries must have career public bureaucracies that are neutral, professional, autonomous, merit-based, regularized, and specialized.[9] Discretion in hiring, they argue, must be severely curtailed. In fact, a major study inquiring into the "Weberian state hypothesis" presents evidence that there is a consistent relationship between economic growth and government systems that hire public officials based on meritocratic principles. The authors conclude that "state bureaucracies characterized by meritocratic recruitment and predictable, rewarding career ladders are associated with higher growth rates."[10] Similarly, according to the World Bank, "Evidence across a range of countries has shown that well-functioning bureaucracies ['a rule-based civil service'] can promote growth and reduce poverty."[11] And discussions of the implications of government corruption routinely advise the creation of a merit-based public service.[12]

As part of the struggle to consolidate new recruitment processes, advocates of good governance promise a transformed public sector from civil service reform. But advocates of greater efficiency, effectiveness, and responsiveness hold civil services to blame for many problems of government and insist that reform of these systems is essential. Chapter 3 considers this experience in the cases of consolidated civil service reform and describes new reformist movements focused more on flexibility and discretion than on stability and neutrality. The book's conclusion revisits the question and asks whether good governance is a reasonable expectation for those countries that have not yet consolidated a civil service system. In putting public sector reform in historical and analytic perspective, this final section of the book considers the tension between stability and flexibility as a way of clarifying expectations about what can reasonably be achieved through institutional change.

The Cases and the Concepts

Jobs for the Boys considers stories of patronage and civil service reform based on the experiences of ten countries. Seven of these countries—the United States, Great Britain, France, Prussia/Germany, Japan, Spain, and Brazil—provide long periods of time over which to observe the development and use of patronage systems and the development and consolidation of career civil services. They thus offer a palette of experiences for a comparative exploration in time of the construction, reconstruction, and deconstruction of Weberian public services. Three countries—Argentina, Chile, and Mexico—provide evidence from contemporary cases in which a wealth of detail about circumstances, motivations, strategies, and challenges could be generated through extensive public records and current accounts and insights of participants in reformist initiatives.

Choosing to approach the issue of public sector reform through a case study methodology was dictated by my interest in exploring the process of reform—process is difficult to study without the evidentiary base of specific cases and the historical record to consult. And if the purpose of this research is to generate general insights into the process of change, then a process-tracing methodology across several countries or experiences makes sense. Comparative cases can be selected on a variety of bases, of course—from those that seem most similar to each other to those that seem most distinct. In this case, I was particularly concerned to select a range of country experiences that could allow for the broadest level of differentiation. To the extent that I might find similarities across cases, then, I would be able to focus in on factors specific to public sector reform rather than the political, social, or economic factors that differ among countries.

Among historical cases, therefore, I wanted to have early adopters of reform represented as well as later adopters; adopters that represented authoritarian regimes and those that experienced reform in more democratic environments; those that represented the state-centric, Napoleonic, or *Rechtsstaat* tradition and those that represented the more polity-centric experience found in the Anglo-American tradition. And, it seemed to me that it would be useful to inquire into the experience of a non-Western historical case. Each of the historical cases, then, falls into one or more of these categories.

From a list of potential cases, I decided that the experience of Prussia/Germany was important not only as an example of one of the earliest transitions to a Weberian civil service, but also because it exemplifies the politics of authoritarian imposition. Thus, it provides a counter to the dynamics of reform in the United States and Great Britain. Prussia/Germany is also a useful case for exploring post-reform regime changes and their relationship to issues of loyalty in a well-institutionalized public service. Japan has much in common with this, and was included as a non-Western site for reform that could allow for generalizing across regions of the world; Brazil demonstrates a somewhat similar pattern, but was also one in which the forces of deconstruction were particularly strong in the post-reform era. France is a fascinating case of the multiple functions of an ongoing patronage system and the capacity to undermine it, as well as the evolution of a highly structured and elitist civil service in a historical context of state-centric development. I included Spain because of my interest in extending the analysis to Latin America, where Spanish patterns of patronage were embedded during the empire. Moreover, it provides an example similar to that of France, in which patronage and highly structured systems can live side by side for long periods of time, and how they survive comfortably in different regime settings, from authoritarian to democratic.

The U.S. case, of course, is very well documented and is often taken as the quintessential example of the politics of civil service reform when a party system has come to rely on jobs for the boys in highly competitive democratic electoral arenas. Although I question the generality of the case in comparative perspective, the United States is critical in terms of the unusual dynamics of reform and the concerted efforts of anti-reformers to undo it in the post-reform period. The public mobilization around reform, as well as the public rhetoric of the reformers, adds an important dimension to comparative analysis. I included the experience of Great Britain in part because historically it provided important fodder for reformers in the United States and elsewhere. More important, however, it provides rich evidence about the importance of patronage to historical contests for power and an alternative model of reform in a context of competitive political parties. It is particularly relevant for demonstrating how particular features of an existing system shape its successor.

For the experiences in Latin America, case selection was easier. The case of Brazil was included because it has the oldest formal civil service in the region, providing not only a lengthy record of the transformation of its traditional patronage system but also more than seventy years of post-reform politics. The three more contemporary Latin American cases— Argentina, Mexico, and Chile—are cases in which serious commitments were made to make a public service transition in the period after 1990. While Brazil made the initial transition to a career civil service under authoritarian circumstances, the others grappled with this change within democratic and competitive political systems.

Of course, other countries might have been selected for study. In the historical cases taken from Europe, the Swedish and Danish examples might have been included as other early histories of the introduction and consolidation of career civil services. In contrast, Italy would have provided a good example of ongoing conflicts in efforts to move to a career-based civil service system in a context in which patronage was useful to many and regionalist and local pressures for the appropriation of public office strong—suggesting some interesting commonalities with Spain. Portugal might have been an interesting case for similar reasons and would have provided a historical platform for the analysis of Brazil. China certainly might have been chosen as a non-Western case; it provides clear evidence of very early transition to a merit-based system as well as a more contemporary case of politicization. India's transformation to a career civil service tells an interesting story of the impact of colonialism, and the parallels to British experience are strong. In Latin America, the other historical case that could have claimed inclusion was Costa Rica, whose civil service system also dates back several decades; Colombia was engaged in an effort to institutionalize a career civil service in the second decade of the 2000s.

In case selection choices, of course, there is bound to be some subjective judgment, and I admit that the absence of China speaks to my concerns about being able to investigate and appropriately analyze a case of such length, depth, and breadth; the Indian case is daunting for similar reasons. In Sweden, Denmark, Italy, and Costa Rica, I decided that the obvious alternatives—Prussia, Spain, and Brazil—were more compelling because of the greater salience of the history of Germany, compared with the Nordic countries, and the greater relevance of Spain, rather than Italy, to the case of Latin America, and the more influential experience of Brazil, than that of Costa Rica. I consider some of the historical evidence of Portugal in discussing Brazil, but the case is understudied and the historical record somewhat sparse, suggesting that documenting its processes of change would be challenging. Colombia remained too new a case to provide sufficient data. Overall, ten cases seemed a reasonable set to explore, even though the same argument might be made for nine, eleven, or some other relatively small number.

These rationales for methodological and case choices do not put questions about approach to rest, of course, but they do suggest that a process-tracing approach is a good option for considering how change happens, that a comparative case approach can generate useful insights, and that the cases included in the study were not haphazardly assembled. Any generalizations that emerge from this study can also be assessed through the lenses of other methodologies and other cases.

Systems and Mixed Models

All contemporary political systems accept the practice of patronage appointments to some public offices. Most often, these positions are at the top level of government and public organizations. Universally, presidents, governors, mayors, ministers, and other decision makers are provided with some—few or many, depending on the country—personal appointments that are expected to provide them with loyal advisers and others who are committed to their political agenda or vision.[13] These officials serve at the discretion of the sponsor—the president, governor, mayor, minister, or other high-level official—although the appointments may need to be confirmed through legislative action. In addition, high-level officials often have the capacity to appoint members of commissions, agencies, and other public bodies without reference to examination, proof of merit, or other feature associated with a career civil service. In most countries, there is an ongoing effort by those who control these patronage appointments—or wish to control them—to expand opportunities to fill positions this way.

In this book, I am not concerned with the kinds of patronage appointments that characterize *all* political systems, although the reasons they exist and persist are important reasons to understand the durability of patronage more generally. Instead, I focus on patronage *systems,* where discretionary appointment for personal and/or political purposes is a principal route to a nonelected position in government for a large portion of those enjoying such positions.[14] Patronage systems are regularized, widely acknowledged as a customary (if not always a legally recognized) form of appointment to public employment, and are independent of any systematic examination or credentialing system. These systems can be controlled and contested by the executive, the legislature, political parties, unions, or economic and social elites. They can be created and maintained for distinct reasons, although they are often found to be functional to political parties that vie for elections in mass democracies. They are, above all, best understood as systems available to political and administrative actors to expand and maintain their power—over a country, a government, an organization, a policy agenda, a party, or a faction. Theirs is the discretion to hire and fire.

Extensive patronage systems sometimes coexist with more merit-based career systems that are specific to particular organizations—foreign services, central banks, and tax and customs agencies are often good examples of these enclave civil service systems. The important point is that large numbers of government offices—not necessarily all of them—are deemed to be patronage posts in the systems I consider. Patronage in the public service, then, is institutionalized in the sense that it is a generalized rule of the game for holding significant numbers of non-elected government positions. Thus, the micro-foundation of patronage—discretionary appointment to a position in government by a patron in what is understood to be a dyadic exchange relationship—is extended to such an extent that this mechanism becomes a strong characteristic of the system, although many systems continue to incorporate mixed models.[15]

Conceptually and heuristically, patronage systems in public service resemble extended pyramids of contracts between superiors and multiple subordinates, in which a job in the public sector is exchanged for loyalty in some form (see Figure I.1).[16] Power in patronage appointments thus cascades downward, while loyalty flows upward, culminating with some ultimate arbiter of employment opportunities—a king, president, parliamentary leader, party official, mayor, or union boss, for example. Loyalty is personal, and its purpose is also defined from above—thus the contract can encompass mutual commitment to the long life and prosperity of the patron, to a dynasty of family or party faction, to a vision of the future or a set of public policy goals preferred by the patron, to the hegemony of a party machine, to an idea of nationhood, class, or life in

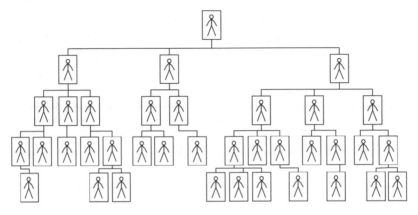

Figure I.1. Structure of a Classic Patronage System.

the hereafter, and so on. The contract is informal and unwritten, but understood by all parties to it.

In reality, of course, patronage systems are riddled with factions and conflict. Loyalties are regularly tested, and contracts for service can be ended at the discretion of the patron in a moment, through means that range from immediate unemployment to prison, poison, firing squad, or beheading, as history amply suggests. While recruitment and career trajectories are controlled from above, contracts can also be broken by subordinates when they seek alternative sponsors, are offered alternative sources of employment, or voluntarily leave service. New contracts can be forged through new appointments. In the real world, then, patronage systems are often quite messy (see Figure I.2).

Patronage systems are extensively present in history and in current reality. Yet almost always they are hedged about by alternative claims to office. Historically, these have been claims about hereditary rights to positions in government, life tenure in a position, or the practice of purchase of office. In more contemporary contexts, legal claims to tenure and constraints on firing often constrict opportunities to dismiss those who have been appointed through patronage. These alternatives can be important means to stabilize claims for precedence and preferment, to fill the coffers of the state, and to create de facto civil services, but they also simultaneously undermine the capacity of patrons to pursue their

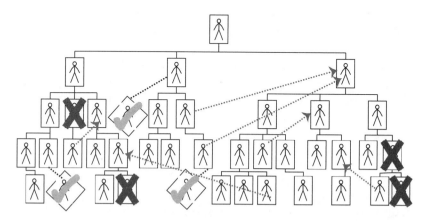

Figure I.2. Patronage in the "Real" World. Xs mark individuals who have left the patronage network; dotted arrows indicate defections to new patrons; checks show individuals who are newly recruited to the network.

political ends through the discretionary use of appointments to public office. These alternative claims are often found coexisting with the extensive use of more traditional patronage appointments.

Patronage systems stand in greatest contrast to career civil service *systems*, in which the preponderance of nonelected public sector jobs are filled through a process of credentialing based on education, examination, or some other test of merit; in which a career ladder exists and is accessed through regularized demonstration of credentials of education, examination, tenure in office, or other form of assessing merit; in which tenure is secure barring malfeasance in office; and in which movement in and out (through retirement, for example) is regulated and compensated.[17] In such a system, the official performs duties for the state or the service, not for the patron. The rules of the game in this system are formal and objectified through regulations and procedures.

At issue in distinguishing between patronage and career civil service systems is the nature of the contract between the employee and the employer. In a patronage system, the contract is based on a principle of political or personal reciprocity between the employee and the employer. In contrast, a career civil service system, rule-bound and impersonal, is based on a contract between an individual and an institution, the state as a system of laws, or a set of formal rules of the game. In Max Weber's terms, modern public service is a vocation, encompassing a duty to the office held and the state more generally.[18] In this distinction between two systems, then, processes of recruitment determine expectations about obligation—to the person and his or her priorities or to the "service," its norms of behavior, and the responsibility of office.

Recruitment to patronage positions defines obligations, but does not necessarily define performance or competence. Indeed, those who are personally appointed to positions in the public sector may be in such positions for a wide variety of reasons. Certainly, the behavior of many feeds the stereotype of incompetence, corruption, and bad governance that is normally assumed to be the consequences of patronage, where many public sector jobs are held temporarily by unqualified political appointees. The spoils of winning office or the cost of cementing political alliances can indeed be dysfunctional public services. Such jobs can be numerous and the subject of intense competition. In these kinds of positions, tenure tends to be determined by the duration of a political administration, a coalition that forms an administration, or the life of a regime.

Performance in office is often minimal, and officials may view their tenure, however brief, as an opportunity for rewarding loyal party members or partisans of a particular leader, or enriching themselves at the public "trough."

Equally important, however, are patronage jobs that are filled with a keen appreciation of the importance of competence in government. Often, technical, professional, or expert personnel are recruited through discretionary appointments, and those who are favored with public positions can be very aware of their responsibilities to serve the policy and political agendas of politicians or parties to whom they owe their positions. Such jobs tend to incorporate many officials at the upper reaches of an administration, at the upper middle levels, and even at middle levels of the public service. The dividing line between appointments that are made without regard to competence and those that are subject to such concerns is variable across countries and across time in particular countries. The line is also permeable in that patronage appointments of those with training or expertise can "infiltrate" positions traditionally filled without regard for competence—and vice versa. In civil service systems, competence is determined through some objective test or competition; in patronage systems, competence can be a criterion of hiring, but whether or not it is depends upon the preferences of the hiring patron.

Similarly, patronage can be used to fill positions that require specialized training, such as in medical, legal, scientific, teaching, and academic fields. While specific qualifications are necessary for such jobs, filling them with those with the requisite qualifications can be accomplished through discretionary selection processes. Certainly expertise is often a requirement in recruitment into career civil service systems, but the appointment of specialists is not enough to distinguish such systems from a patronage system. The contract between the employer and the officials differs, while individuals holding office in both types of systems may have comparable training or expertise.

Moreover, as the experience in a number of countries in Latin America suggests, it is common to find recruitment to public service through patronage but tenure through collective bargaining agreements, through regulatory mechanisms of tenure in service, or through customs of de facto civil service tenure. Public services in the region thus usually contain a large group of people whose employment status is regulated through generalized contracts negotiated between unions and government or government agencies, or who are recognized to have tenure through law, but who are recruited into such jobs through personal and political relationships. The initial contract implies obligations to the personal and the political, even if tenure is regulated through collective agreements or regulatory mechanisms.

The Issue of Performance

As the previous paragraphs suggest, patronage systems cannot be identified simply through an assessment of the competence, incompetence, or "fit" to the job of those who hold positions in government. Thus, patronage is not necessarily incompatible with competence or the accumulation of expertise in dealing with particular types of issues. It is, above all, a form of recruitment and advancement for public service, not a category of performance or competence.[19] As this book indicates, its weakness is its vulnerability to the caprice of those who manage such systems, not that it necessarily leads to corruption or incompetence.

To ensure clarity in the ensuing discussion of patronage systems, it is also important to distinguish notions of the competence of those recruited to government service from the competence of organizations or the competence of a government or state more generally. It is certainly possible to identify competent people who work in dysfunctional organizations or governments, for example. Similarly, organizations or governments that perform well may employ a certain number of people who add little or nothing to their efficiency or effectiveness. Again, patronage systems relate to the personnel systems of the public sector, and may not necessarily have negative consequences for the overall management of organizations or the administration of the state. Thus, the association of patronage systems with incompetence and corruption must be seen as an empirical question, not an assumption of inevitable practice.

Theory and Discontent

Given the questions posed in this book—about persistence, change, challenge, and consequence in institutional development—and a concern with how history and processes of change matter, it is important to be able to explain how the past constrains the present and the future, but also how and when changes in institutions happen. For help in this task, two theoretical traditions have been useful to me.

The issue of persistence over time is helpfully explored through theories of historical institutionalism, a body of perspectives that allows for a discussion of how rules of the game—institutions—emerge and are embedded over time in any particular environment and how they shape the incentives for individuals and organizations.[20] Embeddedness suggests strong impediments to change and indicates that the most likely changes are those that are, in some way, a logical progression of rules already embedded—in short, through path dependence.[21] In this view, legacies of the past help predict the shape of future institutions and narrow considerably the range of options for institutional reform. This perspective explains why institutions are "sticky" and usually well enough rooted to defy accumulated evidence that they should be changed in order to achieve important economic, social, and political objectives.

Historical institutionalism provides a useful means of explaining similarities within countries across time and differences among countires in how societies select solutions to major problems of collective life— new choices are heavily dependent on prior choices, and normal conditions suggest at least near-term equilibria. At the same time, historical institutionalists have adopted the concept of "punctuated equilibria," in which major external events can cause significant change in an institutional status quo.[22] Thus, for example, a war, a revolution, or an economic crisis can open political and historical space for significantly restructuring a set of durable institutions. In this book, historical institutionalism is an important grounding for explaining persistence and the ways in which current and future choices reflect legacies of the past, and is a helpful means of explaining institutional persistence even when it is dysfunctional to an economy, a society, or a polity. It draws attention to possible windows of opportunities to explain change.

But historical institutionalism does not offer enough tools to address how change occurs in specific contexts. Moreover, it may not capture the importance of conflict and strategic action in shaping outcomes. To complement a broad historical approach, then, I have found it useful to adopt concepts from a growing literature on the politics of reform.[23]

This literature focuses attention on the political and economic claims of winners and losers in reform initiatives and their incentives, opportunities, and strategic actions to oppose or support change. It has increasingly noted the importance of policy "entrepreneurs," those who generate ideas for change, lead teams of those committed to new ideas, and adopt strategies intended to overcome resistance.[24] It takes a process-oriented approach, acknowledging the role of distinct actors in conflict and negotiation and the possibility that results of such interactions are often contingent, given that actors can be strategic in ways that alter the incentives and responses of others who are engaged in trying to influence outcomes.

In this literature, contextual and historical factors figure mainly as factors that place constraints on strategic actors as they engage in efforts to promote or resist change. Each situation of reform is a unique setting for conflict and negotiation among actors struggling to influence a change agenda, the interests energized by specific projects for change, strategic decisions about how and when to promote change, and the consequences of action. Thus, the focus of this scholarship is with processes of agenda setting, negotiation, decision making, and implementation in contentious environments.

Explanations that focus on the struggles of reformers and anti-reformers over the introduction of institutional change, however, often fall short in their appreciation of how the embeddedness of prior experience shapes behavior, strategic thinking, coalition formation, patterns of conflict, and even the actors who have stakes in the outcome of conflict. Actors can shape institutions through their actions, but they are also shaped by them. Combining perspectives from historical institutionalism with insights from the politics of reform literature, then, provides a way of appreciating the pull of history and the embedded nature of many institutions while also allowing for an exploration of agency in shaping institutional outcomes.

These issues are also important for assessing previous scholarship that addresses transitions from patronage to civil service systems. In addressing when a civil service system is likely to be introduced, for example, one well-known argument is that rational politicians approve reform when electoral outcomes indicate that parties used to regular opportunities to win elections are no longer assured of repeated victories.[25] Under such conditions, politicians who promise jobs to their followers in the event of an electoral victory might agree to a system in which some of their supporters can gain tenure in public office and will then not suffer the loss of those jobs when power is delivered to other parties by the voters. Alternatively, at the time of an outgoing administration, political leaders may see the benefit of freezing their partisans in office by encapsulating their positions into a new civil service system. Under these conditions, then, politicians who have depended on the promise of patronage to win elections face partisan incentives to regularize jobs for the boys in a merit-based civil service system.

This argument rests on a view of patronage systems tied to party identity in mass democracies and the electoral rationality of those who approve—although they may not have advocated for—the introduction of a career civil service system. It focuses on the legislative moment when new systems are voted into existence, on electoral balances at a particular moment in time, and on the incentives of politicians whose futures are determined by the fates of their political parties. Indeed, these factors are an important part of the analysis of the 1883 legislative moment in the United States and are at the heart of an oft-cited work by Barbara Geddes.[26] The case of Mexico, explored in Chapter 6, also suggests this pattern.

Yet this rational actor model does not deal analytically with legacies of prior choices, the range of political interactions that lead up to important legislative moments, including negotiations surrounding the content of reform legislation, or the actions of those promoting change and those resisting it. Significantly, it may overlook the possibility that political leaders continue to find the ability to appoint their people useful for the pursuit of specific goals, regardless of how parties fare in elections. Even when partisan incentives align for reform, therefore, it may not occur. More importantly, the focus on legislative moments overstates the definitive nature of reform approval, without considering that a new system may be on the books but not actually put in place or that it may be significantly altered or curtailed after its introduction in law. History and process may be short-changed in this approach.

Moreover, party systems diverge significantly in their reliance on patronage for generating votes. In an influential article, Martin Shefter argued that, as historical processes, democratization and bureaucratization interact in distinct ways to create party systems that rely differentially on patronage.[27] First, whether patronage is widely available to political parties rests on whether or not bureaucratization in the direction of ensuring a modicum of insulation from politics (a "charter of bureaucratic autonomy") is established before the introduction of mass democracy. Sequences in the historical development of public and political institutions—bureaucracies and parties—thus shape the way new institutions can be configured. Indeed, in the cases explored in this book, there are important distinctions between the dynamics of change encountered by early adopters of civil service systems and later adopters that had to contend with party-based systems of patronage.

Second, even when it is available, not all parties use patronage to win votes. At times, Shefter argues, political parties are mobilized by "outsiders" who have not had prior access to political power, such as emergent working-class parties in some European countries in the late nineteenth and early twentieth centuries. The lack of access to patronage encourages parties to rely on programmatic appeals to win support, creating a dynamic in which votes are sought on the basis of broad, policy-relevant proposals rather than on the basis of jobs and other favors for the boys. When parties are organized by "insiders" who have enjoyed access to political power, such as those who led initiatives to form parties in the United States and Britain in the nineteenth century, then a very different trajectory is set in motion. In this case, Shefter anticipates the emergence of more clientelistic mass-based parties, reliant on the distribution of patronage and spoils for their support.

Shefter's argument provides valuable insights into issues of timing in processes of bureaucratization and democratization and into factors related to the social foundations of political parties; it also introduces important historical and comparative elements to discussions of patronage, providing an opportunity to explain diverse routes to public sector professionalization. Yet, this perspective collapses patronage into a theory of political party development, linking patronage to electoral strategies but not to a broader history of its utility and flexibility across time. And, like the argument relating to the partisan calculations of politicians, Shefter does not provide insight into the more contingent ways in which career civil service systems are negotiated and constructed, whether this is through what he refers to as an "absolutist" or a "progressive" coalition for change.[28] His argument deals primarily with the party consequences of patronage in the public sector, not with reform initiatives and their dynamics.

A third explanation of the relationship between patronage and reform provides greater insight into the content of reform initiatives, focusing attention on the shape a new system will take. Bernard Silberman argues that highly professionalized and structured civil services—such as found in France and Germany—come into existence when political succession is highly contestable and uncertain. In this view, the absence of a clear sense of how succession will take place encourages political leaders to place a high value on the continuity of the public service. In contrast, where political succession has become well institutionalized, as in the United States and Great Britain, a more open and fluid system of public service is found.[29] Facing decisions about how to rationalize the public service, politicians make "strategic choices . . . in environments of greater or lesser uncertainty."[30] With high uncertainty, such choices favor strong public services oriented to organizational rules, specific training for administrative roles, and high barriers to entry; with low uncertainty, choices will favor more open labor markets for public service, wide scope in individual career choices, and more open and egalitarian recruitment to administrative roles.

Silberman is thus able to explain why different countries develop distinct kinds of public services—the highly elitist variety found in France, Germany, and Japan, in which entry is almost exclusively through structured educational preparation, and the more egalitarian systems found in the United States and Great Britain, where professional expertise is broadly useful for entry at different points in an individual's career. Nevertheless, this perspective, while accounting for institutional outcomes, relies on the considerable prescience of rational politicians who, in their decision making, face up to problems and dilemmas related to broad characteristics of their political systems and issues of political succession. Some caution about such prescience is probably warranted; most political decision making is done in contexts of high uncertainty about many things, considerable pressure to "do something" in a wide variety of policy sectors, and limited information on the consequences of action.[31] The time horizons of politicians do not always contribute to thinking about the dilemmas of ensuring longer-term stability for the administration of the state.

Moreover, although Silberman deals with the content of reform, he is less sensitive to issues of negotiation in the process of change and to the possibility that outcomes are the result of the interplay and conflict of diverse interests and motives among decision makers. My cases, for example, indicate that institutional forms are contested, not simply "chosen" by politicians. His also minimizes the importance of contention over public sector recruitment once choices have been determined. And, as indicated in Chapter 6, the evolution of public services in highly uncertain political contexts in Latin America is remote from this explanation.

Explanations of public sector reform that focus on the mobilization of civil society in demanding change provide yet another way of understanding the transition from patronage to career civil service systems.[32] This perspective focuses on the activities of reformers and their strategies for generating and sustaining support for change. It also provides insight into why politicians would support changes that limit their access to patronage—they must respond to demands from highly mobilized voters or face the possibility of losing office. In a broader perspective, however, only a very few civil service reforms were the result of citizen or voter mobilization. Indeed, as Shefter notes, a number of career systems were introduced long before elections and political parties were significant in political decision making. The cases presented in this book indicate that the broad mobilization of citizens or voter interest in reform was an anomaly rather than a constant in the process of change.

Jobs for the Boys approaches the question of persistence and change through historically informed process-tracing of significant institutional reforms across a variety of countries. It thus combines specific case studies with a search for regular patterns in the persistence of patronage systems in the public service, the development and introduction of modern civil service systems, the ongoing challenges to fragile new institutions in the several decades after they are introduced, and how new rules of the game do not always deliver on their promise. Within historical contexts, then, the stories of reform told here indicate that new initiatives are subject to "on-going skirmishing as actors try to achieve advantage by interpreting or redirecting institutions in pursuit of their goals, or by subverting or circumventing rules that clash with their interests."[33] In general, processes of change are ongoing and indeterminate at any given time.

Weber's Ghost

Max Weber observed the development of the public service in the late nineteenth and early twentieth centuries in Europe and the United States and found a common trajectory—toward a system of public administration that is stable, rule-bound, hierarchically ordered, that maintains permanent records and provides a full-time career opportunity for those with expertise in managing the files and the functions of office, often acquired through specialized training.[34] This system is, above all, rational—objective, impersonal, efficient, specialized, and expert. Weber's enduring insight is that a rational-legal order requires loyalty to the office, not to a person, and implies a clearly observed distinction between the public purpose of government and its "ownership" by officeholders and political leaders.

For Weber, bureaucratic organization, based on the criteria of standardization, hierarchy, objectivity, impersonality, and specialization, inevitably triumphs over more personal and traditional forms of organization. Capitalist development, the demands of modern societies, and the exigencies of providing order and security require it, he argued. Indeed, he was clear that a rational bureaucracy is a precondition for a fully developed capitalist system.[35] Patrimonial states, in which rulers personally control the administrative apparatus and allocate positions based on their own ends and their private control over government, cannot provide sufficient order and continuity for modern societies and economies, he argued eloquently. The "leased prerogatives" of prebends characteristic of patrimonial societies are simply not conducive to such development.[36]

For Weber and for generations of public sector reformers, the inevitable triumph of a modern bureaucracy is ensured through "its purely technical superiority over any other form of organization. . . . Precision, speed, unambiguity, knowledge of the files, continuity, discretion, unity, strict subordination, reduction of friction and of material and personal costs—these are raised to the optimum point in the strictly bureaucratic administration."[37] More than anything else, reformers argue, career civil service systems will depoliticize the public sector. They will turn the attention of bureaucrats from the private orientation of loyalty to person or party to the public orientation of loyalty and service to the state. And, even while Weber anticipated excesses of bureaucracy, he was clear that the emergence of such forms of administration was inevitable.

Political rhetoric surrounding initiatives to introduce Weber's ideal reality is, and has historically been, Manichean. Progressives of all stripes and in all countries promote civil service reform as a tonic for corruption, nepotism, favoritism, partisanship, spoils, incompetence, lack of professionalism, inequity, capture, particularism, mediocrity, malfeasance, and electoral fraud and violence. Patronage systems are reviled as undemocratic and unjust; they are damned as inevitably leading to governments that are dysfunctional. Reform rhetoric promises that a proper civil service system will slay the greatest of public sector dragons—patronage and the pervasive ills that it visits upon virtuous citizens and societies.

In the spin war of public sector reform, civil services are described as professional, merit-based, neutral, uniform, rule-oriented, competent, autonomous, predictable, and continuous—terms that portray reformers' strong beliefs in their evident superiority to patronage. Indeed, patronage in politics has no friends—aside, of course, from the politicians who make appointments based on it and those who are favored with these appointments. While this can be a nontrivial number of people, those who regularly count themselves as opponents of patronage far outnumber them. Woodrow Wilson spoke for many in 1887 when he referred to the struggle between corruption and virtue evident at all levels of U.S. government: "The poisonous atmosphere of city government, the crooked secrets of state administration, the confusion, sinecurism, and corruption ever and again discovered in the bureaux at Washington forbid us to believe that any clear conceptions of what constitutes good administration are as yet very widely current in the United Sates."[38] Civil service reform, for him, was "moral preparation" for more effective government.[39]

The comparative consideration of a number of cases, however, indicates that the oft-repeated notion that patronage is synonymous with corruption, incompetence, and bad governance is simplistic. Historically and in current reality, of the many countries that have had deeply entrenched patronage systems, some have had dismal histories of economic stagnation and volatile politics. Others have demonstrated considerable capacity to grow, to sustain stable political regimes, and to accomplish modern tasks of government. And still others have successfully moved from poverty to significant wealth, to urbanization and industrialization, even while their public services have defied the logic of Weber's expectations. Despite popular and academic opinion to the contrary, then, it is possible that the structure of their public services has not determined their development trajectories.[40]

Yet, by exploring the history of persistence, change, and ongoing contention, *Jobs for the Boys* indicates that the fatal weakness of patronage systems is they are capricious, not that they are inevitably incompetent, corrupt, or incapable of taking on the challenge of modern government. Civil service systems are designed to end capriciousness with regularized rules about recruitment and career development. Thus, civil service systems offer a well-trod path toward ending patronage systems and introducing new standards into the hiring, promotion, and retiring of bureaucrats; they provide the basis for more-regularized government. They also provide foundations for establishing bureaucratic autonomy, when loyalty to the ends of the patron ceases to be the measure for job holding, replaced by a commitment to rules of performance. The change from one recruitment system to another is highly consequential, although advocates of reform may err in their expectations of what a career civil service system can deliver.

Thus, at the broadest level, this book seeks to infuse discussions of public sector reform—often framed in black-and-white terms—with shades of gray. Gray is not a popular color when reformers press the imperative for change. Indeed, the ghost of Max Weber actively stalks politicized public service systems and colors the rhetoric of reform. The specter's voice is clear: modern states have modern—that is, professional, merit-based, career-oriented, stable—bureaucracies. It looms large in discussions of public sector reform and continues to offer stark alternatives—a dark world of patronage, corruption, and incompetence or a well-governed world in which public positions are allocated through merit judged on the basis of examination and/or education and skills.

I do not seek to lay Weber's ghost to rest in *Jobs for the Boys*. The conflict between good and evil is a useful way for reformers to cast their struggle for change; it is less useful in providing perspective on how change happens across time. In this book, I seek to clarify the enduring attractiveness of patronage systems for those who hold political power, trace the often lengthy political construction of their replacement in public administration, and address the performance consequences of civil service reforms. My objective is not to take a position on the conflict between good and evil, but to recognize the importance of politics in constructing systems for the management of the state.

PART I

The *Longue Durée*

CHAPTER 1

A System for All Seasons

Geoffrey Chaucer held office as comptroller of customs in the Port of London, clerk of works in the royal palace, and commissioner responsible for maintenance of the Thames, each position allocated to him through the "grace and favor" of John of Gaunt, his patron. John Milton was appointed "secretary for foreign tongues," a reward for loyalty and a position he used to defend the resurgence of Parliament in the seventeenth century. Daniel Defoe, Joseph Addison, David Hume, Edward Gibbon, and John Locke all held public office through the intervention of powerful patrons; Matthew Arnold and Anthony Trollope were also among those serving government as a consequence of their personal connections.[1] The extent to which English literature, philosophy, economics, and history were advanced by the use of patronage appointments to public office is thus open to speculation.

In the early days of the U.S. republic, John Adams repeatedly (if dourly) sought preferment for his son-in-law, Colonel William S. Smith, found a position for another son-in-law as superintendent of the stamp office, and of course appointed "midnight" judges just prior to leaving office.[2] During the heyday of the Jacksonian spoils system, Nathaniel Hawthorne was named a customs official in the port of Boston (a position he found "a very grievous thralldom") by George Bancroft, and subsequently Charles Sumner was instrumental in his appointment as a port surveyor in Salem; he secured another appointment as consul in Liverpool in the 1850s.[3] Interestingly, in the late nineteenth century, those who worked to establish more effective government bureaus in Washington usually owed their appointments to the discretion of those who hired them.[4] In turn, they used their own powers of appointment to colonize these bureaus with those who had professional and technical qualifications they deemed important to the progress of governance.

In more recent times, when Mexico's President Carlos Salinas redefined a broad range of policies to govern the nation's economy, he did so by hand-selecting a team of technocrats who in turn selected their former students, colleagues, and political allies to become "probably the most economically literate group that has ever governed any country anywhere."[5] In Argentina, economy minister Domingo Cavallo personally appointed bright, well-educated technocrats at high and middle levels to bolster his initiatives to reform government and economy in the early 1990s.[6] Chile's state modernization in the same decade was led by those personally appointed to serve at the convenience of their modernizing bosses, in alliance with a governing coalition of political parties.[7] Under Alberto Fujimori in Peru, Vladimiro Montesinos became head of the national intelligence service and used his patronage power in this agency, the armed forces, and other parts of government to build an extensive network of corruption and political intrigue.

These historical examples of patronage begin to suggest its ubiquity. Kings and parliamentarians, oligarchs and democrats, Luddites and technocrats, the honorable and the crass have all been implicated as its practitioners. Patronage systems have been resilient historically in part because they can be impressively responsive to the objectives of those who control them—despots, criminals, modernizers, and progressives alike. Indeed, those who have controlled patronage networks have sought a variety of ends—from cementing absolutist rule, to building competent states, to ensuring the hegemony of class elites, to amassing private wealth and power, to determining the fortunes of political parties, to promoting significant policy change. A catalogue of its practice indicates that patronage has proved useful in achieving some of the ends of modern government, even while it is widely held responsible for extensive corruption and inefficiency, damned as a throwback to premodern and patrimonial government.

My purpose in this chapter is not to extol the virtues of patronage, however, but to argue that what is often dismissed as a mechanism of corruption and incompetence is in fact a flexible means of managing power and, as such, has been used to achieve a variety of ends—good, bad, and indifferent. Moreover, seeing patronage in history indicates that the issue of who controls appointments figures at the core of a number of major historical struggles over power. The clash between king and Parliament in seventeenth-century England, efforts to implement governance reform in colonial Spanish America, the hegemony of Paris over the regions in nineteenth-century France, the struggle for power between Congress and the president in the late nineteenth-century United States—the contest between patronage and the introduction of civil service systems is but part of a larger conflict about who controls recruitment and advancement in the public service. Inevitably, the uses of patronage influence how the larger purposes of government are achieved.

Here, I explore the history of its uses in six countries that now boast well-institutionalized civil service systems—Britain, France, Japan, Prussia, Spain, and the United States. While demonstrating the flexibility and variability of patronage in each of these countries, the chapter shows that the purposeful employment of patronage contributed to significant macropolitical ends in each country. In Prussia and Japan, patronage was a mechanism for building centralized authoritarian states; in France, Britain, and Spain, it was instrumental in ensuring the hegemony of class elites in public service; in the United States, it was a principal means for building mass-based political parties. As will become clear in Chapter 2, which deals with how civil service reforms occurred in these same countries, these consequences also shaped reform initiatives in each. Thus, the utility of patronage as a mechanism for recruitment to office and the objectives sought by those who control it are important to understanding the ways in which new systems of public service recruitment are constructed as alternatives to patronage.

Patronage and Purpose

Employment contracts for loyalty are the consistent mechanism through which patronage systems work. In medieval European history, early kings sought to establish and extend their lands and wealth not only through marriage and warfare, but also through appointments to civil, religious, and military positions in royal households that did not distinguish private from public property.[8] Loyalties were purchased through the distribution of lands, rents, and positions. Such loyalties often proved fragile, however, as rivalries among those who held land and position

encouraged the emergence of contenders for kingly status, and as retainers shifted loyalties in the expectation of greater wealth, power, or
security, often taking their own retainers with them.[9] Efforts to centralize
power were also hedged about by hereditary claims to land, titles, and
positions.

As king succeeded king (and a very occasional queen), and as warfare
and the requirements of royal life necessitated more resources, the availability of positions and the utility of using patronage appointments for
specific purposes increased. To the requirements of loyalty to a household
or lineage, patronage appointments needed to incorporate those who could
provide relatively reliable administration of lands, warfare, and treasury.
Early conflicts over the control of these appointments often centered on
whether the assignment of positions carried with it hereditary rights.[10]
Clearly, if the positions were made hereditary, kings and subordinate
patrons lost the power to control recruitment to them, and incumbents
gained in independence. In feudal Europe, where positions were counted
as property, the power to allocate them could not help but be contentious.
Much of the construction of centralized and absolutist monarchical states
in the seventeenth and eighteenth centuries dealt centrally with a conflict
over rights to office, as well as to titles, land, and other forms of property.[11]
While such conflicts were frequent, evidence of the spread of royal absolutism suggests that kings often gained the upper hand in determining
recruitment and tenure.

More specifically, however, purpose and contention were a function
of time and place, and even though the practice of patronage was ubiquitous, its history is varied. In Prussia and Japan, for example, state building was facilitated through the consistent manipulation of patronage, tied
to the control of the state by an educated elite and eventually the control
of this elite by the state. In France, a broad history of patronage appointments demonstrates their use in state creation, the establishment of royal
absolutism, later in the consolidation of state centralization, and still later
in the maintenance of structures of power and privilege. In Britain,
state building was similarly an apparent objective of patronage, but the
country's history demonstrates important contention over the power to
control it, as well as in embedding structures of class and education in
public life. In Spain, the quest for state and empire was facilitated through
royal appointments, but control over patronage was frequently insufficient

for fully achieving domestic and imperial ends. In the United States, patronage first served a patrician elite interested in honest and gentlemanly government, then a party-based mass democracy focused on electoral mobilization, but also a reformist group intent upon professionalizing the public service.

Those who dispensed patronage with purpose were not universally successful in achieving their ends, of course, at times due to the poor judgment of its dispensers, at times due to the weight of alternative claims on such resources, and at times due to the complexity and difficulty of the ends being sought. And, obviously, patronage was not the only factor that accounted for the destruction of feudalism, the construction of royal absolutism, the development of modern states and their administrative machinery, or that created conflict between nobles and kings, kings and parliaments, or presidents, legislators, and parties. Wars, plagues, religious conflict, technology, and a variety of other factors litter any historical explanation of change. Yet patronage was an important mechanism in how these larger processes shaped historical outcomes. Common across space, patronage was used to distinct purposes or to no purpose at all and was frequently an important factor in conflicts among those who sought to monopolize power.

Ubiquity, flexibility of purpose, and contention—these are the themes that unite distinct histories of patronage as a mechanism of power. What distinguishes these histories from each other are the specific purposes of those who controlled the mechanism and the contextual factors that shaped the effectiveness of its use and the larger struggles for power that determined control over it.

Building Authoritarian States

CENTRALIZING RATIONALITY IN PRUSSIA.   The decisions of kings and emperors, the actions and inactions of armies, the terms of treaties, and the purposeful use of patronage transformed a small and insignificant Prussia into a centralized and efficient state with claims to significant power in Europe. Efficiency and order were at the core of the state apparatus that emerged in the seventeenth and eighteenth centuries. As this state emerged, patronage was married to loyalty and efficiency to give impetus to the first consolidated career civil service system in Europe.[12]

The power of the state-building Hohenzollerns was limited until the seventeenth century, and while their acquisitions were substantial, their capacity to rule depended on the acquiescence of a hereditary class of wealthy landowners, the Junkers, who held sway over local administration and government in the east and north of what was to become Prussia. Here, the "squirearchy was on the verge of holding a virtual monopoly of political power."[13] Taking advantage of the dislocation and economic decline caused by the Thirty Years' War, Frederick William of Brandenburg (the Great Elector) set about crafting the lands of the Junkers into a centralized and expanding state. By the 1660s, he had stepped into a leadership position by assuming the right to make foreign policy for the various provinces, to tax their inhabitants, and to establish a standing army. A centralized administrative system for revenue collection was established at the end of the seventeenth century.[14]

The patronage wielded by Frederick William and his successors was deliberately focused on encouraging the established and relatively independent nobility to take up positions in the military and the state administration.[15] Over time, patronage filled both military and civil administration with "new bureaucrats" who gradually replaced traditional and aristocratic claims on public positions with criteria of efficiency and loyalty to the monarchy. "Supervision, regulation and routine" were characteristics of this bureaucratic establishment, and military bureaucrats enjoyed considerably more power than civil ones.[16] Unlike other centralizing monarchs in Europe, the Prussians carefully avoided the sale of office and the loss of power over appointment that it implied.[17]

This new bureaucracy in the army and the civil administration, obsessed with order, hierarchy, and predictability, led the expansion of Prussia toward all points of the compass in the following century.[18] By 1748, the Hohenzollerns of Brandenburg had control of Brandenburg, East Prussia, Farther Pomerania, Silesia, and patches of land bordering the Elbe and Rhine rivers. The lands were widely dispersed, offering a challenge to the royal servants who administered the many noncontiguous territories on behalf of the king; they concerned themselves with quashing local laws and practices and consolidating a central bureaucracy and army able to tax and command.

Thus, over the course of the eighteenth century, the government of a poor and largely rural state focused enormous energy on building and maintaining an army that demanded the attention of other European countries. The long reign of Frederick II (the Great, 1740–1786) cemented personal and absolute royal rule based on the ascendance of his military, and he "taught his administrators the virtue of conscientiously performing their duties for the good of the state."[19] His obsessive concern with order and administration, along with a pervasive distrust of the administrators, encouraged ever-greater vigilance and regulation of the state apparatus.[20]

With the powers of absolutism at their service, Frederick William and his successors had clear objectives and criteria in mind as they filled positions in the military and the civil administration. They consistently appointed landed aristocrats to commissions in the army—to take advantage of a heritage of military service among this elite and of what were perceived to be traditional capacities of those who managed lands and commanded serfs and to co-opt those who represented traditional claims on positions of authority.[21] The clarity of purpose is suggested by legislation that prohibited the sale of landed estates to those without claims to nobility. At the same time, members of a dependent middle class were widely appointed to positions in the administration; places in the higher administration were reserved for aristocrats, cementing a bond between army and state.[22]

This patronage system did not result in a lax regime, although corruption was ongoing. The rules were clear—the army was to be disciplined and efficient, and the purpose of the government administration was to ensure that there was sufficient funding for the army.[23] At an individual level, competition for promotion—and the favor that would bring it—led to an abundance of officials who made "careful calculation of personal chances and the adoption of rules of behavior designed to outwit and trip up rivals by shrewdness, superior performance, intrigue, or eel-like maneuvering."[24] This, in combination with the discipline, duty, and hierarchy of a militarized state, meant that characteristics like efficiency and skill mattered, just as class status did.[25]

The providers of patronage—the Great Elector, Frederick I, Frederick William I, and then Frederick the Great—each of them devoted to the army, to discipline, to rights and obligations stratified by class, to centralization of decision making, and to austerity, encouraged an implicit exchange of performance for position.[26] "Patronage with Purpose" might have been their motto. In an evolving bureaucratic state, education gradually became a proxy for recruitment based on competence, and officialdom took on a dynastic caste as sons often succeeded fathers in administrative roles.[27] Early on, Frederick William I put this orientation in place by requiring officials to have education in practical skills.[28] Frederick II followed suit by emphasizing legal education, believing that the structure of the laws would enhance monarchical autonomy. As a consequence, it was difficult to distinguish " 'spoils' from 'merit,' privilege from proficiency, patronage from appointment for competence only, and 'artificial' from 'natural' aristocracy."[29] Patronage was dispensed from the top, and with time it became a form of "regulated competition," with "growing emphasis on fact-finding procedures in screening candidates for commissions."[30]

STATE AND WARRIORS IN JAPAN.   The recruitment of officials in premodern Japan was a deliberate affair, focused on promoting loyalty to an imperial household whose power rested on claims of religious leadership and military acumen.[31] Despite very early efforts to mimic the imperial service of China—selecting officials from a specially trained class of mandarins committed to Confucian ideas of moral integrity and learning and who passed entrance examinations—uses of patronage powers in Japan for military and civil purposes focused on drawing feudal barons into the imperial orbit. In a country characterized by warring clans and a fragmented geography, these were clear objectives with uncertain outcomes, however, and a strong imperial state proved difficult to maintain. Imperial and then aristocratic power yielded increasingly to the military might of feudal lords, who turned to the court to legitimize their territorial hegemony.[32]

Thus, from the ninth to the beginning of the seventeenth century, a gradual process of increasingly decentralized rule undermined the political role of emperors, leaving them with largely religious and ceremonial roles. By the sixteenth century, power had become fragmented among a multitude of large landed domains and the military lords *(daimyō)* who ruled them, and they were frequently, even constantly, at war with one another.[33] Not surprisingly, those who served these early military chiefs were appointed largely because of their skills as warriors who pledged loyalty to the *daimyō*. Even during periods when there was more centralized coherence, most administration of the state was local and under the control of the domain lord. Appointments were personal and dependent upon loyalty and military prowess.

Under the rule of the Tokugawa shogunate from 1600 to 1868, Japan developed a more stable, centralized state.[34] In the mid-sixteenth century, strong feudal lords took the first step toward greater unity through military domination of diverse domains; a second step involved buying off, through stipends, warlord control over land; a third step involved restricting the use of arms to a specialized caste of warriors, the samurai.[35] Through such mechanisms, *daimyō* power was curtailed, as was that of the emperor, and the shogun rose in power.

As domain lords were required to swear allegiance to the shogun and they lost ultimate control over their lands to the Tokugawa clan leadership, they were incorporated into an elite system of greater centralized power. Further, the *daimyō* were required to reside in the capital city during alternate years and to leave their families in residence when they returned to their domains, further strengthening central control. Appointments to court and the allocation of land were increasingly subject to Tokugawa patronage. Many samurai, in turn, were delegated the principal administration of the lands of the absentee *daimyō* and then were gradually incorporated into the patronage network of the shogunate.

With the gradual success of greater central control under the Tokugawa, military administration was joined by greater bureaucratic capacity to extract taxes and ensure some degree of common practice across disparate domains—even while access to positions of authority remained based on ascriptive criteria of caste and rank.[36] Initially, important officials were drawn from the Tokugawa clan and given responsibilities for civilian administration. Over time, the demands of taxation, control, and administration lessened the importance of clan, but appointments remained personal and rooted in hereditary rank.

Under the Tokugawa, officials also gradually became more subject to claims for competence in carrying out their duties.[37] Samurai were encouraged to maintain their skills in the martial arts but also to study a variety of subjects if they wished to rise in importance within the administration of the state. Those fitted for high-level office attended a training academy, which, in the late eighteenth century, introduced examinations meant to ensure greater competence.[38] Clearly, these factors limited the patronage pool for the shogunate, but encouraged its greater control over administration. Nevertheless, public service in Japan remained closely tied to clan and rank within castes and to geography, where clans were rooted.[39] "Appointments to office, promotions and dismissals were made at the discretion of superiors. The powers and responsibilities of offices were poorly defined and there was a great deal of room for inefficiency, imbalance, and the personal interpretation of official duties."[40]

Despite limitations, the Tokugawa introduced a period of greater centralization of power and almost two centuries of unaccustomed military peace in Japan. Their rule, however, rested on a delicate balance between the power of the shogun and that of *daimyō* who might combine to challenge that rule. Indeed, the rights of samurai and *daimyō* were considered hereditary, and the stipends received from the state were deemed to be entitlements.[41] By the nineteenth century, challenges to Tokugawa power had become more frequent; efforts at reform, including opening up administrative positions to more diversity of background, proved insufficient, and the rigidities of caste and rank undermined the capacity of the regime to respond to gathering discontent of samurai and domain leaders. In part, a patronage system based on an increasingly closed hierarchy of rank and caste weakened the capacity of state leaders to use it effectively to maintain the state.[42] The 1853 arrival of American warships in Tokyo Bay emphasized to the Tokugawa rulers the importance of a more effective system and encouraged a series of initiatives to improve the quality of those appointed to office, although mechanisms of appointment remained constant.

With the Meiji Restoration in 1868, led by disaffected samurai from non-Tokugawa domains, titles and public positions from the eighth century were resurrected, and the capacity of the feudal *daimyō* to temper centralized control was eliminated; the return of imperial rule was celebrated by reformists who used ancient roles and mythologies to modernize the government. Some 280 domains were consolidated into 72 prefectures, and gradually their control shifted from traditional *daimyō* to reform-oriented samurai.[43] Traditional elites lost their claims to land, were forced to move to Tokyo, and became officials or pensioners of the state. Eventually, they became bondholders whose future would be determined by the success of the state.[44] Samurai could no longer wear swords simply as a result of their hereditary right; the state became strong enough to limit this privilege to police and military officials. Gradually, what remained of locally autonomous administration was melded into a single system of government, with authority clearly located in the central state, although administration continued to be decentralized.[45]

With the Meiji Restoration, public officials were declared to be "servants of the emperor," to ensure loyalty to the new state, and, under a banner of "make the Country rich and powerful," a new generation of better-trained public officials appeared.[46] The ministry of finance was at the center of this new generation, recruiting intellectuals to fill senior positions. Despite the use of ancient and imperial rhetoric and offices, these authoritarian nineteenth-century reformers clearly distinguished positions in government from their origins in the royal household.[47]

In the same period, a series of official missions to Western countries brought back knowledge of administrative structures and processes, and the construction of a modern bureaucratic state was undertaken, with particular reference to the German experience under Bismarck. In 1882, the establishment of the Bank of Japan served notice of the modernizing orientation of this new state. The Meiji reformers sought out administrators who brought talent, even when accompanied by more modest background than those of the past, and incorporated them in provincial and central government. Early on, the emphasis on clan and rank was maintained, as the Meiji rulers personally appointed those from clans central to their successful coup in 1868. Thus, the modernizing leaders of the new state found the powers of patronage useful for constructing a centralized state and a means to build loyalty to a system focused on the importance of effective management for maintaining and expanding their power.

Embedding Privilege in State Service

KINGS, REVOLUTIONS, ELITES, AND PATRONAGE IN FRANCE.   In France, the flexibility of patronage to achieve a variety of ends was clear. In the medieval period, the union of church and royal household was one such purpose, as kings sought rights over religious patronage. State building was also advanced when positions and the power that came with them were exchanged for fealty to a royal clan. The success of this royal claim came at the expense of the feudal nobility, whose own claims to hereditary rights and autonomy were overcome through war, marriage alliances, penury, cooptation, or exhaustion. Aristocratic claims died slowly, however, and resurfaced repeatedly to threaten the advance of central power. In the late sixteenth century, for example, Henri IV struggled to maintain his right to allocate positions in the face of demands by powerful princes that the honors of position be made hereditary. The limits of his capacity to achieve central control were clear when he used money or rights over less powerful cities to buy off these demands, which he feared would lessen his capacity to dominate provincial governments.

In the following century, state building was advanced by Louis XIII through the exchange of military commissions for loyalty to the king. His son further cemented fealty to the crown by bringing "the great of the kingdom around his person, where he could see and control them. Those who came were richly rewarded—and thereby domesticated and made dependent."[48] This centralization made peace and an expanding economy much more possible. High-level officials were able to recruit family members into service, reinforcing central power.[49] The resulting life of the court was anything but straightforward, of course. By the time of Louis XVI, it was "an endless pursuit of advantage, status, pensions, offices, and perquisites from those whom royal favor endowed with power to bestow them."[50] As ministers of the king came and departed, they brought their relatives and clients with them into office, and then took them along when they left.

Absolutism is never thoroughly so in practice, of course, and even at the height of royal power, those who were appointed to court were able to resist changes in public policies when these were seen to threaten their privileges. The need for increased taxes—and the attractiveness of selling offices in order to fill public coffers—acted as constraints on the majesty of French kings, and provided some room for new commercial wealth to find a place at court. By the eighteenth century, some fifty thousand offices were up for sale, at times by the king, at times by those who owned the positions from previous purchase. This was an important source of capital for the royal state, but one that seriously undermined its ability to wield patronage for political purposes.[51] "Traffic in offices" assumed extraordinary proportions, making effective administration increasingly difficult, and undermining the state-building purposes of patronage.[52] Indeed, the sale of public offices—characteristic of most early modern governments—reached its zenith in France.[53] Once sold, these offices were essentially private property, and officeholders sought to pass them on to their heirs. The problem was clear: "If the king sold offices, he could no longer choose his servants according to their capacities or reliability."[54]

Then came the Revolution.[55] Beyond the bloodshed, the drama, the new ideology of *egalité,* and the consequent undermining of the privileged position of aristocracy, the French Revolution introduced a clear notion of public office as public rather than private property.[56] As the state took on new responsibilities for *egalité,* it significantly increased the size of its public sector and the number of laws and regulations that were to be carried out. This did not make the public service noticeably less ascriptive, however. Loyalty to the new state—and to its rapidly rotating leadership—became an evident litmus test for public appointments; wholesale purges of government personnel became part of politics-as-usual.[57] While this period introduced some rationalization of positions and territorial divisions, it was also notable for a significant increase in the number of public officials at all levels, and thus the extent of positions that could be exchanged for commitment to the revolutionary state—or to its leaders.[58]

Under the Revolution, some offices were filled by local elections, but many positions continued to be filled through personal appointment; ministers became centrally important patrons in the recruitment process. At the same time, the founding of the École Polytechnique in 1794, which served as a feeder institution to the previously established elite schools that played a large role in training the organizers and builders of the state, the École des Mines and the École des Ponts et Chaussées (the *grandes écoles*), signaled the increasing importance of technical qualifications for those needed to carry out the engineering and logistical tasks of state building.

Under Napoléon, appointments to public positions were put even more in the service of centralization, hierarchy, control, and stability, critical components of the Napoleonic state. Positions that had been elected under the Revolution—mayors, for example—became subject to appointment again. The sale of offices came to an end, and law became uniform and universal with the introduction of the Napoleonic Code.

Centralization, through a process of "centralized decentralization," began in 1800, and Napoléon's departmental prefects were personally appointed by central authorities at the highest level and then gained the reputation of being "emperor[s] in miniature," serving as patrons to more local elites and aspiring administrators.[59] Indeed, the France of Napoléon had a "mania for regulating everything from Paris down to the smallest details."[60] Administration was subject to order, procedure, files, and reports, and the power of administrators was uncoupled from the strictures of privilege that constrained them in the prerevolutionary period. An incipient career system was established for those appointed with the expectation of rise to senior appointments.[61]

Loyalty to appointing ministers and to the state, increasing emphasis on educational credentials, and concerns for social status underlay official appointments of the Napoleonic era.[62] Once officials were in office, the activities they carried out increasingly resembled those of more modern bureaucracies, with regular processes, professional standards, and rational organization of work. Foreshadowing later conceptions of the duties of officials, statistical reports were increasingly required from those who were recruited and appointed by the emperor and his ministers.[63] In this period, patronage had a clear purpose: to organize and systematize the state administration. This, then, was a mixture of "formalism and personalism" in the management of government.[64]

Early nineteenth-century conflicts over patronage reflected appeals for preference from aristocratic survivors of the Revolution and the rising bourgeoisie. By 1830, the place of new commercial wealth was assured, but its assault on positions in the state was hedged in by increasing insistence on the possession of a *baccalauréat*—evidence of successful completion of a *lycée* education—and then a diploma in law (preferably from the University of Paris) or from the École Polytechnique and then attendance at one of the *grandes écoles*, for aspirants to positions of importance. Informal but increasingly clear requisites for appointment and advancement were strong testimony to French emphasis on capacity as a requirement for office, and significantly narrowed routes of entry into public service. In 1872, the École Libre des Sciences Politiques became the primary recruiting ground for responsible positions in government, and prepared applicants at high levels of proficiency. Thus developed a strong corps of specialized and well-trained public officials whose appointment—after suitable training to an appropriate level at a *grande école*—continued to be based on connections, patronage, and class. Those not completing the rigors of this educational process were eligible for good positions in government, but also more subject to the vicissitudes of preference and patronage.[65]

Gradually, by the end of the nineteenth century, a clear career structure based on criteria of training and competence had developed within a system that continued to rely on personal appointments to fill government office and to ensure that those rewarded with positions would be loyal to the ministers who provided them the jobs. The majority of posts continued to be allocated through patronage because "no government, and no regime, was willing to rationalize and professionalize the bureaucracy, which despite its Napoleonic reputation, and the thorough training of its technical branches (bridges and highways, and mines) was far less well organized by the mid-19th century than that of Germany or Britain, because the only way to keep it under ministerial control seemed to be to continue with arbitrary appointment, favouritism and occasional wholesale purges of the politically unreliable."[66] At the same time, some units of government introduced examinations to assess competence in technical fields, even though the information gained was put at the service of patronage rather than replacing it.[67]

A significant consequence of the combination of educational requirements and reliance on patronage for appointment and promotion was the predominance of class elites in the middle and upper reaches of French public administration. Entrance into the *grandes écoles* was limited by the *baccalauréat*, which in turn relied on the completion of an elite private education, generally eliminating access of those who did not come from privileged conditions. Similarly, the development of a period of unpaid apprenticeship for many public positions ensured that those who aspired to such positions were enabled to do so only if they had private wealth.[68] While politicians in nineteenth-century France competed in increasingly unstable governments, the public administration, cemented by ties of class and training, gradually developed an ethos of professionalism and elitism. In this case, patronage incorporated a principle of merit for public office, but merit determined by advancement through a narrow door of privilege.[69]

KING AND PARLIAMENT, CENTRAL AND LOCAL IN BRITAIN.   As for 1066 and all that, the Domesday Book notes that William the Conqueror had in his service Henry the Treasurer, esteemed for loyalty to the financial well-being of his patron.[70] Such loyalty was important to early kings of England, but so were other skills. When in need of administrative assistance, they recruited from the ranks of the literate clergy, to take advantage of the ability to write in Latin and to monitor accounts. Preference in royal and church service was intertwined, and the cost of employing and promoting loyal officials was shared between the two institutions.[71] By the thirteenth century, an increase in the complexity of administration encouraged the assignment of a permanent body of officials in Westminster. Those selected for office, whether of royal or aristocratic origin, were charged through the "grace and favor" of the king; clearly, they could lose such grace and favor as well as gain it.[72] In addition to the church, there was little other calling for the literate than the law and royal service. And, as for making a living, official posts came with grants and opportunities for generating fees.

Over time, and particularly under the Tudor monarchs, as the affairs of state grew, so too did the number of dependents of the crown, to the point that the palace at Whitehall was claimed by Henry VIII to become the home of the English administration.[73] Duties were not clearly defined, nor was there any regular system of salaries, standards for promotion, or common understandings of tenure in office.[74] Indeed, the importance of personal service in grace and favor appointments is clear in the favor and then loss of grace suffered by two of Henry VIII's most competent officials, Thomas Cromwell and Thomas Wolsey.[75] The centralizing tendency of royal patronage, however, was constrained by local claims to make appointments as crown agents.

Under Elizabeth, initial inroads to a distinction between private and public careers emerged, but only faintly.[76] By the seventeenth century, the sale of public offices, which in practice usually conferred positions for life, became a significant way to raise revenue for the crown and contribute to the livelihoods and social status of purchasers, even though it was never considered a legitimate way to obtain office.[77] At the same time, offices obtained in this way undercut royal authority to control positions of importance and, by the eighteenth century, were undercutting the ability of government to govern.

Moreover, and gradually over several centuries, the importance of filling and dispensing royal and then government coffers, and the necessity to employ large numbers of people to accomplish at least the first of these tasks, enhanced the role of the Treasury as a manager of public office and the rents derived from them.[78] In this system, patronage was not averse to competence; it could be a versatile means for encouraging loyalty and improved governance at the same time.[79] Nevertheless, a preference for gentlemanly amateurs in government made its appearance long before the nineteenth century, when it became a principle that was characteristic of the Victorian reform of the civil service.

As these general trends unfolded, increasingly apparent—and at times violent—struggles between crown and Parliament invoked control over appointments, along with large and complex issues of religion, rights, and obligations, as central issues of conflict. In the eighteenth century, Parliament, emerging powerful and firmly in the control of landed aristocrats who had long been granted the capacity to appoint local officials, was intent to gain ground in filling a greater number of offices at the national level.[80] These efforts, local and national, and the tensions they created between king and Parliament, limited the extent to which royal absolutism could fully control access to public office, although they did little to broaden the social basis of office holding. Incipient parliamentary parties in the eighteenth century laid additional claim to senior offices in the Treasury and thus brought Treasury control of many appointments under the purview of Parliament. Eventually, an official in Parliament, who was later anointed the patronage secretary, was charged with ensuring that as many appointments as possible helped increase party discipline and construct party loyalties.[81]

The end result, by the late eighteenth century, was a system parceled out to an amalgam of local notables with a virtual monopoly over naming local officials to crown service, a king with control over a large number of prestigious appointments, demands by parliamentary parties for control by Parliament of public offices, and an increasing number of executive departments seeking to control recruitment into office as the size and responsibilities of government increased. Over the course of several centuries, then, archaic informal rules, changing demographics, and tempestuous relationships between executive and legislative bodies led to a government that carried out much public business haphazardly and with significant corruption. Moreover, the continuing practice of selling offices reached the level of public scandal by the early nineteenth century.

Eighteenth- and early nineteenth-century wars increased pressures on government to become more organized and efficient, yet the patronage system prevailed, adapting itself in important pockets of policy to become more effective in the selection of better-qualified people for office.[82] At the same time, numerous commissions investigated the workings of government in the late eighteenth century, and reform became synonymous with a search for economy in government, at times accompanied by abolition of particular positions. Purchase of office and profiting from office were outlawed early in the nineteenth century, and the size of government declined.[83] Some departments introduced probationary periods in the employment of officials, and the Treasury, given its fiscal role, grew in importance in recruiting public officials.

Moreover, by the early decades of the nineteenth century, Parliament and the Treasury had far outpaced the importance of the crown as sources of patronage.[84] Still, "the notion of careers in offices simply did not exist. . . . Individuals were simply appointed to them without any basic criteria other than the individual's place in constructing an edifice of deference, status, loyalty, and parliamentary power. . . . No specific education standards were required . . . in some of these offices, no real duties were required."[85] Famously, Edmund Burke railed against the low level of public employment in the late eighteenth century, citing the Board of Trade and Plantations as "a sort of temperate bed of influence; a sort of gently ripening hot-house, where eight members of Parliament receive salaries of a thousand a year, for a certain given time, in order to mature at a proper season, a claim for two thousand, granted for doing less, and on the credit of having toiled so long in that inferior laborious department."[86] The extensive network of patronage rights and appointments came to be associated with the corruption of government, of the monarchy, and of Parliament.

As a consequence of such concerns, the nineteenth century was characterized by another series of commissions selected to look into the practice of public administration in the country and to explore the ways in which public officials were reimbursed—often in unorthodox ways—for their services. Report upon report, and growing public annoyance with the way the business of government was carried out in a rapidly industrializing country, eventually produced greater pressure on recruiters and officeholders to improve the level of competence. Still wedded to patronage, the nineteenth century witnessed increased attention to the educational qualifications of those selected for government position and a gradual modernization of the ways public business was carried out. Offices of government became more subject to uniform procedures and more coherent in terms of salaries and conditions of work.[87]

Thus, as in Prussia, Japan, and France, early solutions to problems of administrative incompetence were not to do away with patronage but to ensure that patronage was adapted to competence. Educational attainment at elite schools and universities became the measure of competence, and British discussion of reform focused great attention on higher-level civil servants. In the class-based society of the nineteenth century, only those whose educations and backgrounds qualified them for leadership positions were considered fully competent to be in influential roles in policy making and administration. Moreover, reform discussion was carried out primarily among political and educational elites, and they were aided by what was at the time only an incipient party system.[88]

CLAIMS OF EMPIRE IN SPAIN.   Don Alonso Pérez de Guzmán el Bueno, the seventh Duke of Medina-Sidonia, was selected by Philip II to lead the Spanish Armada in 1588. In a letter to the king, Don Alonso protested that he had no military experience, was unable to pay for any part of the expedition, and was prone to ill health and seasickness. The king insisted, and the duke did his best as the Captain General of the Ocean Sea, but was certainly not very successful as a sailor or commander. Philip II's motives for the appointment are opaque, although the duke had a reputation as a competent administrator. Perhaps more important, he was known to be a good Catholic.

There was, certainly, a close connection between royal patronage, the Catholic Church, state building, and empire expansion in Spain. The union of Aragon and Castile in the fifteenth century, represented by the marriage of Isabella and Ferdinand, was cemented through loyalty to the church, where common identities were focused, and the recognition of Catholicism as the official and only religion. Indeed, what melded the two kingdoms together was commitment to religion and the institution of the Inquisition, not unified government.[89] Over the centuries after the reconquest of the Spanish heartland from the Moors in 1492, aristocrats, gentry, artisans, and peasants learned that to be Spanish was to be

Catholic. Kings and queens claimed rights to patronage in secular affairs as a private benefit to be bestowed on good Catholics.

Moreover, patronage in the church was as important as patronage in court to the building of a Spanish state and nation, and religious officials were at times appointed to official positions in government.[90] In the sixteenth century, Spanish kings demanded, and were ceded by the pope, rights to name officials of the church in Spain and in its colonies. In 1574, Philip II declared that religious patronage in the form of appointments to positions in the church at home and abroad was his personal right to bestow. The Inquisition was a ready handmaiden to the union of church and monarchical power as it terrified Spain into religious and political orthodoxy and legitimized central authority.

Councils to advise the king and to manage affairs for the crown were the typical bureaucratic form established in Spain, and as these organs matured, they took on increasing administrative and decision-making responsibilities. Domestically, creating order and peace allowed them to cut away at local autonomies. Indeed, much thought was given to how to ensure that traditional institutions—often diverging from one principality to another—could perform effectively in changing circumstances.[91] These strategies worked effectively for Ferdinand and Isabella, largely because the empire was incipient under their reign, and they were noted to be extremely careful in naming capable royal officials.[92] Like other monarchs in Europe, they were inclined to select those with lesser claims to nobility, thus gradually undermining the traditional aristocracy and cementing loyalty to the monarchy.

Under Charles V (1519–1556) and Philip II (1556–1598), the empire grew significantly, and with it, a larger bureaucracy was inevitable, and patronage became important for knitting distant lands to the government.[93] The Council for the Indies was established in 1524 to regularize the administration of the American territories, and with it came increasing need to make decisions and fill positions for the king, important among them the various viceroys given extensive power in the Americas but also closely monitored by the council.[94] Gradually, in the hands of these centralizing kings, the administration of empire introduced greater stability into the bureaucracy, to the extent that the "age of the conquistador" gradually became the "age of the Civil Servant."[95] These were sixteenth-century civil servants, of course, requiring an influential patron to make appointment possible, and the willingness of a king or a council responsible for a particular area of governance or territory to make a position available. Appointments to high-level office privileged legal education and prior experience, a practice that generally resulted in well-qualified people holding office for considerable periods of time, even if they came from a very restricted social strata.[96] At more subordinate levels, competence was often less important than the strategic goal of responding to elite pressures.

Indeed, "No States were more governed in the sixteenth century than those of the King of Spain, if government can be measured by the amount of discussion devoted to any individual problem and by the quantities of paper expended on its solution."[97] In the sixteenth century, this system helped Spain hold vast power in Europe and claim lands in Europe, North Africa, and the Americas. Complaints of malfeasance and corruption were frequent, but given the administrative technologies of the day, government functioned fairly well when monarchs and their closest advisers were serious, focused, and intelligent and the system was effective in building loyalty to the crown. The system created a modicum of hierarchy, order, orthodoxy, and a regularized pattern for administering empire, creating patterns of governance that continue to echo in the public service of many Latin American countries.

Yet an ongoing royal obsession with religious orthodoxy, an empire that was possibly too far-flung, and enduring claims of local autonomy ultimately hindered the ability to create competent administration and eventually weakened the state.[98] Additionally, high-level officials, many of them from the minor nobility and municipal gentry, at times passed positions on to the next generation of a family.[99] The sale of offices was considerable, largely to pursue wars, although some types of offices—judicial ones—were largely protected from this practice, and some kings were noted for their emphasis on the professionalism of their servants in public office.[100] Nevertheless, on such bases, it was difficult to construct either efficiency or effectiveness in the bureaucracy in any durable fashion.

Thus, even with extraordinary wealth flowing from its empire, especially the Americas, dependence on the preferences of those at the top was the critical weakness of the administrative system. The Spanish crown was unable to ensure the leadership to administer well on a consistent basis and to use the wealth to build a strong domestic economy.

When inflation, underdevelopment, and overconsumption threatened the solvency of the crown in the seventeenth century, the sale of offices increased and contributed significantly to royal coffers, but not to royal efficiency or the coherence of government.[101] By late in that century, the Spanish crown was a shadow of what it had been under Philip II, and its monarchs demonstrated considerable capacity for poor judgment in their selection of advisers, spouses, and wars.[102]

The eighteenth century brought some respite when the Bourbon king, Philip V, was placed on the Spanish throne and ushered in an era of administrative and colonial reform. Appointments to public positions took on a clear purpose in the hands of the Bourbons—to establish a more fiscally sound state—and officials were held to higher standards of competence and work in order to increase royal revenues and deal with official corruption.[103] General rules and regular processes of administration based on the French pattern of ministries replaced the Hapsburg system of councils.[104] Salaries and positions became more standardized, and a professional corps of salaried officials became more evident.

For a time, then, when they employed their right to patronage, including the right to name officials of the church at home and abroad, the Bourbons used it with clear and modern purposes of better administration.[105] Reform, and increasing vigilance of imperial affairs, however, also increased the size and expenses of government. Improvements in efficiency were thus consumed by a larger bureaucracy. There was also an ongoing tension between the rights to public office of those born in Spain and those born in the New World; while discrimination against those born abroad was not as rigid as often portrayed, petitions for office clearly favored the *peninsulares*.[106]

Empire also weakened domestic capacity to govern domestic affairs. By the nineteenth century, unresolved issues related to royal absolutism and constitutional monarchy, liberalism and Catholicism, centralism and localism, republicanism and traditionalism, democracy and order, party platforms and personalist leadership, and a variety of related tensions significantly reduced efforts to build a modern state administration. Indeed, from a formidable imperial power in the fifteenth and sixteenth century, Spain became a virtual failed state in the nineteenth. The ancien régime was destroyed, but it was replaced with an unstable and weak state that was constantly challenged by new constitutions, insurrections, military encroachment into politics, fraudulent elections, shifting and ephemeral parties, and government-by-decree laws.[107]

A system of partisan spoils, enshrined in the constitution of 1812, characterized half of government positions until 1918. Under this system, with each new government—and they were frequently changed—a system of rotation in office ensured that government employees would have to resign. This system of *cesantía* prohibited those leaving office from finding employment elsewhere in government.[108] Positions in new governments were offered on the basis of service to political parties, and actual and prospective officeholders were important actors in mobilizing votes in elections. So intense did competition become that the constitution of 1876 established two political parties that would alternate in power, bringing their partisans into public offices as their turn came, while ensuring that the previous "ins" lost their hold on such positions.[109]

Such instability meant that much of government administration retreated to the municipal and provincial level, where it depended on the orientations of local political elites, or *caciques*.[110] Local magnates dominated local government and political parties, and although they were appointed from the center, their central patrons were merely recognizing the local basis for political stability in the country. The bargain between local and central was sealed through the distribution of benefits and appointments to office.[111] In reality, this system functioned through a time-honored process of local bosses who could deliver votes and claim rewards for followers.[112] The network of the *cacique* was carefully constructed. "He created his clientele by handing out jobs—from night watchmen to judge—and by favoring his client."[113] Election results preceded extensive changes in public positions. "By the twentieth century, the state's considerable capacity to offer employment and distribute and redistribute resources was an irreversible trend."[114]

Even as the country adopted many aspects of liberalism, including a modern central bank, a national currency, and secularization of government, the monarch at midcentury still appointed ministers, and they, in turn, appointed their subordinates. "The court functioned . . . as a powerful propeller of patronage, favouritism, and corruption."[115] Lines between military and civilian administration blurred in the context of insurrection and revolution. Efforts to improve the quality of public officials through more merit-based appointments systems were short-lived, and public administration reflected the politically managed alternation of political parties in power. Although constitutions recognized a formally centralized state, "in order to accomplish even the most elementary of tasks—such as tax collection or conscription—ministers needed to act through local notables."[116]

Moreover, administrators at local and central levels, despite revolution and counterrevolution, continued to be drawn from traditional elite families with their roots in provincial centers. Thus, "what characterized this society was its oligarchical nature. . . . The notables—as the members of this oligarchy were called in the language of their time—possessed the political, economic, and social power within the community and managed to retain it by means of a social system based on patronage, loyalty and personal dependence."[117] Ongoing political turmoil meant that the weak Spanish state and its inefficient administration endured well into the twentieth century.

Building a Party System

THE TRIUMPH OF PARTY PATRONAGE IN THE UNITED STATES.   Among countries discussed thus far, the U.S. experience best demonstrates the extensive capacity of the "spirit of party" to expand the reach of patronage for political purposes. Well before the Jacksonian era, all public positions were awarded on the basis of personal appointments. In the early years of the republic, those controlling patronage focused considerable attention on ensuring the "fitness of character" of potential officeholders. Even in those early years, however, the spirit of party encouraged Federalists and Republicans to be concerned about the allocation of public positions, and they kept track of which faction received how many of what kinds of appointments.

Under George Washington, who, as president, sighed in annoyance that he found "the selection of proper characters an arduous duty," the task of appointment to public office was considered seriously as setting in place the standards for public conduct in the small new republic.[118] Indeed, Washington and his first cabinets set high standards for appointments—character, industriousness, education, conduct, prudence, respectability, marriage.[119] The task occupied considerable time of the president and his department heads, even though the government of the 1790s was small—the two rooms that housed the Department of State 1792 contained the secretary and six officials, among them a messenger and a doorkeeper, and this was a tripling of officials from three years before.[120] At the time, there were fewer than eight hundred people working for the federal government in Philadelphia and in the field service, largely made up of customs officials and postmasters.[121]

While filling top positions was at times difficult in the new republic, appointments were largely made in response to letters of application, most of which were directed to the president or top-level executive officials.[122] Beyond advising and consenting to high-level positions, Congress was not involved, nor does it seem that senators and representatives were much bothered by appeals for public office. The standards were set by the president and echoed by the orientations of his cabinet. Appointed without terms of tenure, most officials below those at the top echelon were expected to remain long in their positions. While in some departments there were opportunities for advancement, in general there was no career ladder or expectation of career development, and the president early on acquired the ability to remove officers at will.

Although fitness of character consistently outweighed other criteria of appointment, early leaders regarded such criteria as military service, regional origin, and loyalty to the new state. Nepotism was rare, although not unknown, as the case of John Adams suggests. It was, of course, not long after the founding of the republic that the spirit of party and factionalism emerged, but appointing officials of the first generation of leadership were generally averse to recognizing it publicly or making it a criterion for officeholding. Given the overriding concern with character, the business of government was the business of gentlemen. This business was carried out in ways that were slow and inefficient, but they were not noticeably corrupt in operation.[123]

Nevertheless, by the early nineteenth century, the Federalists were weighing political orientations more seriously. Of considerable concern as Thomas Jefferson became the third president was whether his appointments would subordinate character, as defined by the Federalists, to Republicanism. After some uncertainty in the first two years in office, Jefferson made clear that the idea of a governing elite of gentlemen—stable and respectable—would hold strong, even while he gradually appointed more Republicans to office as positions held by earlier appointees became vacant. For Jefferson, respectability was a central criterion for public office, at whatever level.[124] Leonard White, who chronicled the administration of government in the first century of the new republic, concludes that, "Party did not seriously affect administration from 1801 to 1829; there were no changes in party control and the Federalist conception of a permanent public service was already strong enough . . . to keep party demands upon administration under control."[125] In Jefferson's two terms, however, about one-quarter of presidential appointments changed hands.[126] Meanwhile, members of Congress were gaining increased ability to manage patronage at the state level for electoral gains, even as at the federal level the army and the navy began administering examinations as part of the recruitment process for service.[127]

By 1820, and despite the maintenance of Jeffersonian principles, patronage appointments had emerged as issues of contention between the executive and the legislature, and were a heavy burden for presidents and other officials in positions to make appointments. For John Quincy Adams, office seekers were "wolves of the antechamber, prowling for offices."[128] By the election of Andrew Jackson as Adams's successor in 1828, concerns about personal loyalty combined with political orientation became haunting issues in the appointment of officials for all levels of office.[129]

Yet under Jackson, and contrary to popular belief, recruitment to office based on partisanship was restrained, although debates and anxiety about acquiring and losing positions were legion.[130] Contemporary accounts suggest that about 10 percent of positions changed hands in the first years of Jackson's presidency, increasing to a total of about 20 percent when he left office in 1837.[131] These proportions are significant, but do not reach the level of party "purges" often assumed. Yet, the era of party government, emerging under Jackson and becoming full-blown in the 1830s, did much to increase the identification of patronage with party and corruption, and the notion of "spoils of war" as a consequence of electoral victory became widespread.[132] The spoils system—as a basic characteristic of public life, linking elections to the colonization of public administration by partisans—was an artifact of nineteenth-century politics in the United States.

While currently "spoils system" is explained in terms of winning and losing elections and the crass necessity of paying off political promises and rewarding the faithful, the term's inception in the United States contained an explanatory logic that was less scornful and more seductive. For Jackson, in particular, government in a democracy could and should be carried out by democrats, ordinary citizens who had an opportunity to be part of the government of the day. The work of government was relatively simple, Jacksonians claimed, and "In a country where offices are created solely for the benefit of the people no one man has any more intrinsic right to official station than another."[133] Moreover, the principle of rotation in office held that it was a good and beneficial thing that the management of government administration should change hands on a regular basis; public office should not be considered the property of incumbents.[134] If almost everyone (every male, that is) is capable of carrying out the business of government, and if rotation in office is a reflection of democratic values as well as a hindrance to an entrenched and possibly corrupt elite of officeholders, then it would make sense to provide as broad an opportunity as possible for citizens to engage in government and have an opportunity for public service.

The rationale for everyman's administration, of course, was easily converted into selection by party. Jackson's successor, Martin Van Buren, presided over appointments that became increasingly, if only gradually, put to the test of party and personal loyalty. A change of party in the presidency in 1841 ushered in a period of extensive rotation in office as criteria of party and party activism became the critical determinants of appointment. In the largest employer of federal officials, the post office, some 84 percent of postmasters were replaced in the second half of the 1840s.[135] Under John Tyler, one-third of government positions changed hands; James Buchanan turned party patronage into an explicit objective of office holding.[136]

As the system grew in size and acceptance, the terms of the exchange clarified. Obligations to local party machines—the engines behind not only local but also federal appointments—involved, of course, the need to vote for the appropriate party, and also electioneering responsibilities and regular contributions to party coffers. By the time of Lincoln, who, as a candidate, promised to do something about the partisanship of public appointments, the clamor for public office had become notorious. Yet he, like his predecessors, was hard pressed to avoid its claims. He turned seventeen hundred of his predecessor's appointees out of office.[137]

Understanding its more positive consequences, however, Lincoln used patronage judiciously to build support within a fractured Republican Party and Congress. Slowly, forces of reform began to emerge, but even after the passage of the Pendleton Act in 1883, some fifty thousand postal positions changed hands under President Benjamin Harrison.[138]

The reach of the partisan patronage system expanded in part because government itself was expanding. Particularly as the country grew in population and expanse, offices in the post and tax offices grew. In 1800, some three thousand officials worked for the federal government; by 1860, they numbered fifty thousand, and over one hundred thousand by 1880.[139] And, given the decentralized nature of the American government, with state and local governments responsible for many public functions, patronage appointments at the federal level were compounded by much more numerous appointments—increasingly controlled by party machines—at state and municipal level. In general, the salaries were low, but the opportunities for appointment were legion, and the connection between party and patronage was increasingly clear. Loyalty to party was central to midcentury politics, and in practice this included increasingly clear obligations on officeholders to contribute to party coffers and to the hard work of getting out the vote at election time. The stakes were accordingly high for elections, even as the number of elected positions was also growing along with the nation.

While under the Federalists control of public office was a claim of the executive, the issue of whether presidents or Congress would control patronage emerged as a critical conflict in the years after Jefferson. Beginning in 1820, more executive appointments required confirmation; by the mid-1850s, congressmen held vast powers of appointment for federal officials assigned to their districts and states.[140] The Tenure of Office Act of 1867 claimed senatorial prerogatives over the removal of department heads and anyone in the executive whose position required the advice and consent of the Senate—this was a clear statement of congressional capture of the patronage system.[141]

And Congress, in turn, was generally the creature of local party organizations; positions in government belonged to the party winning elections, a contest determined by the mobilization of local voting. Indeed, presidents from John Quincy Adams on complained of the incessant lobbying they endured for this person or that to fill this or that position. Yet senators and representatives equally complained of the pressure they were under from state and local party officials, those who stood at the grass roots in the distribution-of-offices chain. Daniel Carpenter argues that the spoils system "thoroughly yoked national officers to state and local party machines."[142] And this network of local, state, and national office holding steadily increased the powers of Congress—and the decline of the executive—until the presidency of Rutherford B. Hayes, when the trajectory was reversed.[143]

Yet even as the patronage system expanded and became notorious, some offices, especially those involving comptrollers, auditors, some clerkships, the military, and some employees of specialized technical agencies, were characterized by greater permanence and continuity in office.[144] Patronage and rotation in office were the hallmarks of the Jacksonian era of party government and the Republican era that succeeded it, but underlying it was a small but relatively stable system of officialdom that maintained office and kept the work of government going.[145] For some such offices, examinations existed at the departmental level. Gradually, in some offices and bureaus more than others, competent, professional, and focused administration and administrators emerged, as Daniel Carpenter has documented.[146] Moreover, important infrastructure, services, and regulatory regimes emerged in this period, often staffed by competent and committed public officials, many of whom held appointed office.

Despite these caveats, outrage at the manifest evidence of instability, incompetence, and corruption in public office accompanied the expansion of the patronage system. Even before the Civil War, energetic citizens—particularly those from emerging professional classes of doctors, lawyers, clergy, journalists, professors, and businessmen—criticized the emergence and growth of party-based patronage. With the founding of the American Social Science Association in 1865, reformers could count on a national organization whose purpose was to promote probity in public office.[147] Reform proposals abounded, put forth by citizen associations, congressmen, and presidents. None gained serious support among parties or Congress, however.

Then came the assassination of President James Garfield by an unsuccessful office seeker and the generation of enough demand from a range of reformist groups and citizens for the passage of a civil service reform.

Yet the Pendleton Act of 1883 had only a marginal impact on the spoils system. In the post office under President Grover Cleveland, some 40,000 postmaster positions changed hands, a number that reached 50,000 under his successor, Benjamin Harrison, and 78,500 by 1896.[148] In 1900, the majority of over two hundred thousand federal government positions remained available for patronage appointments.[149] Interestingly, the creation of modern cities in the United States, the construction of great works of physical infrastructure, and the application of science to improve public health coincided with a period of massive party-based patronage and notorious urban machines, where patronage reigned supreme.[150] The association of patronage systems with premodern political systems is certainly belied by this and other examples.

Yet the party-based appointments system in the United States did much to cement popular—and scholarly—opinion that patronage is synonymous with corruption and incompetence. A longer history suggests that the extent of patronage in the United States was not always a measure of bad governance. The first forty years of the republic witnessed a patronage system in the service of government by "gentlemen," chosen with an eye to issues of character and commitment to public service, as well as loyalty to the new government and its leadership. In addition, even at the height of a spoils system that fully met definitions of corruption and incompetence, important and effective new bureaus emerged, cities acquired extensive new physical and social infrastructure, and roads, canals, and railroads spread across a huge continent. Each of these accomplishments required some competence in administration, and at the bureau level, patronage was often employed to produce it.

Conclusion

Patronage is ubiquitous in the history of the emergence of the modern state. Its extended history would no doubt return us to the emergence of early efforts to organize human society, but this adds too much to the tale. Its ubiquity in public life may point to the essentially sinful and self-interested nature of human beings through evidence of sloth, corruption, lack of accountability, unresponsiveness and irresponsibility, graft, favoritism, and much, much more. But it may just as easily suggest that patronage in public life is an eminently flexible mechanism for achieving leadership goals. As indicated, it was an important tool used in concentrating power in authoritarian states, enhancing the survival of class elites, and providing for the expansion of mass democracy. Among mechanisms for organizational management, it is unique in providing very direct incentives for loyalty to the objectives of those who control it. In many ways, it deals effectively with the principal-agent problem that captures so much scholarly concern about government. The cases of Prussia, Japan, and France can even be used to indicate that patronage is not incompatible with the evolution of high standards of performance in public service.

This is, in fact, the difficulty of assessing the impact of patronage on government. If the Prussians and the Japanese could adapt the use of patronage to the creation of strong and absolutist states and, as with the French, use it as a foundation for an elitist and competent public service, and if the British could employ patronage to help wrest control of government from absolute monarchs to be used by Parliament and elites to uphold local powers and privileges—not to mention those of class—and if Spain could build and destroy empire through its use, and if leaders in the United States could adapt it first to government by gentlemen and then by mass political parties, what can be said about its purpose and its contributions to public life? Indeed, the nature of patronage itself is that it serves the extremely useful purpose of allowing those who control it to mold its impact to their own purposes, whether these be noble and exalted or sinful and perverse.

Table 1.1 provides a summary of this historical survey of patronage in the development of six modern states. It indicates that it was used for distinct ends across and within countries and that its use was consistently constrained by alternative forms of staffing the public service—through claims of heredity, sale of office, and restrictions related to education, clan, and caste. In each case, patronage systems were challenged, and they faced limitations in what they were able to achieve. Yet they supported stability, competence, and state-ness as often as they introduced incompetence and instability.

Clearly, then, patronage systems are diverse because those who manage them have diverse purposes and because such systems have considerable capacity to be molded to these purposes. Thus, the utility of patronage is simultaneously enhanced and diminished by its capriciousness. In

Table 1.1. Patronage systems in history: diversity, limitations, and achievements

Country	Ends sought through patronage system	Constraints on use of patronage	Important system limitations	Important system accomplishments
Prussia	State building; state unification; military hegemony over state; subordination of independent nobility; royal absolutism; order, stability, efficiency; loyalty to the state	Claims of hereditary rights to office; variable capacity of monarchs to supervise; gradual development of administrative autonomy	Elite bias in appointments; corruption	Stability, efficiency, and competence of public administration; technical and professional expertise; loyalty to abstract conception of state; high status of public officials
Japan	Clan and territorial control; state unification; centralization; consolidation of power of clan and class	Clan and territorial boundaries and commitments; focus on skills of warfare rather than administration	Elite bias in appointments; narrow recruitment pool; customary laws and loyalties	Stability and competence of public administration; technical and professional expertise; loyalty to abstract conception of state in guise of emperor; high status of public officials

France	Union of church and royal household; state building; centralization of power; royal absolutism; revolutionary change; technical and professional expertise in government; organized state administration	Claims of hereditary rights to office; sale of offices; intense competition for office	Competition for control of system; elite bias in appointments; corruption; competition among ministers	Stability of administration in an unstable polity; technical and professional expertise; loyalty to abstract conception of state; high status of public officials
Britain	Union of church and royal household; state building; control of government by crown; control of government by Parliament; control of Parliament by party; hegemony of Treasury over appointments	Claims of hereditary rights to office; sale of offices and life tenure; local control of administration; party development and discipline	Elite bias in appointments; corruption; ongoing competition and occasional violence over control of system; localism and competing claims to positions; haphazard public administration	Gradual evolution of Treasury control of appointments; high status of public officials; competence based on education as criterion

Table 1.1. (continued)

Country	Ends sought through patronage system	Constraints on use of patronage	Important system limitations	Important system accomplishments
Spain	Union of church and royal household; religious and political orthodoxy; state building; royal absolutism; administration of empire; fiscal reform and improved administration	Sale of offices; claims for local autonomy; claims for hereditary rights to office; variable capacity of monarchs to supervise	Corruption; lack of efficiency, effectiveness; elite bias in appointments; power of *caciques*; incompetence and disarray	Creation of hierarchy and order; administration of far-flung empire
United States	Consolidation of government by gentlemen; consolidation of government by party; rotation in office and democratic values; party and party machine building; bureau-based development of expertise and professionalism	Long terms in office; competition for control of appointments; intense competition for positions	Corruption; inefficiency; incompetence; localism and federal government captive to local and state interests	Electoral engagement of citizens; some opportunity for upward mobility; development of bureau-based competence; support for industrialization and urbanization; mobilization of citizens to oppose the system

the short term, it is a responsive mechanism for leadership, one clearly worth fighting to retain; over a longer period, its instability can become embedded in government and in policy, a mechanism that cannot be trusted for the ends it seeks. It is too easily bent to political and personal ends.

This chapter has emphasized the enduring quality of institutions that serve as mechanisms for staffing the state. In the six case study countries, the institution of patronage as a basis for recruitment to public office was relatively stable over time, yet it was used to distinct purposes. In appreciating the "stickiness" of such rules of the game, then, it is also important to recognize the extent to which they can be adapted to the concerns of powerful actors and can be useful for for important macropolitical objectives when skillfully employed. Patronage systems appear to have considerable capacity to endure and to adapt.

Yet, given what we have seen about the flexibility and utility of patronage systems, an appropriate question is not why they endure so long and in so many different places, but how they come to be replaced by other systems of recruitment into public office. Each of the countries surveyed in this chapter traded patronage for formal civil service systems in which recruitment is managed by an organization that is relatively far removed from the purposes of politicians. They did so, however, in distinct ways. This is the topic of the next chapter.

CHAPTER 2

Politics in the Construction of Reform

Patronage systems flourished in distinct patterns across history, across countries, and within countries. So, too, did reform initiatives. The countries considered as historical cases in Chapter 1 all established career civil services in the nineteenth and early twentieth centuries. Given the embedded nature of the institution of personal and political appointment to staff the public sector, reforms did not "just happen." They were the result of deliberate initiatives that created conflict among potential winners and losers, played out within constraints and opportunities set by the past. Often, reforms that put new rules of the game into practice were preceded by failed initiatives to achieve the same goal, suggesting the importance of contingent political moments and the ability of political agents to take advantage of them to introduce new structures and strictures for the public service.

This chapter explores the construction of reform in the six countries whose histories were just reviewed for what they could illuminate about the institution of patronage in the public service. It shows that legacies of the past influence choices for new institutions, but that such choices also depend on negotiation among strategic actors, the way in which reform projects are envisioned, and the moments selected for introducing change. Moreover, as will be indicated in the next chapter, the consequences of the change initiatives reviewed here drove subsequent efforts to introduce reform. Legacies of the past help frame stories of reform, yet the past is also layered by long histories of choice and consequence.

In terms of broad patterns, the cases of Prussia, Japan, Britain, France, the United States, and Spain suggest some important similarities and differences in the dynamics of reform. Prussia and Japan, for example, followed a path of imposing change from the top down, using the potential of centralized and authoritarian political structures to co-opt potential losers into new rules of the game. Britain and France were characterized by lengthy processes of evolution that worked to legitimize prior patterns of elite control over the public service. The case of the United States indicates a pattern of extensive public contestation marked by ongoing negotiation over wins and loses, and the Spanish experience demonstrates that institutional change within the context of a weak state is extremely difficult, prolonged, and inconclusive. Five of the cases—the exception is the United States—demonstrate relatively closed political processes in which those engaged in conflict over the shape of the public service were primarily insiders in government.

Reform and Co-optation from the Top Down: Prussia and Japan

In Prussia and Japan, the emergence of career civil service systems was characterized by top-down reforms that increasingly emphasized education and examinations as means to enter public service. In these processes, aristocratic elites with traditional claims to public office were privileged in the acquisition of the educations that meant success in the examinations. In this sense, then, civil service systems were imposed, and the claims of traditional elites to patronage were managed and transformed through an educational buyout that enshrined competence and loyalty to the state as traits that characterized successful bureaucratic careers. The prior authoritarian monopoly on patronage thus paved the way for statist civil services that were relatively well insulated from partisan pressures. In these two cases, reform was managed by state actors concerned primarily about the consolidation of regime power.

Prussia and the Servants of the State

Long before transitions to career civil services in other countries, administration became a stable career and a profession in Prussia. Examinations for entry (1771), tenure in office (1797), promotion based on seniority (late eighteenth century), a schedule of salaries (late eighteenth, early nineteenth centuries), declaration of a profession open to talent (1807), and pensions (1825) clearly indicated the direction of change. Indeed, Max Weber's ideal type of a rational-legal bureaucracy was largely fashioned on what the Prussian/German bureaucracy had become by late in the nineteenth century, and his view that such a system emerged inevitably with industrialization, capitalism, and urbanization was deeply influenced by the German case. So, too, were his fears about the power of bureaucracy in modern societies.

In Prussia, the consolidation of an autonomous career civil service was traditionally constrained by the strong claims of aristocracy for preferment in government positions. While monarchical absolutism had been clearly established in the eighteenth century and professionalism in the public service was strongly emphasized, social elites had not relinquished their rights to public office. Thus, for example, when recruitment by examination to high-level office was introduced in 1771, entrenched privileges were acknowledged through the exemption of those with claims to nobility. Given the very strong presence of those with noble backgrounds in the public service at the time, especially at higher levels, this was a significant exception. Nevertheless, by instituting such examinations, the criteria for admission to officialdom were narrowed and made more autonomous from the preferences of monarchs; the right of the state to set such criteria was reinforced.

Even in acknowledging the rights of elites to public office, Prussian reformers helped insulate them from monarchical power. In 1794, for example, civil and military officials were recognized as corporate estates, fitted for lifetime careers of service to the state.[1] Gradually, then, "royal servants" began to refer to themselves as "servants of the state," and considerable patronage power devolved to ministers and other high-level officials.[2] At the same time, such changes further imbued officials with a sense of caste and social entitlement.[3]

Napoléon put an end to the status and privileges of the Prussian army and the authoritarian state bureaucrats in 1806, however. In the ashes of the battles of Jena and Auerstädt, Prussia almost ceased to exist. Subsequent reformers sought to restructure the state in the image of its efficient and well-ordered past. Reacting against its insignificance in Napoléon's Europe, Prussian leaders recast the army in a more nationalist mold, further wedding it to the state, and revamped the civil administration to embrace a renewed sense of duty and service to the state. Central to these reforms were initiatives to open commerce, government, and the military to greater social mobility—putting a formal end to the class system that had been frozen in time through public policies in earlier centuries, and ending hereditary serfdom and entitlements to office.

Interestingly, those who were the lead architects of the new Prussia in the early nineteenth century, and who significantly curtailed the role of patronage and aristocratic claims to public office, were raised to prominence through the old aristocratic patronage system. Baron Heinrich vom Stein had enjoyed a series of appointments under King Frederick II and Frederick William III, and Count Karl August von Hardenberg was also privileged through the former class-based patronage system.[4] Acting in the name of the monarch, they restructured the government around organizations focused on tasks rather than geography and introduced more efficient decision-making structures.[5] They strongly promoted the reform and expansion of education as a criterion for entry into the public service.[6]

The reformist initiatives of Stein and Hardenberg further encouraged a view of the state as supreme and the importance of competence for positions in the state.[7] Competence, in fact, should trump noble status, declared Hardenberg, known as the "first dictator of the bureaucracy." "Every position in the State, without exception," he opined, "is to be open not to this or that caste, but to the service and the skill and competence from all strata," and even liberals applauded the role set out for the state, based as it was on progressive principles of order and law.[8] Thus, by midcentury, one scholar has suggested that the state bureaucracy in Prussia emerged to have a role "comparable to that of Plato's guardian class."[9] And, accordingly, "the system of royal absolutism [was] replaced by a system of bureaucratic absolutism."[10] Through a series of laws, decrees, and regulations—and through the gradual replacement of aristocratic claims by those of education—the Hohenzollerns were replaced in all but name by powerful ministers and their bureaucratic empires.[11] This was largely accomplished through the co-optation of those who held alternative claims to public office.

This period of reform and its aftermath was not without its tensions, of course. Within the bureaucracy, for example, traditional aristocratic claims to office vied with those of emergent social classes. There were also tensions among generations as education became more important to recruitment, and the claims of birth became less so. In the relationship of the bureaucracy to the society, public officials were drawn into midcentury debates and conflicts over political representation and liberal reform.[12] Similarly, the right of public officials to be active in politics and government was tested and repressed.[13] Despite these tensions, changes in the criteria for recruitment were gradual and almost imperceptible, and the state that emerged from the political crises of midcentury increasingly demanded absolute loyalty from its servants and empowered those servants to act for the state.[14]

The transformation of the Prussian bureaucracy—which then modeled the German administration after formal unification in 1871—began early and was characterized by a gradual limitation on the personal power of the monarch, often brought about by the actions of monarchs themselves, and then by the gradual co-optation of elites who claimed traditional rights to office. Examinations increasingly served to provide entry to public positions, and in 1846, administrators were required to have university educations, and legal education above all else.[15] While those able to acquire such educations were scions of wealthy families, they no longer had to be of aristocratic origin.[16] High-level state actors managed the particular moments in which credentialing for public service became more formal and constricting.

Yet even as the proportions of those with noble backgrounds in the bureaucracy shifted downward over the course of the century, their elite status was ensured. Inherited attitudes of superiority, together with the expense of the study of law and the long period of unpaid apprenticeship that followed it, gave the sons of social elites an upper hand in what became a very competitive recruitment process.[17] They could no longer succeed by ascription, but their social and educational backgrounds ensured that they had privileged access to positions of importance. Even as the proportion of those from the nobility—and those with fathers in administrative office—declined, the proportions of the wealthy increased, and wealth tended to become conflated with education.[18]

As with prior initiatives that affected the composition of the state, changes in preferences for recruitment were imposed autocratically. The process was effective; Prussia had the most efficient and least corrupt public administration in Europe by midcentury.[19] The *Rechtsstaat*, embedded in the education system and the focus on law for entry to public service, became an overriding ideology of a public service. And, through the nineteenth century, amid struggles for liberal reform and conservative resistance, nationalist claims and the consolidation of Prussia and the German states, the bureaucracy followed a roughly continuous trajectory toward greater insulation in educational credentialing and recruitment. Reflecting the focus of unification as a federation, however, the civil service continued to be organized in terms of the federative units, or *Länder*.

Across time, then, what is evident in the development of a professional civil service in Prussia was its imposition from above, its co-optation of aristocratic elites, and the paucity of open struggle over patronage. There was no evident engagement of public opinion or interest groups, no parties contesting whose partisans could hold office; no civil society demanding reform. Monarchical control ceded to an autonomous bureaucracy colonized by an elite of status and education in a process that was instigated and institutionalized by officials of the state, acting at the behest of regime leaders.

Japan and the Transformation of a Restoration

The Meiji Restoration that began in 1868 introduced the critical era in the creation of a professional civil service in Japan. Within three decades, a formal set of rules based on access to education, entry by examination, and a career system ending with provision of a pension was created and consolidated. It established a social and economic elite in public office and encouraged the emergence of educational qualifications specific to particular government organizations, constraining lateral movement in the bureaucracy. Like the case of Prussia, the Japanese public bureaucracy developed in relative insulation from the claims of party politics, the parliament, or public demands for improvement in the functions of government. As in Prussia/Germany, a career civil service system was largely the creation of authoritarian imposition.

As indicated in Chapter 1, rank and birth determined recruitment to public office under the Tokugawa dynasty; stipends were a recognition of inherited rank, not a payment for services.[20] With the restoration in 1868, loyalty to the emperor (initially determined by the timing of adhesion to the cause of imperial reinstatement) and experience in the struggle were primary determinants of access to government positions, discriminating among elites, and engaging many from the lower ranks of the samurai. In 1871, as traditional rank and heredity were officially eliminated when domains were replaced by prefectures, the stage was set for the centralization of government power and, with it, government service.[21] Governors, appointed by the central state, replaced the relatively autonomous lords of the domains who had held local power under the Tokugawa. Governors in turn took charge of appointments of all officials at local levels, underscoring the extent to which local power had succumbed to central power. "By 1878, there was a seamless thread of hierarchy that stretched from the offices of the new leaders down to the smallest village by way of the prefectural governors."[22] This hierarchy continued to be based on personal appointments and ties of loyalty to superiors.

To establish their legitimacy to hold public office and to discourage challenges to their control of government, however, the samurai of the Restoration soon established a set of rules that determined who would hold office, what duties characterized different offices, and how offices related to each other in a formal hierarchy, all of this long before they were pressured into establishing a constitution.[23] Thus, an emphasis on process came to distinguish the emergent Japanese bureaucracy and administrative system. And, like the early Prussian bureaucracy, the state in the guise of the emperor—who granted the constitution of 1889—became the object of loyalty. "In bestowing these powers on the emperor, the Meiji leaders ensured for themselves and their civil bureaucratic colleagues the isolation of the political parties from effective control over policy-making and administration. These were in the hands of the emperor and his administrators, who were legally his servants," and who expressed his will.[24] In this way, public administration came to be subordinate to the state yet superior to the population and to emergent political parties.

Until the 1880s, however, although there were examinations to determine literacy at lower levels in the bureaucracy, little constrained the appointment power of upper-level administrators and leaders. Moreover, political leadership was generally selected from these levels of the bureaucracy.[25] Cliques and factions abounded in the first years of the Restoration. As the Meiji leadership searched for a more stable basis for legitimate claims to public office, however, they increasingly empha-sized education. Unlike the British and the French, who had ancient and agreed-upon educational structures to define qualifications for public office, the Meiji leadership had to identify appropriate educational prepa-ration for public office. Their task was made easier by the preeminence of Tokyo Imperial University, but more difficult by the incursion of West-ern knowledge, acquired in a variety of ways from a variety of sources, that had come to influence government decision making in the 1870s and 1880s.[26] In 1884, Western education became a necessary requisite for higher-level public servants in some departments. More generally, the most important preparation was graduation from Tokyo University with a degree in law.

Concerned about the public service, the Meiji leadership sent Itō Hiro-bumi to study European constitutions in 1882. Later, as he became head of the Bureau for the Investigation of Public Institutes, established in 1884, his remit included drafting a constitution; and in 1887, while Hiro-bumi was prime minister, examinations as a route to entry into the public service were established. His views, as well as those of the Meiji oligarchs, were clearly on the side of imperial rather than democratic principles in terms of how the public service should be formed.[27] In particular, study in Germany had underscored his prior belief that public servants should serve the emperor rather than respond to a parliamentary government.[28] The 1889 constitution declared that Japanese "subjects" were eligible for appointment to the public service, on the condition that they had neces-sary qualifications. Formally, then, this constitutional moment, managed by state elites, established the civil service system.

The qualifications required for public service, however, severely re-stricted actual access to it. Initially, when rules ensuring examinations for entrants at both higher and lower levels were established, graduates of Tokyo University were exempted, increasing incentives for its graduates to enter the public service; as their numbers swelled, extending the examinations to this group was one way of dealing with demands for employment.[29] Examination of general rather than specialized knowl-edge further privileged the study of law for prospective civil servants.[30] By 1894, an examination system was fully in place, although appoint-ments to the level of bureau chief and governor continued to be personal.[31] Then, in 1899, direct appointments in the name of the emperor were restricted to ministerial levels and like positions.[32] The introduction of pensions further encouraged the emergence of a stable career system, providing incentives for remaining in service for long periods of time.

Thus, the examination system clearly benefited those who were able to acquire specific forms of education in specific schools, from the elementary through the university level—indeed the system severely constrained others. "Tokyo University students were confined in fact if not by statute to the sons of upper- and upper-middle class families (of civil bureaucrats, military officers, landlords, rich farmers, businessmen, and industrialists), except for a very small number of students holding scholarships provided by former feudal lords and other rich people."[33] A strong preference for seniority in career advancement as well as increased emphasis on specialized education encouraged the development of careers within one department or ministry. In a sense, then, an appointment system for a stable and professional civil service held at its core an ascriptive character based on education and class.[34] By increasingly defining the educational criteria needed for public office, Meiji reformers coopted those with class-based claims to preference into a new career system.

Each of the steps that led to the institutionalization of the career civil service in Japan was imposed by the Meiji leadership, in the name of the emperor, with no active engagement of those beyond the leadership. Their purpose was clearly to insulate the bureaucracy from the parliament and party influence. At the turn of the century, when an emergent party system sought to use patronage for access to government positions, the still-active Meiji leadership responded by further insulating the civil bureaucracy from party influence. "In sum, the phalanx of civil service regulations put into force between 1884 and 1899 produced a career structure that was characterized by its emphasis on an objective test of knowledge for entrance and on seniority, hierarchy, highly organization-specific specialization and differentiation, and career as integral elements of the role."[35]

The development of a career civil service system was one face of the "revolution from above" crafted by the leaders of the Meiji Restoration. A consolidated, centralized, and authoritarian state with a powerful executive was clearly a goal of the Meiji reformers, allowing Japan to experience a "transformation of society from a system of fixed statuses to a more fluid, merit-based social order."[36] Over three decades in the late nineteenth century, then, an elite civil service was the well-organized, well-trained, and competent heir of the elite patronage system that predated it.

Reform through Elite Compromise: Britain and France

In Britain and France, the transformation of a patronage system into a merit-based career civil service involved a process of the gradual exclusion of patronage appointments. In both cases, the principal actors were found within government, although the engagement of elites across government was broader than in the cases of Prussia/Germany and Japan. In contrast to the authoritarian imposition of new rules and criteria for recruitment, the cases of Britain and France indicate a gradual process of elite compromise with new standards for the public service. The professional civil service in both countries was the result of a long process of evolution in which claims to patronage were first narrowed by increasing emphasis on education, then examinations gradually determined competence for office, and eventually structured systems for appointment were introduced. In both cases, this evolution ensured a clear connection between educational qualifications and examinations for entry.

Britain and Its Suitably Educated Gentlemen

As indicated in the previous chapter, control over patronage was at stake in conflicts between king and Parliament in Britain for several centuries; Parliament had clearly triumphed by the early nineteenth century, and with it, the capacity of local elites to allocate positions of influence and to play a central role in determining parliamentary representation. The result of an ongoing struggle over the right to appoint was important in providing individual members of Parliament, especially backbenchers, with greater power in government, particularly in the absence of a well-defined party system.[37]

Well into the nineteenth century, then, patronage provided the cement of an informal allocation of power between central and local and between a parliamentary executive and the administration of government, and was the fundamental process through which higher-level positions in government (and in Parliament itself) were allocated. The counterpart of this decentralization for the staffing of important positions in government was the devolution to relatively autonomous department heads of the right to recruit their subordinates. Characteristically, they adopted distinct criteria and procedures to hire such officials, who then were virtually certain to be retained in the same position for a lifetime.[38]

Within this broad-brush history were other struggles that became more apparent as the nineteenth century wore on: between the local interests that controlled Parliament and the cabinet that controlled the government; and between the departments of government and a Treasury eager to claim primacy over recruitment into and management of the public service. Ultimately, the widespread practice of patronage was a victim of this struggle, losing out to merit by examination for recruitment, a lifetime career with promotion based on performance, and pensioning after a given term of service. With only few moments when the volume was turned up loud, however, these struggles were quiet ones, engaging relatively few people and only occasionally alarming Victorian gentlemen and gentlewomen about the possible undermining of a government and a society based on class and "fit" for public office.[39]

Thus, the evolution of a professional civil service system in Britain was very much that—evolutionary. Gradually, the idea that a position in government was a sinecure gave way to a notion of a contract for public service. Gradually, the idea of fees gave way to the notion of salaries. Gradually, the principle of merit was introduced side by side with patronage at the departmental level, and political parties gradually became more organized at the central level to claim a place in determining policy that would be adopted by the government of the day, represented in the cabinet. Gradually, the Treasury gained greater capacity to set standards for public employment, and gradually, the departments of government relinquished to the Treasury their appointive power. When the moment for the introduction of government-wide standards and procedures for the civil service were introduced through Orders in Council in 1870 and 1871, much that was officially established was already in place. What differentiated the evolution of the British system from that of Prussia/Germany and Japan was intense competition over appointment power, a lingering preference for patronage, and the role of social class in constructing an elite compromise.

In this evolutionary story, however, key actors moved the process along and made critical decisions at particular moments. Central among them were Charles Trevelyan and William Gladstone, who spent twenty years pushing and pulling Parliament and government departments toward reform. Trevelyan's role was that of the zealot, and Gladstone's was primarily to signal when the timing was right to push forward with reform.

The Treasury Department, where Britain's professional civil service was eventually housed, was also where it began. In the 1830s, the Treasury introduced a basic examination system for its officials in which three individuals were presented for each position; the highest scorer—an outcome that could be managed to preserve patronage through the selection of the three contestants—was hired.[40] In the same period, some departments began administering literacy tests to those who were appointed to office. In addition, by the 1850s, many departments had introduced a period of probation for newly hired officers.[41] At the same time, the Treasury, through its control over a number of appointments, its role in funding activities of government, and its capacity to manage an incipient pension system, was in a good position to lead the process for institutionalizing a career civil service, and this position was strengthened as it seized the initiative to claim preeminence in appointment power.

Propitiously, Trevelyan, raised to prominence in the exceedingly well-organized civil service of the East India Company, became permanent secretary of the treasury in 1840. Firmly self-righteous, "a cocktail of evangelism, intelligence and family connection," he was zealous in his commitment to change.[42] His initial aim was to ensure the proper functioning of the Treasury; soon, the reform of the civil service became his life's purpose. He was guided by his understanding of the Indian Civil Service, at the time a service that boasted a training institute (Haileybury College), insistence on competence in local languages, law, history, and other topics, as well as pride—or outright arrogance—in believing that generalists were well fitted to tackle most problems of governance.[43] According to Lord Macaulay, who was instrumental in institutionalizing entry examinations in this service, "We believe that men who have been engaged, up to 21 or 22, in studies which have no immediate connection with the business of any profession, and of which the effect is merely to open, to invigorate, to enrich the mind, will generally be found in the business of every profession superior to men who had, at 18 or 19, devoted themselves to the special studies of their calling," a statement echoed a century later in terms of the importance of developing "mental muscles" through the study of any topic of sufficient difficulty.[44]

First appearing in Parliament in 1848 to promote reform, Trevelyan brought together two ideas that would underlie the effort to improve government—individual merit judged on the basis of examinations, and efficiency based on a division of tasks determined by educational attainment.[45] Thus, he proposed, some work was mechanical or routine in nature, and other work required "intellect" to carry out; each type of work necessitated a distinct educational background. For all his initial efforts, however, he evoked little sympathy for his scheme in Parliament. His fallback was to pursue his objectives at the level of individual departments, most of which resisted prodding to become more efficient through attention to the training and activities of their employees.[46]

When Gladstone became chancellor of the exchequer in 1852, the prospects for reform brightened; he shared Trevelyan's perspectives and also sought to centralize more power in the Treasury. Throughout the early 1850s, parliamentary and cabinet mandates of reviews of government departments served as opportunities for inquiry into their poor performance and lack of economy and for recommending thoroughgoing reform in recruitment and promotion of public servants. In addition, Gladstone ordered an extensive administrative review of the public service as it then existed, to be written by his appointees, Trevelyan and Sir Stafford Northcote.

Very shortly, the famous twenty-page Northcote-Trevelyan Report of 1854 outlined the need to draw the most well-educated young men into government service and to provide them with work befitting their intelligence and education, along with a steady path of promotions based on how well they accomplished this work. The shadow of recruitment into the Indian Civil Service was evident in the report. A Civil Service Examination Board would certify all entrants into the public service (which at the time numbered some forty thousand people), whether they did "mechanical" or "intellectual" work. To those who were deeply uncomfortable with opening the public service to merit through examinations—including Queen Victoria, the existing public service, and much of the Victorian establishment—examinations would set a barrier to entry that only those educated in public schools and the ancient universities of the country were likely to be able to pass.[47]

In Parliament, however, the proposal made little headway against the desire to maintain members' rights to patronage, a right that increased their independence of party and cabinet and connected them firmly to local elites.[48] When Gladstone introduced legislation to institute an examination board that would serve all departments, he was not able to marshal support for it. Trevelyan later reflected few illusions about the popularity of his proposals with those who mattered, writing that in 1854, those who favored reform *"might be counted upon the fingers,* and if the matter had been put to the vote in London society, or the clubs, or even in Parliament itself *by secret voting,* the new system would have been rejected by an overwhelming majority."[49]

Contingent events helped his cause, however. Reports of gross negligence and incompetence in the conduct of the Crimean War carried the discussion of improving the performance of government—discussion that had been confined to the halls of Parliament and Whitehall—outside to more general public opinion. In 1855, the Administrative Reform Association was established, with a roster of impressive members, Charles Dickens and William Makepeace Thackeray among them.[50] The press was clear that the fault lay with an inefficient Parliament and a failure to observe business practices in the management of government. This public discussion provided an opportunity for Gladstone to initiate plans for a Civil Service Commission of three Treasury officials to certify that anyone entering a junior position was "fit" for office, a plan that was established through an Order in Council, not requiring parliamentary approval, by his successor in 1855.

Although falling short of what Trevelyan wanted for the commission, the certification of "fitness" was a step forward in that it encroached on parliamentary members' privileges by placing greater power in the hands of department heads.[51] Nevertheless, the design of examinations that were required for certification remained with individual departments, giving them opportunities to ensure that favored candidates came out ahead in competitions. Moreover, this Treasury commission could not force departments to comply with this process, and though the Order in Council shifted control over patronage away from Parliament, it did not seriously impinge on the use of patronage to fill offices. In the late 1850s and into the 1860s, the Treasury continued to strengthen its capacity to be central to an evolving civil service system, but without significantly challenging the social basis of the bureaucracy. By 1860, pass examination for fitness had been supplemented by a more competitive model of examination.[52] Certification and control over pensions further cemented the preeminence of the Treasury in the evolving civil service system.[53]

Evolution remained the currency of change until Trevelyan had long departed to be governor of Madras in 1859 and then Indian finance minister. Gladstone assumed the prime ministership in 1868, and Robert Lowe became chancellor of the exchequer. A self-righteous and committed zealot like Trevelyan, Lowe took up the banner of reform, leading in time—and through lack of support in Parliament—to the drafting of the Orders in Council of 1870 and 1871.[54] This administrative action instituted a list of public positions that would be filled by examination, placed the Treasury and Civil Service Commissioners in charge of the civil service, and established intellectual and mechanical levels of work with distinct educational qualifications as well as examination requirements—later a technical or specialist category was introduced. Only the Foreign Office and the Home Office were able—by arguing the confidentiality of their activities—to remain exempt.[55] Formal departmental power over appointments was thus significantly narrowed. Some patronage positions continued under the control of the crown and Parliament, and field offices of agencies such as the post office and customs continued to make lower-level appointments on the basis of patronage, but the overall system now responded to a centralized and ordered career system.

Over the next thirty years, the business of government in Britain became more subject to routine and process, regularity and standardization. Parliament was not invoked for the establishment of a civil service, nor was the civil service created by a single act of legislation. Emerging political parties played a minor role in the reform initiative.[56] Instead, the civil service system of Britain was created by a slow accrual of requirements for "fitness" for office, defined by level and type of education, and managed through a system of examinations. With time, issues such as career development, retirement, and pensions were sorted out and added to the stability and regularity of public office, and the preeminence of the Treasury in managing this system was affirmed.[57] The expansion of government provided continued opportunities for patronage, while the career civil service took form and expanded at the same time. The evolution of this compromise engaged political and intellectual elites, and drew strength from similar views on education and class. Public opinion encouraged reform from time to time but did not lead it, nor did groups mobilized around reformist initiatives outside of government significantly shape the dynamics or outcome of reform.

With the reform moment of 1870–1871, liberal education became a formal requisite of office; birth would no longer determine position. Yet in practice, just as in Prussia and Japan, education and birth were often proxies for each other, ensuring the exclusivity of appointment to responsible office in government. The central notion of what it takes to hold office for a lifetime career as a public servant—broad knowledge of a variety of subjects that would aid in reasoning and decision making for upper-level offices and general knowledge of basic subjects for those whose work would be routine—was the invention of Victorian zealots who were building on solid foundations of class prejudice and an exclusionary educational system.

Thus, this new civil service was one that, in practice, did not lead to a composition of government much different from that under the patronage system. Those appointed to high-level office were those who had access to elite educations at Oxford and Cambridge. Skills for public office emphasized the general and the classical, and duties in public office were consistent with such generalist skills. The higher civil service, when created, claimed positions at the highest level within ministries—the permanent secretary, under-secretary, and deputy secretary—in large part because of the continuation of the elitist orientation of the new service. Social status was retained as a central component of recruitment, although now disguised as educational attainment. The Northcote-Trevelyan Report and its aftermath, the emergence of the professional civil service in Britain, was thus "a means of extending, confirming, cleansing, and legitimizing an existing elite."[58]

France and the Patronage of Merit

A competent public service in France was well on its way toward construction in the Napoleonic period, when the prefectural system—with prefects carefully appointed from the center to promote an emphatically centralized administrative system—was instituted. Prefects in turn had liberty to select their own staffs of administrators and lower officials, with the understanding that patronage was to be allocated in the interests of the center.[59] After Napoléon, however, a full century of institutional and political instability in Paris encouraged considerable decentralization of de facto power over local affairs, given the enormous power of central officials assigned locally but their incomplete regulation from above.[60] Local elites were able to reclaim many of the posts—and their rights to patronage—that had been centralized in Paris. At central levels, with the restoration of the Bourbon monarchs in 1814, political criteria became more important in appointments.[61] Indeed, in the four decades that followed the Napoleonic period, local elites claimed a number of political posts, and politicians at the center periodically purged the ranks of administrators in the interests of party.[62]

Nevertheless, and despite considerable accommodation to regionalism and party, the recruitment pool for public office grew steadily more exclusive.[63] As indicated in the last chapter, the *baccalauréat*, which could be acquired only through a rigorous educational process, was increasingly the filter applied to recruitment into responsible positions in government. With time, the *baccalauréat* was joined by the importance of a law degree, and then, an examination that led to one of the *grandes écoles* providing technical training for the state service. In 1872, the École Libre des Sciences Politiques was established to prepare career aspirants for the examinations that would give them entry to one of the *grandes écoles*, which in turn made them eligible to compete for entry into the public service.

Those who ascended this steep ladder of achievement could anticipate being appointed to positions in the higher public service and a career that would advance by seniority. For those who did not make it all the way up the ladder, positions were available within ministries and the regional administrations, where patronage appointments tended to have greater weight, but where seniority was also an important principle of advancement.[64] Patronage appointments were largely a political response to senators and deputies with relatives and party favorites to recommend, and negotiation over the destiny of patronage appointments was generally managed within ministries and regional administrations.[65] As a consequence, patronage and increasing reliance on rigorous educational requirements and examinations lived side by side in France.

Eventually, this led to a patronage system that tested for merit based on educational credentials, in the context of a party system that was unstable and incipient and political leadership that was insecure. The consequence was that control over positions was relatively open to claims by the executive administration.[66] Eventually, patronage was channeled to a narrow elite, whose merit had been tested—and tested again—in the development of a professional career. Access to elite education, of course, tended strongly to reify class relationships and produced public officials of similar backgrounds. Once in service, having passed through the educational gauntlets for qualification and having served an often lengthy apprenticeship and found promotion tied to time in service, officials were likely to use their patronage powers to select people with like educational backgrounds to fill the offices they controlled. Those who held administrative positions frequently sent their sons into service.[67] Ministries and prefects had long controlled powers of appointment, so patronage was specialized as ministers and other high-level officials brought in "their people."[68]

At the same time, specialized education and recruitment bolstered the expertise and relative autonomy of corps of high-level officials and several of the ministries, particularly those that had more technical tasks such as public works, mines, and finance. In some fields, notably law and engineering, there were few alternatives to state employment, further drawing education and public service together. Thus, for those seeking high-level positions in administration, "by about 1850 entrance into one of the *grands corps* meant an early commitment to an educational career which, in turn, led to a life career of a very organizationally specific kind."[69]

Political executives maintained greater control over ministries whose responsibilities were primarily administrative, political, or diplomatic.[70] Yet these organizations also became more professional by way of educational requirements and examinations. In ministries of war, justice, agriculture, interior, and commerce, for example, examinations became mandatory and were focused on the specific expertise needed in each of the recruiting ministries.[71] Moreover, given the focus on specific expertise, it is not surprising that, within ministries, seniority became an increasingly important requisite for promotion. With time, also, distinct organizational processes characterized each ministry, staffed as it was with those whose specific skills and knowledge made them "fit" primarily for employment in the same ministry. Ministers and heads of the *grands corps* had come to control recruitment and advancement.

In 1872, a law reorganizing the Conseil d'État from an executive organization to a judicial one laid the basis for greater homogeneity across recruitment and promotion activities of the *grands corps* and the ministries. And it significantly enhanced the autonomy of the Conseil to regulate examinations and the career system more generally.[72] Careers in public service thus became more stable and more uniform. Meanwhile, politicians who might otherwise have been interested in jobs for the boys focused on securing other forms of local benefits for their constituents. Throughout a century noted for political turmoil and the rise and fall of numerous political regimes, the evolution of the French public service from its basis in patronage to its basis in education and structure evolved in a fairly steady trajectory. Along with the increased professionalization came significantly increased power of administrators and ministries in influencing public policy. It was the state and the *corps* they served, not necessarily the government of the day.[73]

Thus, in France, the power to recruit through patronage was not directly confronted with the alternative of a professional civil service. Instead, its reach was gradually narrowed through emphasis on structured education leading to structured careers. Moreover, patronage was transformed into an examination-based structure of recruitment and promotion bit by bit, as the *grands corps* and the ministries acted to institute examinations and to recruit almost exclusively from particular schools. At the same time, the idea of classes or types of work—requiring distinct levels of education—became more common at the ministerial level.[74]

In comparison to the other cases, what is striking in this history after Napoléon is the absence of a major reformist figure or group such as found in other counties and the absence of civic engagement of any kind in efforts to improve or make administration more autonomous from politics. No grand act of legislation or administrative order created this service—it evolved piecemeal and at the level of specific organizations of government. No clamor from reforming citizens, the press, or reform-focused organizations accompanied this development. The obstacles to this development in France—decentralized administration, an extensive franchise, localized political parties needing to provide benefits to voters—were all weak. Indeed, it was not until 1946 that a civil service law, ensuring common rights and benefits, was passed.[75] Prior to this, formal moments for reform advance were decentralized and piecemeal.

Reform through Party-Based Contestation: The United States

The introduction of civil service reform in the United States, often taken as emblematic of the process through which such changes are introduced, differed greatly from the experiences of Prussia, Japan, Britain, France, and Spain. The effort was an extraordinarily protracted one and engaged a series of presidents, a number of representatives and senators on different sides of the issue, local machines of both major parties, and a broad mobilization of civic elites who railed against the corruption of the spoils system. The proponents of change were numerous and vociferous, while the opponents were dogged in their resistance. In the end, it took over thirty years and the assassination of a president to move the political system toward the acceptance of a professional civil service. It would take an additional forty years before this system was fully institutionalized.

In contrast to the experience of other countries, civil service reform did not legitimize an existing elite of officeholders. Moreover, the focus was less on the higher civil service that characterized the European cases and Japan than on clerks and other middle-range officials. The reform was not imposed; it was negotiated at length. And in those negotiations, the interests of executives, legislators, parties and their electoral machines, and prominent citizens and their organizations of reformers were almost always at odds. The press was deeply engaged in making the reform of public service a public issue in the years after the Civil War. Although presidents and many congressmen had come to find it burdensome, giving up the patronage system was a very high-stakes proposal that involved proponents and opponents in ways not duplicated in other countries. Thus, the U.S. struggle for civil service reform was unique among other developing countries at the time; the ways in which the patronage system had served the interest of party ensured that it would be.

As indicated in the last chapter, patronage in the United States was a bone of contention between presidents and Congress through much of the nineteenth century. Initially, almost all patronage fell to presidents, who used it in accordance with their particular objectives—bringing men of character and birth into government, balancing political claims of emergent parties, building party constituencies, pursuing policy objectives. Increasingly, however, patronage appointments, particularly for the growing field service of the post and customs offices, were claimed by Congress, in fact by individual congressmen in the service of their local party organizations. Indeed, by the time of the Civil War, congressmen and senators had come to play the role of middlemen in the allocation of federal employment for local party leaders.[76] Central to this extensive patronage system was the notion of rotation in office; partisan loyalties determined recruitment and also length of tenure. They also created a public service that was little more than a collection of jobs, with varying responsibilities and salaries established in an ad hoc way, with little structure and very little regulation.[77] Those within the system were often torn between loyalty to party bosses and administrative superiors.[78]

By the second half of the nineteenth century, the patronage system was regularly decried, even as Jacksonians and their successors praised its democratic impulses and consequences. It was publicly known as a spoils system and publicly attacked for corruption and incompetence. "At present, there is no organization save that of corruption, no system save that of chaos; no test of integrity save that of partisanship; no test of qualifications save that of intrigue," as one proponent of reform had it.[79] Interestingly, and in contrast to the low level of public interest in public sector reforms in Europe and Japan, civil service reform in the United States was a topic that captured public attention during election campaigns and was central to political discourse from the Civil War era to the first decade of a new century. In addition to the organizational dysfunction attributed to the spoils system, critics were clear that the partisanship that resulted in open assessments of officeholders was an evil that encouraged even greater corruption from those assessed for the party coffers. Given the increasingly well-institutionalized rotation system, criticism was more frequent from those out of power than those in office. Yet there were many reasons for patronage to remain an important currency of politics: it was a useful tool for local party machines, for senators and representatives, for presidents, and for interest groups such as the Grand Army of the Republic.[80]

The contest between patronage and a career civil service was early cast in Manichean terms—by both sides. For example, the Indiana Civil Service Reform Association was excoriated in print in 1887 by anti-reformers for being full of "Republican moral lepers, who, if capable of distinguishing between the truth and a lie, always chose the lie, just as a buzzard prefers carrion to fresh meat. The representatives of this aggregation of Republican ulcers, warts, tumors, sties, and fistulas constituted . . . the dregs of partisan malice . . . a moving, crawling, breathing pestilence."[81] The rhetoric in favor of reform was also strong and blunt. According to reformers, spoilsmen—found in greatest number in local party machines—were "a class of greedy adventurers, without conscience, or honor, or shame, or decency, or patriotism, or fear of God or the devil, or any strong spring of action, except love of money, and who go into politics and repeat the party war-cries for the same reason that other men pick locks and forge bills—to avoid honest labor, fill their bellies with rich food, and adorn their bodies with rich clothing."[82] Harsh words indeed, but ones that suggest the extent to which the battle over civil service was joined in the latter part of the nineteenth century.

Initiatives in midcentury spoke also of a concern to bring greater competence into office; much discussion centered on the importance of examinations for entry into public service. In 1853, Congress went so far as to vote a law requiring that all clerks be examined for competence, a result of a negotiated settlement among reform and hostile congressmen.[83] In 1864, Charles Sumner, Republican senator from Massachusetts, championed legislation for examinations and a civil service commission.[84] Moreover, a number of Washington insiders knew of and admired the evolving civil service systems of Britain, Prussia, and France—some could also describe China's system.[85] In 1865, the British civil service, and the famed Northcote-Trevelyan Report, served as the basis for a law proposed by Thomas Jenckes, a Republican congressman from Rhode Island, to establish a career civil service based on examination and a civil service commission that would be charged with the examinations.[86] These early proposals made no progress in Congress, nor did other reform initiatives. Throughout the 1860s and 1870s, while many attacked the patronage system, and presidents, congressmen, and senators alike complained bitterly about what a burden it was, it was equally difficult to find many politicians willing to give it up.

Although initial agitation for reform came from individual congressmen and from presidents attempting to wrest appointment powers away from Congress, a group of individual reformers—radical Republican editors, lawyers, ministers, professors, a few businessmen—gradually began to cross paths as they promoted reform in the years after the Civil War. In 1866 and 1867, they were in regular contact with Congressman Jenckes, who continued to propose civil service legislation, and they found a voice in periodicals such as the *Nation,* the *North American Review,* and the *New York Times.* The issue came to life around the initiative to impeach Andrew Johnson, when efforts were made to curtail his patronage power.

Organizations such as the American Social Science Association, the National Manufacturers' Association, the American Free Trade League, and a variety of reform clubs such as the Republican Civil Service Club of Boston and the American Civil Service Association, took up the call for reform. Bar associations in a variety of cities were important in representing the interests of professionals in government reform.[87] The election of Ulysses Grant gave these still disparate reformers hope that the new president would support and promote civil service reform. Indeed, in 1871, Grant established the first Civil Service Commission through an executive ruling; recalcitrant lawmakers retaliated by keeping the commission chronically underappropriated, so while it remained in existence, it was not able to carry out activities for lack of funding after 1874.[88] Beyond this initiative, however, reformers were disappointed with Grant; the clamor of local and congressional party stalwarts for jobs for the boys proved too much for his commitment to a civil service. Once "in," this Republican reformer found patronage to be a valuable resource; more Democrats, now "out," were found among the ranks of the reformers. Although party platforms of the period routinely called for the end of the rotation system, there was stalemate between president and Congress and between reformers and the reviled spoilsmen.

Initiatives for reform were not lacking, however. President Rutherford Hayes repeatedly lobbied for legislation that would provide for an effective civil service, but to little effect. A few nonlegislative advances were made; in the Treasury Department, a committed secretary introduced regular examinations of those recruited into the department, less to replace the patronage system than to ensure that it put forth competent people.[89] The Interior Department followed suit. But their achievements were slight. In contrast, the opposition was obdurate. Those who wished to preserve patronage attacked the workability of civil service legislation and regulation, raised questions about its antidemocratic consequences, and continued to vote down reform initiatives. Indeed, "Tradition, habit, and democratic theory joined with the sentiments of practical politicians to support an almost impregnable assumption that patronage was both necessary and proper."[90] One opponent of change argued that civil service was "against the genius of our republican institutions, and only fit for the iron heel of monarchical despotism."[91] Infamous party machine boss George Washington Plunkett called it "the curse of the nation" and argued that anarchists were recruited from those who failed civil service examinations.[92]

In this seeming impasse, public scandal played a role in advancing the cause for reform. In particular, the New York Custom House, controlled through the patronage power of Republican Party boss Roscoe Conkling, was an important arena where battle was engaged—and won by the reformers—in 1877.[93] Scandals related to the post office and assessments levied on appointees by party machines brought further attention to the issue.[94] Equally important, the public organizations supporting reform began to coalesce into a coalition of support for civil service reform and for an end to the preeminence of party politics in staffing the public service. Civil service associations were organized in major cities—Boston, New York, Philadelphia, Cambridge, Milwaukee, Providence, New Orleans, Buffalo, St. Louis, Baltimore, St. Paul, San Francisco, and several others.[95] By 1881, they were well established and their scope was national; their weapons were the press and the distribution of pamphlets. They studied other systems of government and proposed options for reforming the public service. They drew up model laws. Through their activities, pressure built up on the president and Congress to promote reform. But still the path was not clear. The "ins" lost enthusiasm for reform, and the "outs" found it impossible to marshal enough congressional support for reform.

Like presidents before him, James Garfield waxed hot and cold over reform. Nevertheless, he was a key to its ultimate success, after being shot by an office seeker in mid-1881. Garfield's subsequent death united exceptional public opinion behind the need for change.[96] Memorials to the slain president, broadsides, editorials, pamphlets, conventions, and petitions made it difficult to ignore the issue. Reformists made Garfield a "martyr to the fierceness of factional politics and the victim of that accursed greed for spoils of office . . . the gravest peril that threatens the future of the country."[97] The Pendleton Bill was finally passed by Congress, signed into law on January 16, 1883, by Chester Arthur, a protégé of New York's Conkling machine. In the end, it took increasingly intense party competition, highly mobilized groups of influential citizens, the legitimate and the muckraking press, and the assassination of a president to make this happen—a far more public stage than was needed elsewhere.[98]

The Pendleton Act (re)established a Civil Service Commission, firmly within the executive branch, undermining congressional and local party control over appointments. Competitive examinations and the creation of a career structure were part of the legislation, and party assessments were outlawed. The most important consequence of the new legislation, however, was the criterion of merit through examination (as opposed to a clear career structure) and the requirement that the quality of scores on these examinations be used in the hiring process. Its primary focus was on "ordinary" jobs rather than on the higher civil service.

In the aftermath of the success of the reformers with the Pendleton Act, significant reformist zeal focused on municipal governments, where party machines were most adept at creating and filling jobs for the boys. As indicated in the next chapter, for the next several decades, civil service reform at the national level crept forward through the gradual incorporation of positions into the examination system, but its very existence was also frequently challenged. Certainly the expanding size of the federal government offered an opportunity to pursue both reform and patronage at the same time. In addition, because the Pendleton Act focused on the middle and lower levels of the public service, appointments to high-level positions in government continued to be claimed by presidents and their parties. And even while the federal government eventually became more organized through a civil service recruitment process, federal largesse that found its way to states and municipalities could continue to be used to provide benefits and jobs.

Corporatism and Clientelism: The Case of Spain

Spain was a latecomer to public sector reform. In the early nineteenth century, the administrative system, long organized along regional and judicial lines through *cortes,* or advisory councils, was reorganized during the Napoleonic period into a French system of functional ministries, but appointment procedures for public officials were based on patronage. Throughout the century, liberals and monarchists of various hues created and destroyed governments, introduced and discarded six constitutions, sought out and rebuffed military insurrections and interventions, and oversaw a century-long destruction of empire, from independence wars in the 1810s and 1820s to the Spanish-American War of 1898. Moreover, the nineteenth century witnessed an ongoing conflict between state builders who favored a republic and those who remained true to monarchism and absolutism.[99] Coups and civil wars were frequent, and when stability reigned—as it did for most of four decades after 1875—it was achieved through a careful parceling out of parliamentary seats and government leadership, alternating regularly in party control of the parliament, and the distribution of public positions in the administration.[100]

At the center, kings continued to make and unmake ministers and ministries through personal control over appointments. Emergent political parties made the most consistent claims on the king for representation in the public service, and much of their influence involved the selection of mayors and governors, a royal prerogative. The system thus combined an extreme form of centralism with decidedly decentralized political control. "Civil servants and army officers in the larger towns were, for the most part, birds of passage, gracing the local clubs and forming, with landowners, the provincial town elite."[101]

Yet behind this chaotic system of spoils, another process encouraged the development of an administrative elite that acquired tenure in office and that was limited by the establishment of examinations for entry. Between 1808 and 1813, when Joseph Bonaparte reigned as king (thanks to his brother Napoléon), Spanish public administration was molded on the French model of *corps,* corporatist bodies of professionals with training in particular topics. This model long outlived the Napoleonic period. During the nineteenth century, in fact, it grew to incorporate more positions and became consolidated in power. Two types of *corps* developed in a haphazard and uncoordinated fashion—a general *corps* of administrators and the *grands corps* of specialists in particular aspects of public administration such as law, finance, and public works.

Members of these *corps* occupied the most important positions in the public administration and came to be clearly distinguished from public employees who were selected through the spoils system. Membership in the *corps* was conditioned by education and specialization, and with time, the various *corps* developed guildlike autonomy over their memberships as well as considerable power in the political system because of the privileges they were able to command from weak and unstable governments. There were numerous *corps*, often within the same ministry and often with similar bodies of expertise. About half of the public administration was incorporated into these semiautonomous bodies by the end of the century.

Although there were initiatives in 1827 and again in 1852 to establish a system of public administration independent from the parliament and the spoils system, the *corps* were powerful enough to exempt themselves from such initiatives and thus to foil any effort at system-wide reform.[102] Over time, the *corps* were also able to insulate themselves from demands for change by charging for the services they rendered citizens, thus reducing the power of those who managed and approved public budgets.[103] They became, in the words of one analyst, "closely knit social groups," and their "common training and community of professional interests . . . a natural channel of expression of their joint aspirations."[104] As part of their autonomy, they were able to dissent and defect from any reforms instituted on public service. In the meantime, extreme political instability and the engagement of the military in political decision making undermined efforts to improve the competence or efficiency of the public service more generally.

As World War I came to an end, Spain was beset by extensive political instability and military engagement in politics. In the summer of 1917, in the face of what appeared to be a collapse into anarchy and possibly revolution, military and civilian officials organized self-governing juntas to protect their positions and make claims for improved salaries and conditions.[105] These corporatist groups became the units that faltering and rapidly changing governments tried to appease. Political attention, of course, was focused primarily on the military, on various political factions that represented views from monarchism to revolution, and on the extreme volatility of a society that had been subject to the privations of war if not to its pursuit. But it was a strike of the juntas representing postal and telegraph workers in February 1918 that brought all other public servants together to demand reforms in pay and conditions of work. By royal decree, the government of the day had shifted posts and telegraphs from the interior to the war ministry and dissolved the juntas in these services and in the ministries of finance, interior, and public works.[106] In response to this hard-line stance, public officials across government and their juntas went on strike, leaving public services in disarray and paralyzing the country.

Eventually, in an effort to deal with the breakdown of government, an *Estatuto de Funcionarios* was introduced in 1918 to grant salary increases and job security to public officials and to establish open competitive exams for those not in the previously existing *corps*.[107] This, then, was the first important initiative to introduce a civil service system in Spain, and it excluded the elite of the system, who continued to respond to the recruitment and career opportunities established by the *corps* they belonged to. The spoils system was abolished, and public officials at middle and lower levels not belonging to a *corps* acquired job security.[108] Nevertheless, this system only lasted until a regime change in 1923 led to a purge of government officials in the interest of consolidating the dictatorship of Primo de Rivera (1923–1931); similar actions accompanied the authoritarian regime of General Francisco Franco between 1939 and 1975.[109] Those appointed to the public service were tested for their loyalty to these regimes, and under Franco, "civil servants of the grand corps had become the masters of the system."[110]

Through a reform in 1964, the Francoist regime sought greater coherence in the public service by creating a central commission for managing personnel issues in government, introducing a career system while still respecting the autonomy and political ascendance of the *grand corps*.[111] In fact, despite such initiatives, at the end of the decade of the 1960s, a review of the Spanish public administration indicated that "the Administration now appears as a complex assemblage of organizations with ill-defined boundaries and that, as a result, it is not always easy accurately to define the extent and characteristics of the group of persons which serve it, or to reduce the complex relationships to which their services give rise to any simple pattern."[112] The review noted not only a ministerial organization, but also "several hundreds of administrative agencies . . . endowed with a legal personality separate from that of the State and employing their own personnel."[113] No official count of how many people worked for the state, or in what capacity they did so, existed at the time.

Considering how such a corporatist system of relatively independent and self-regulating organizations could be reformed and organized into a coherent civil service system continued to defy those who sought such an end. As each of the *corps* and autonomous agencies could resist incorporation into a single system, the introduction of change appeared to be stymied. The body of laws and regulations affecting the status of each of the units of the public service also grew to extraordinary size as each of the corporate bodies generated its own specific structures and procedures related to personnel. Even setting salary levels proved beyond the capacity of those seeking uniformity.[114]

A change did occur, however, but not in the direction that might be anticipated based on the experience of other countries. A regime change in 1975 and a referendum on a new constitution in 1978 provided an opening for the introduction of new rules of the game and new actors, as well as the sidelining of the military from public decision making. The new constitution, negotiated among political parties of left, center, and right and claims for distinct "nationalities," recognized seventeen newly established "autonomous communities," composed of groups of provinces, and formed the basis of a radical decentralization of government and the public sector.

With a complex and at times ambiguous set of guidelines for transition to autonomous status and home rule, the new system gave powers of education, public works, health, agriculture, tourism, commerce, and transport, among other responsibilities, to more local levels of government. Consequently, over half of the national civil service was transferred to the autonomous regions, and the national civil service became significantly smaller and less powerful.[115] Indeed, by 2002, only 34 percent of public sector employees worked for the central government, including the armed forces and security personnel.[116] More than any other effort of the government, this new constitution had the effect of dispersing the traditional power of the *corps* widely across regional and local governments, constricting their capacity to resist reform.

In the wake of a constitution that undermined the national power of the corporatist groups that had so long resisted change in Spain, an additional reform in 1984 was focused directly on reducing the power of the *corps* by limiting their capacity to recruit, set salaries, and control promotions. A new civil service law of that year narrowed the range of positions that could be hired under labor contracts and separated positions and salary levels from the *corps* that had formerly controlled them. Numerous *corps* were also combined, based on their functions, limiting the extent of fragmentation in the system. The *corps* continued to exist and to exert influence over the public administration, but the combined impact of radical decentralization, downsizing at the center, and curtailed powers over careers significantly reduced their weight, an achievement sought but not gained by all prior initiatives at reform.

Legacies, Moments, and Actors

Career civil services do not emerge in a uniform way. In Prussia and Japan, authoritarian leadership authorized reformers to bring greater order to national public services by co-opting those with traditional claims to preferment through patronage. In other cases, civil services were not so much created as encouraged to evolve from prior patronage systems based on the nexus between education and social class. Most clearly in evidence in Britain and France, reformers gradually claimed rights to appointment powers and managed the introduction of formal standards and processes for recruitment; gradually, claims for patronage were excluded. In the United States, reform of patronage in the context of mass-based party machines was a much more open conflict between reformers and the politicians who benefited from the existing system, characterized by a prolonged process that gradually undermined the hold of the patronage system. And in Spain, efforts to introduce a uniform public service system were numerous and unsuccessful due in part to the resistance of powerful insiders; change was only possible through deep structural changes in the organization of government power that undermined the capacity of those insiders to resist.

Thus, some civil service systems were imposed from above, some through gradual accommodations among elites concerned about conserving their rights to public office, and some through open and uncertain contests between party politicians and reformers. Clearly, transitions were deeply affected by the context in which they developed, and the management of prior patronage systems affected how the new systems emerged. Thus, in Prussia and Japan,where patronage was instrumental in constructing competent and authoritarian states, the creation of a civil service was an artifact of those authoritarian states; in Britain and France, patronage was a mechanism helping ensure that important levels of government employment would be reserved for well-educated elites, a system reflected in the subsequent shape of their civil services; in the United States, patronage was fundamental to the emergence of mass-based political parties, and reform had to be painfully negotiated through them; in Spain, the failure of reform was a consequence of a strong preexisting corporatist and clientelist political system and a state that did not really control either.

Yet these reforms were also affected by the aims and concerns of the reformers who sought to put them in place and by the capacity for resistance of those who opposed change. In particular, change is rarely an event of a moment, but rather a long process of political construction. This process provides many opportunities for reformers and anti-reformers to contest the timing and shape of the public service, reducing the extent to which a new system is the direct consequence of its predecessor.

Thus, Stein and Hardenberg consciously shaped the profile and the organization of the Prussian civil service; the Meiji reformers based their civil service on prior elitist principles, but introduced significant change in terms of the centralization of the civil service and the definition of what it meant to be a member of the elite; the step-by-step approach in France required the organization-by-organization agency of multiple actors. In Britain, it is clear that persistent struggles by actors such as Trevelyan, Gladstone, and others significantly shaped the institutionalization of the civil service around principles of education and fitness for office. Certainly, among the cases considered here, reform was most publicly contested in the United States, and its outcome was most clearly affected by the nature of these conflicts and the strategic actions of politicians and reformers. In contrast, for long periods of time, reformers in Spain were unable to make any progress in the face of the power of the *corps*.

With the exception of the United States, the creation and introduction of civil service systems was the work of small groups of reformers, most of whom had elected or appointed positions within the governments they sought to change. In Britain, there was some public engagement in the discussion of the need for reform, but this was but a pale precursor to the much more open conflict around reform in the United States.

This chapter, then, responds to the variety of perspectives laid out in its introduction. It suggests that reform is constrained by the extent to which prior patronage systems were coherent and then by the capacity of state leaders to have centralized control over them—differences in the cases of Prussia and Japan on the one hand, and Britain, France, the United States, and Spain on the other are clear in this regard. But the chapter also indicates that in addressing reform, theoretical perspectives that were discussed in the book's introduction often do not account for a wide variety of initiatives. For example, it indicates that a focus on the legislative moment of the introduction of a civil service does not provide a comprehensive understanding of the dynamics and process of reform; that reforms are often partial and gradual; that political parties are not always in control of patronage systems or their transformation; that much of the politics of reform happens within the hallways of government with little resonance outside them; and that path dependence is punctuated by creative and variable agency over and over again. In the next chapter, the struggle for a modern civil service is viewed from a post-reform perspective, and indicates that the politics of public sector reform continue long after the establishment of such services.

CHAPTER 3

Après Reform

Deconstruction and Reconstruction

Career civil service systems were constructed in the United States, Europe, and Japan in the nineteenth century. In some cases, their introduction was established through laws or regulations that set up commissions to oversee the recruitment, promotion, monitoring, and pensioning of public servants; in other cases, the systems evolved without a single legitimizing moment, but became accepted fact through gradual accretion of practice and regulations. However they emerged, reform initiatives were everywhere subject to questioning and contestation, and they took shape in ways that reflected these conflicts.

In addition to the difficulties of their birth, new systems faced further challenges, and as the nineteenth century gave way to the twentieth, political construction of the public service continued apace, albeit often quietly. This chapter indicates that four issues marked post-reform contention about the civil service—its continued existence, the power to control it, the criteria that would define its composition, and the focus of its loyalty. Countries differed in terms of the salience of these conflicts, and in the pages to follow, I use cases of high salience to demonstrate how and why each issue of contention played out. In Chapter 7, a discussion of *après* reform in Latin America indicates the range of strategies that opponents of change employ in their efforts to constrain opportunities for change. In this chapter, I focus on general issues of contention.

In addition, I raise the issue of performance. As the consolidation of Weberian civil services proceeded, they in turn became subject to a host of criticisms. Indeed, the characteristics that nineteenth- and early twentieth-century reformers most cared about—stability, neutrality, hierarchy, consistency—became the whipping boys of new generations of reformers who recast them in a much more negative light—immobilism, unresponsiveness to leadership, formalism, resistance to new demands. Thus, while much of the twentieth century was engaged in contests over existence, control, criteria, and loyalty, the end of the century marked much more focused initiatives to improve performance and responsiveness.

Contesting Four Issues

Existence, control, criteria, loyalty. In the case of the United States, the very existence of the career civil service was clearly in doubt for several decades after the Pendleton Act of 1883. Equally evident was the ongoing struggle about who would control the public service, a conflict that also characterized the consolidation of the British and Japanese civil services. The issue of the appropriate credentials for recruitment into the public service likewise remained a highly salient topic of contention for over a century in Britain. In Germany and France, on the other hand, struggles over the existence, control, and composition of the public service took second place to the question of how loyalty to the state translated into service to political regimes.

Despite ongoing contention over these four issues, the overall trajectory favored the consolidation of career civil services that were professional, neutral, and well trained. This development altered the politics of public sector reform in important ways. Among other factors, the "new bureaucrats" recruited into the career systems developed corporate identities related to their roles and became active in organizing and representing their own interests in the furtherance of professionalism, stability, pay, pensions, and autonomy. Moreover, organizations set up to oversee the new public services—such as civil service commissions—became adept in protecting themselves against unwanted change and partisan politics. Thus, new protagonists became engaged in conflicts over the complexion of the public service, and worked to deepen and entrench the characteristics defining these new public officials.

Post-reform history also indicates that, even in the context of increasing consolidation of new career systems, the claims of politicians for patronage appointments were never fully vanquished. In particular, these claims gained traction during periods of political and economic stress.

During such times, politicians were aggressive in reasserting power to recruit those who would serve in government—bringing in "their people" to advance new public agendas, to staff new programs, and to prod those who had become "old bureaucrats" within the career system. Ironically, then, modern Weberian administrations were often challenged by traditional claims of patronage when governments were called upon to take on new or difficult tasks and to pursue new definitions of the state.

And even as the new career civil services and the organizations that supervised them became more entrenched—the triumph of modernity over traditional practice, many believed—they became more subject to criticism for their failures. Designed and negotiated to bring efficiency and professionalism to the operation of government, these services were increasingly decried for their immobilism, conservatism, and aloofness. Their very modernity became a public Achilles heel, as citizens, scholars, and politicians echoed Franz Kafka's observation that "the chains of tormented mankind are made out of red tape."[1] Indeed, by the late twentieth century, fundamental questions emerged about the wisdom of institutionalizing career civil services. Methods of recruitment and career advancement were on the table again, a century and a half after reformers insisted their proposals would effectively resolve these issues. In time, and in all countries, consolidation of a Weberian bureaucracy was attacked at the most fundamental level, and a new generation of reform-mongers became concerned, not with the existence, control, composition, and loyalty of the public service, but with its performance.[2]

Will the Civil Service Survive?

In the United States, the very existence of the career civil service was seriously threatened after its establishment through law, a pattern replicated in the case of Brazil to be considered later. The timing of the development of political institutions had much to do with this unique situation. Among other countries whose modern public services were also taking shape in the nineteenth century, the United States was far in advance in the extent to which a party system had emerged and grown through the appropriation and distribution of public positions. More than in other countries, then, the emergence of a career civil service was intertwined with the experience of mass-based political parties from the

1830s through the 1920s. In a related fashion, the transition from a government by gentlemen to a government by party in the first fifty years of the new republic limited the extent to which an elite public service— a mandarin system such as emerged in other countries during the same years—could take hold.

As noted in the previous two chapters, patronage and rotation in office had been standard procedure in the U.S. government for half a century before 1883, long enough for many to regard it as natural and legitimate and for parties and politicians fully to appreciate its political value. Commitment to this characteristic of the political system meant that in the decades after the Pendleton Act, the career public service system was embroiled in ongoing efforts to strangle its existence and limit its reach. Indeed, fifteen years after this important legislative moment, reformers who fought hard for it in the 1870s and 1880s lamented that "the conviction of the country in regard to the soundness of the principles of civil service wabbles about, so to speak, in such a way that creates in the hearts of many of us the keenest apprehension."[3]

These reformers had good reason to be apprehensive. Although much lip service was paid to the importance of a regularized civil service, the crowning achievement of the reformers, the Civil Service Commission, barely survived its initial two decades of existence. It was repeatedly investigated and kept short of money and staff by Congress. Presidents encouraged the weakness of the commission by appointing commissioners who were at best lukewarm about the Pendleton Act.[4] The commission was declared un-American in the Senate in 1891, and numerous bills were introduced to abolish it.[5] Unconvinced of the political virtues of a career public service, the platform of the Democratic Party in 1896 supported merit, but with term limits on public servants, reintroducing the banished system of rotation.[6]

Presidents repeated the rhetoric of reform in their campaigns, and still more when they "blanketed in" their patronage appointments at the end of their terms in office, including them in the civil service tenure system. Nevertheless, they continued to rely on patronage to fuel electoral organization and mobilization, and they actively appointed party stalwarts once they acquired office. Parties continued to rely on the promise of jobs to fill positions at local, state, and national levels as they campaigned for office; their ability to keep these promises was considerable—the expansion of government in the late nineteenth and early twentieth centuries continued to create new opportunities for public employment. Figure 3.1 indicates that the expansion of the size of government was an ongoing challenge to the proportional expansion of the civil service in its first six decades.

Federal positions closest to the state and local party machines—particularly the post office—were most valued by the politicians. Many such positions could be allocated without much regard for educational background, and they could be allocated locally through the intervention of congressional representatives. At the same time, local party machines found extensive opportunities for patronage at a time when urban infrastructure was a significant focus of investment.[7] As a consequence, reformers singled out the post office and municipal governments as particular targets of their attacks on patronage in the public service.

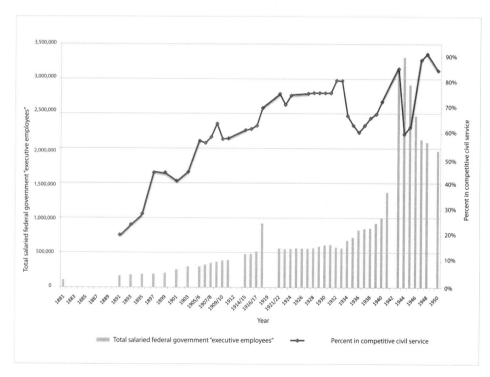

Figure 3.1. The Federal Public Service and the Civil Service System.

Back in Washington, department heads were sometimes friendly to the new system because they hoped to curtail the political pressures that made their jobs more difficult, but at the same time many sought to avoid the intrusion of the Civil Service Commission into personnel matters.[8] Even those bureaucratic leaders who were recruited to expand the activities and competence in the federal government in areas such as weather, census, food, drugs, and reclamation preferred to bring in their people to help them; the expansion of a series of public organizations noted for their competence owed much to continued opportunities for patronage. Thus, resistance came not only from politicians and party machines, but also from departments that sought to maintain their autonomy from the commission and the oversight of the president.

Against this difficult set of obstacles, the Civil Service Commission had limited capacity to push its agenda forward.[9] Enforcement of much of the responsibility for civil service rules was delegated to department heads, each of whom had distinct views on the importance of the new system. Regardless of where they stood on the issue, they were committed to enabling their departments to maintain control over examinations and recruitment. Moreover, the commission's initial activities focused on examinations for "fitness" that established a relatively low bar of educational attainment and assessed practical skills, leaving considerable room for department heads to use their discretion in filling posts.

The commission was also chronically short of staff and had difficulty carrying out its responsibilities to investigate failures to conform to the new law, again leaving considerable leeway to department heads in personnel matters. To add to the problem of enforcement, the most stalwart of the civic organizations promoting public sector reform were now primarily focused on state and local patronage systems, and it was difficult to resurrect the moral outrage of citizens that had met the assassination of President Garfield in 1881.[10] Not surprisingly, then, "The spoils system . . . fully maintained its vitality for many years after the passage of the Pendleton Act, and constituted a covert threat to the life of the merit idea."[11]

Nevertheless, many jobs for the boys did eventually become incorporated into the career civil service. Significant steps forward in its consolidation occurred on the eve of party changes in the executive—when the "ins" became the "outs" and it became important to ensure one's own people were safe by incorporating their positions into the civil service "blanketing" the jobs in, as the practice was called. Ironically, then, the patronage system fueled the advance of reform as presidents blanketed in more positions when they left office. Low barriers to entry also meant that many potential political appointees could enter public service via the career system, a route to office that was also strongly pursued at state and local levels, where party machines were strongest.[12] In addition, the low bar and focus on job-specific skills meant opportunities for those with experience in public service—that is, those who had been hired under the patronage regime—to acquire certification and entry into the new civil service.[13] As a consequence, by 1900, most clerical jobs in Washington were within the new system, and opportunities for patronage were increasingly found in field positions in departments such as the post office and customs, and in higher-level positions in Washington.[14]

At times, skillful and persistent public leadership pushed consolidation forward, even in the face of a significant set of obstacles. A crusading Theodore Roosevelt, chosen in 1889 to head the Civil Service Commission, certainly advanced the reformers' cause. As commissioner, he traveled widely to expose abuses of patronage. Among his allies were a number of newspapers and journals, a few department heads who sought relief from political pressures in appointments, and the remnants of the civic organizations that had fueled the fight for the Pendleton Act. Among the departments that figured most prominently in Roosevelt's war was that important employer of party regulars, the post office.

When Roosevelt became president in 1901, he continued to crusade for the career service. His leadership was instrumental in giving the new service a more secure life, and he was joined by the National Civil Service Reform League and the press in keeping up the pressure for implementation of the Pendleton Act, revising rules to give it greater power. Most important, he provided the Civil Service Commission with greater resources, and thereby greater capacity to enforce its mandate and rulings; henceforth it could count on a field staff and regional offices for carrying out its responsibility.[15] In addition, the Progressive Era featured numerous commissions concerned with issues of efficiency in government, keeping the theme of the importance of public sector reform alive in public debate.[16]

The politics of the public service also shifted as the Civil Service Commission gained strength and as the career service became more organized. Indeed, as more officials became part of the career service, they joined with the reformers to press for greater stability, regularity, and equity in salaries and benefits.[17] For the beneficiaries of the new system, stable careers and the end of party assessments were important selling points for a less partisan system.[18]

Over its first decades, then, although the career civil service system in the United States advanced slowly and haltingly, it did advance. Certainly, legislators sought to destroy it, and politicians found numerous ways to continue to use patronage to their advantage. Certainly, patronage remained a staple of local- and state-level politics, and presidents and congressmen were regularly reminded of its importance in a competitive party system. Yet, as a result of blanketing in, reformist leadership, organizational strengthening, and the support of the emergent career service, the reformers were able to ensure the survival of the new system. Indeed, in 1909, nearly 64 percent of the federal public service was part of the career civil service, and new legislation in 1912 guaranteed public servants rights to organize and represent their interests to Congress.[19] The existential challenge that figured so prominently in the aftermath of reform gradually abated.

Who Will Control the Administrators?

What part of government should be responsible for the management of civil service systems? The history of the nineteenth- and twentieth-century public sector reforms suggests that this was not a purely technical question. Indeed, intense competition over the control of new civil service systems characterized post-reform politics. At stake were issues of the budget for personnel—surely a major slice of any government's expenditure—and the capacity to select commissioners; set regulations and recruitment criteria; make decisions about whether the system should be expanded or minimized and centralized or decentralized; decide whether the autonomy of the system should be advanced or curtailed; and focus the attention of public servants on particular priorities or goals. Behind these instruments of management, of course, lurked larger and often unspoken issues such as the seesaw of intergovernmental power relations and leadership in setting the course of public policy.

These issues were of particular salience in three countries. In the United States, the extent to which the president or Congress would be the principal branch to claim rights to manage the administrative personnel system was at issue for several decades after 1883. And, as presidents gradually gained the upper hand, the extent of their capacity to oversee the new system was challenged by the growing autonomy of the civil service system and its consolidation within the executive branch. In Britain, Parliament had ceded much control over the new system to the Treasury as the system evolved in the nineteenth century, but the twentieth century witnessed an ongoing conflict between prime ministers, the Treasury, individual departments, and associations representing civil servants over the management of the civil service. In Japan, the strength of the public service, rooted in specific ministries, gave it the upper hand in managing alliances with the private sector and ongoing relationships with political parties. The experiences of these three countries indicate the contentiousness of the issue of control.

PRESIDENTS VS. CONGRESS IN THE UNITED STATES.   Central to Theodore Roosevelt's commitment to a career civil service was the desire to gain presidential control over the personnel system and sideline Congress and local party machines. Thus, as the civil service gained presence in Washington, it became part of a larger—and much longer—conflict between the president and Congress about who was in charge of the direction of government.[20] As this conflict worked itself out, the "bureaucratic advance of power" was, to Congress, the advance of the hegemony of the presidency.[21] Over time, however, presidents had to try to protect their gains from the increasingly autonomous action of public administrators, now protected from political pressures by the civil service and the commission that regulated it.

After Roosevelt, the advance of presidential power was aided by wars and economic crises. World War I, for example, with its need for centralization, planning, and enhanced resource allocation capacity, played into the hands of presidents. At the same time, presidential leadership of the administration, the management of increased power, and the organization of the war effort were also marked by intense conflict and factionalism within government, and this, too, helped advance presidential power in the aftermath of war. At that point, President Woodrow

Wilson was able to secure from Congress the discretionary authority to reorganize the executive branch, largely because of criticism of the inefficiencies of the wartime government apparatus.[22] Moreover, with an expansion in the size of government, the president had new resources to offer in the regularization of careers and salaries. An important law in 1923 established a classification system that allocated positions among classes, grades, and services primarily for lower-level positions, bringing more coherence to the system and thus enhancing executive authority over it.[23]

In this contest between presidents and Congress, recourse to patronage also played a role. The creation of specialized agencies and bureaus and the selection of those to staff them, tactics well practiced by Theodore Roosevelt, were taken up by Wilson during the war and used again extensively under Franklin Roosevelt during the Depression and World War II. In all three cases, presidential control over the public service expanded, often through the extension of presidential patronage. This was most apparent under the presidency of Franklin Roosevelt. At the outset of his first administration, federal executive employees incorporated into the civil service dropped from 81 percent of the total in 1933 to 63 percent in 1937, at which point the percentage began to climb again. During World War II, a newly robust 85 percent incorporated into the civil service dropped to less than 60 percent.[24]

Ironically, many of these patronage jobs were used to bring new professionalism to the public service, in the guise of well-trained and energetic proponents of the New Deal and managers of the war effort "a kind of Phi Beta Kappa version of Tammany Hall," as one beneficiary put it.[25] Then, by blanketing-in many of his appointees, Roosevelt effectively incorporated more positions into the civil service. In retaliation for what it saw as the partisan role of some New Deal agencies—especially the Works Progress Administration—Congress, which had spent considerable energy in the preceding decades limiting the scope of the career system, championed the system's neutrality in 1939 with the Hatch Act, which restricted the political activities of federal employees.

By the mid-1940s, presidents had become acknowledged leaders of the federal civil service. They also had some thirty-five hundred full-time high-level patronage appointments at their disposal, and contention over these appointments continued to characterize a dance between Congress and presidents.[26] The bulk of the civil service, however, was off-limits to partisan appointments until the 1980s, when President Reagan sought to expand the number of appointments available to presidents. In addition, patronage lived on in the use of part-time and temporary positions in government—in the hiring of census takers, for example—during the 1970s and 1980s. Indeed, at particular moments, crusading presidents found much to like in patronage, congressmen sought to acquire control over the civil service from presidents, and civil servants became more organized. In the end, a career civil service system was consolidated in the United States, but the issue of who would control the administrators remained an important conflict for at least six decades after it was established.

TREASURY VS. PRIME MINISTERS VS. DEPARTMENTS IN BRITAIN.   In Great Britain, questions of who would control the civil service marked the evolution of the career system before and after it was formally established by Orders in Council in 1870 and 1871. As we saw in the previous chapter, Parliament and the Treasury Department tussled over this issue prior to the reform. Treasury triumphed in this conflict. After 1890, however, its capacity to lead the civil service was challenged by the emergence of public service associations.[27] Gradually, these unions gained the capacity to represent civil servants' concerns about salaries and conditions of employment. Such associations were unwelcome by Treasury as voices urging changes in conditions of employment, yet these associations, eventually coalescing into large service-wide unions, lobbied for consistent service-wide policies that were best ensured by a central personnel agency in the Treasury.

The relationship between Treasury and civil servants' unions, however, was periodically upstaged by events that allowed prime ministers to gain ground in the contest for power. During World War I, for example, Lloyd George took the lead in recruiting experts in engineering, logistics, and science to government as temporary civil servants on an emergency basis. The prime minister also appointed numerous advisers, bypassing civil service regulations to bring his people into the public service. Wartime leaders were clear that such appointments were necessary to the performance of government precisely because new recruits did not share the education or values of those who made it through the examination system, particularly the "gifted amateurs" who staffed the upper reaches of the government.[28] The war, then, provided opportunities to use patronage for increasing the availability of expertise in government on a significant scale. And Treasury's power waned as that of Number 10 Downing Street waxed.

In the aftermath of war, however, Treasury was able to reassert its hegemony, consolidating the grip of the civil service over affairs of government. The so-called "mushroom departments" were eliminated or brought under Treasury control in an effort to establish order from the chaotic management of the war years.[29] Then, in 1920, an Order in Council gave Treasury virtual carte blanche to "make regulations for controlling the conduct of His Majesty's Civil Establishments, and providing for the classification, remuneration, and other conditions of service of all persons employed therein, whether permanently or temporarily," and making the permanent secretary to the treasury the head of the civil service. This put paid, at least for a time, to the capacity of the prime minister and the departments to have significant impact on recruitment and promotion policies.[30]

Nevertheless, when another war threatened, the balance tipped against the accretion of power in Treasury. On a scale surpassing that of 1914–1918, outsiders were brought into government at all levels during World War II, new organizations flourished—the Ministries of Supply and Food were good examples—and greater power was assumed by the prime minister in the structure and performance of government. History repeated itself again at the end of the war, however, with a reversion to politics-as-usual. Treasury regained preeminence as emergencies abated and the civil service was able to reassert its boundaries and prerogatives. The reassertion of Treasury power at this time also encroached on the remaining capacities of ministerial departments to recruit their own through examinations.[31] Similarly, Treasury preeminence limited Britain's Civil Service Commission to the management of examinations.[32]

Prime ministers did not give up the fight, however. In 1968, the Fulton Committee, set up by the prime minister to address problems of the civil service, called for a new civil service department—separated from Treasury and under the Prime Minister's Office —a greater role for departments in recruitment, more career flexibility, and increased opportunities for ministers to appoint special advisers for policy, among other changes.[33] The recommendations were put in place, but since the Treasury maintained control over personnel expenditures, its considerable power in the civil service system remained strong.[34] The Fulton Committee Report and its implementation only sharpened the conflict about control—the ability of prime ministers, cabinets, and departments to set and carry out national policy vs. the capacity of Treasury and the established civil service to maintain an alliance for control and autonomy.

In a similar initiative to expand prime ministerial control over government, Margaret Thatcher abolished the Civil Service Department, established a Management and Personnel Office in the Prime Minister's Office as a balance to Treasury, and raised the specter of privatization of many of government's administrative functions.[35] Famously, Tony Blair sought to move government toward New Labour policies through the extensive recruitment of political and policy advisers, gaining opprobrium for his presidentialism in office. Thus, just as in the United States, conflicts about control of the civil service in Great Britain long outlived the introduction of a career public service. Indeed, even in a century characterized by gradual consolidation of the civil service systems, contention over control was never fully resolved.

POLITICIANS VS. THE SYSTEM IN JAPAN.   The Meiji leaders managed to put in place a hierarchical, legally-oriented, centralized, and professional system very similar to that developed in the eighteenth and nineteenth centuries in Prussia. By 1900, the Japanese civil service had become a mandarin bureaucracy, based on recruitment by tough examinations that reflected the curriculum of a very few elite universities, particularly law faculty of the Imperial University in Tokyo, later the University of Tokyo.[36] As in the Prussian model, the idea of the state, as embodied in the emperor and in law, was the focus of official action and loyalty.

Not surprisingly, the ability to direct this professional and hierarchical system was of concern to party politicians. In the late nineteenth century, they sought access to higher-level positions in the system through special decrees. The civil service trumped this initiative when its upper-level officials became explicitly subject to examinations.[37] Somewhat more than a decade later, in the face of more organized political parties, vice-ministers and other high-level positions became open to members of the parliament, and the prime minister gained wider scope in top-level appointments.[38] Early conflict about recruitment to the civil service, therefore, tended to focus on where the line should be drawn between political and administrative personnel, and how broadly the recruitment process should cast its net. In the 1910s and 1920s, "the two camps, the elected and the non-elected, battled ceaselessly for control of the cabinet and public policy."[39]

It was not easy for politicians to win much power over the system, however. For most of the period leading up to World War II, "party politicians serving as ministers had to choose from among officials who had similar training and service backgrounds. There was no autonomy of choice as in a patronage system."[40] In place of loyalty to the government of the day, public servants in Japan focused their aspirations at the ministry level because the highly centralized examination system was married to appointments and career development systems that were ministry specific.[41] Moreover, little during the prewar period, during the war, or after it increased the prestige of politicians or political parties; "progressive bureaucrats" of the prewar and war period focused on regulation and efficiency, with little regard for the voices of elected politicians.[42]

Under the occupation at the end of the war, principles of recruitment continued even as the bureaucracy was reorganized and decentralized.[43] A new civil service law of 1947 made public officials responsible to "the whole community," breaking the tradition of primary allegiance to the state in the guise of the emperor.[44] The prestige of the service continued to be high, its training rigorous, and its powers considerable, even though parliamentary government and the role of political parties were strengthened.[45] Moreover, a postwar purge of elected government officials associated with the war meant extensive opportunities for bureaucrats to run for public office, thus infusing the political parties with their expertise and networks within government.[46] For a considerable period, cabinets were headed by ex-civil servants.

Over time, and through such mingling of roles, the administrative apparatus was able to build a long-term alliance with the reigning Liberal Democratic Party. Within the bureaucracy, a strong preference for seniority and few opportunities for lateral entry also meant that the tenure of public servants was much longer than that of elected politicians, further enhancing the power of the administrators. Indeed, the policies of government became noted for their frequent promulgation as ordinances—a mechanism of administrative regulation—rather than as laws, which were the output of Parliament.[47]

The ministry-specific nature of the career system also encouraged another kind of alliance—between ministries and clienteles in the private sector. Certainly, the experience of the 1930s and World War II increased the engagement of the public service with industrial development, providing many opportunities for close engagement between administrative power, state power, and the private sector. In the postwar years, retirement from elite positions in government often meant reintegration into policy relevance through service on public, autonomous, and private sector boards, undergirding a "a maze of ties that connect ministries and major industrialists."[48] This condition made Japan a prime example of the interactions of state and society that Evans called "embedded autonomy."[49]

In Japan, then, battles over control of the civil service systematically favored the bureaucratic apparatus, securely tied to ministries and strengthened through carefully managed alliances with the private sector and the Liberal Democratic Party. The resulting system was extraordinarily stable for the five decades in which the Liberal Democrats dominated politics almost uninterrupted between 1955 and 2009.

What are the "Right Credentials" for Recruitment?

The educational backgrounds and training of civil servants was another bone of contention in the evolution of civil service systems. In the initial construction of the new systems, this was a significant issue—experts or generalists was debated in the United Kingdom, Western vs. traditional knowledge a subject of concern in Japan, elite schools or democratization discussed in France, Japan, Germany, and the United Kingdom. In the decades after reform, the civil services took shape around these choices, but often the issue of the appropriate criteria for recruitment remained a source of debate and struggle.

The experience of the United Kingdom is perhaps the most emblematic of the struggles to define credentials for admission into public service. On the one hand was an elite service characterized by educational advantage, with training that emphasized general skills. On the other was the increased need for expertise as government became larger and more engaged in the management of economic and social issues. The debate about proper credentials for public service was often public and also part and parcel of the conflict between prime ministers, departments, and the Treasury for control over the public service.

As indicated, the Orders in Council that institutionalized the Northcote-Trevelyan Report were not revolutionary documents. They enshrined much of existing practice in ensuring that those with "intellectual" jobs in government would be qualified for them by virtue of their elite educations, verified through examinations based on the curricula of Oxbridge institutions, and that other kinds of jobs would be similarly staffed by people with educations thought appropriate for implementation and clerical work. The sons of the upper and upper middle classes no longer needed to rely on patronage—they, along with an increasing number of the professional middle class, now had privileged access to such positions by virtue of their educational advantages. So, too, the generalist orientation of those called to government service at all levels was formalized through the Orders; Victorian reformers were convinced that the skills needed for top-level administrative leadership were the result of a liberal education and class background, and that these skills could be usefully employed across departments, regardless of the responsibilities of specific organizations or jobs.

Despite the strong conviction of these reformers, in the years and decades after the Northcote-Trevelyan reforms, a continuing stream of criticisms and commissions raised and discussed the subject of what credentials were most appropriate for those staffing the civil service, particularly at its higher levels. Two issues in particular were debated—the impact of the examination system on the composition of the service, and the fitness of generalists for the evolving tasks of government. In both cases, opinions varied widely, and concerns about appropriate recruitment criteria were often married to discussions of efficiency and performance in government.

The examination system clearly produced an elite civil service of impeccable educational backgrounds, particularly in the Treasury, in the first decades after the reform. Higher civil service positions were filled by those who had first-class degrees from Oxford and Cambridge; they were joined by a smattering of those who had graduated from Trinity College, Dublin, and London University.[50] As the examination system took hold for new recruits into the service, the size of government was also growing, leading to increased differentiation between those who did "intellectual" and those who did "routine" work, the two great categories of the Victorian reform.[51] But by the early twentieth century, the higher civil service had acquired the reputation of a caste that reified the old boys' network of the public schools and elite universities.[52] Those consigned to routine work did only that—routine—with little hope of rising to elite status. Early efforts to assess the biases of the examination system did little to alter its increasing reputation as castelike and aloof.[53]

Consistently, in attacking the apparatus bequeathed by the nineteenth century, later generations of reformers charged that it had resulted in a system that was out of step with the responsibilities and tasks of modern government and unresponsive to policy makers and citizens alike. One high-level civil servant committed to changing the nature of recruitment railed against the system that relied on the induction of young men as they finished university. "If you [recruit such people], they will then get to work and take their little pens in their infant hands and they write away little criticisms of every sort and kind, very clever ones no doubt, but there is no training for constructive work, or work that would enable them to get the practical experience that might make them Heads of Department."[54] In general, responses to such grumbling were answered at the level of individual departments, some of which undertook focused internal initiatives to encourage efficiency.[55] Yet forty years after the Northcote-Trevelyan reform, as the country contemplated a major war, the public service was considered "a convention-bound, precedent-laden, secretive society."[56] The profile of a successful high-level public servant was generally that of a "gifted dabbler."

This left little room for the systematic application of specific expertise to the functions of government, particularly at higher levels of the service. While the debate between amateurism and expertise was a constant of the twentieth century, the introduction of greater in-government expertise, often through the skillful use of patronage, was most noticeably advanced when government was under pressure to perform more rapidly or effectively—when the state took on new functions, mobilized for war, or addressed deep economic crises. Thus, when in 1906 the tasks of government expanded to include the initiation of the early welfare state, Lloyd George used successive positions in the Board of Trade, the Treasury, and the Prime Minister's Office to recruit more activist and specialized civil servants. He established commissions to administer new systems of pensions, labor exchanges, and national insurance and staffed them with those who had specialized expertise in government and academic institutions.[57] These efforts were overtaken by a more critical problem for government, mobilization for war, a situation that also provided political leaders with extensive room to bring in outsiders—particularly businessmen and experts in a variety of fields—to run the machinery of government from 1914 to 1918.

The reassertion of Treasury control over the civil service in the postwar period again elevated the role of the generalist and the amateur in managing the affairs of government.[58] Criticism of the efficiency consequences of civil service recruitment also resurfaced during these years, as the civil establishment "recruited its new blood young and kept it until well stale."[59] Predictably, World War II radically expanded the need for more hands and particularly for those with specialist training, often at the expense of generalists. The rigid barriers to bringing in outsiders gave way during the wartime emergency and allowed a reversion to patronage for expertise, speed, and more-efficient management. Women became a greater presence in government service—although their careers were not made easy by either the old or the new boys. And even civil service diehards admitted to the energy and commitment that characterized government activities during the war when so much "new blood" helped drive the system.[60] One consequence of this period was a blurring of the Northcote-Trevelyan distinction between those who did intellectual work and those who did routine work.[61]

After the war, the issue of how to provide sufficient expertise to government remained open. Prime ministers and others experimented with official think tanks and policy review teams when they were stymied by the persistence of the generalists. Some encouraged secondments from outside organizations, a practice that had some success in returning appointment power to departments.[62] In response to the Fulton Committee Report, Prime Minister Edward Heath established a Civil Service College to provide additional training for higher-level public servants, a task its first head claimed to be a combination of "All Souls and a mechanics' institute."[63] Despite many such efforts, critics continued to argue that Northcote-Trevelyan "had saddled Britain with an entrenched administrative class of non-specialist dabblers renewed, generation after generation, by a recruitment process 'favouring the smooth extrovert conformist with good connections and no knowledge of modern problems.'"[64] In other countries, extended debates continued about the appropriate credentials for those recruited into public service, but perhaps nowhere so dramatically as in the United Kingdom.

What Does Loyalty Mean?

As career civil services were consolidated in the decades after they were introduced, an important issue emerged uppermost in those systems that had, in their creation, extensively emphasized the importance of loyalty to the state. These countries were simultaneously characterized by strong, autonomous, and elitist public services and considerable political instability.[65] Thus, in Germany, France, and Japan, where political regimes were less stable than in the United States and the United Kingdom, the early development of public service legitimacy and autonomy raised questions about how loyalty to the state would translate into loyalty to shifting political regimes. Each country had evolved professional and elite public services that were highly regarded, even feared, and that demonstrated strong capacities in the well-organized management of public affairs. In each case, the power, status, and coherence of the public service made it a threat to those who assumed leadership of new political regimes. Could these powerful and autonomous civil services be trusted to carry out the priorities of politicians? In Germany and France, this question was particularly salient.

REGIMES AND TRUST IN GERMANY.   As the civil service in Prussia and then Germany evolved in the nineteenth century, quiet contention within its ranks focused on the extent to which noble birth would be a condition of entry and the extent to which professionals of the middle and upper middle classes could join the service as a result of their education and performance on examinations. The balance was clearly tipped in favor of the latter by midcentury, and educational attainment—most easily acquired by those of comfortable social status—became the key to entering the public service.[66] Increasing specialization of function in the structure of the state administration further solidified the role of education and the study of law as the most important credentials for a civil service career.[67] The evolution of the German system from its beginnings in Prussia ensured a federation of *Länder* services that remained supremely sensitive to hierarchy, rank, and the authority of the state, even while they emerged from the political challenges of the mid-nineteenth century committed to distancing themselves from day-to-day politics.[68]

Thus, the Prussian state, and the German empire that incorporated it, established a fully professionalized and legitimized civil service with a strong esprit de corps and highly regularized requirements for entry, promotion, and retirement managed at the *Länder* and departmental levels. Civil servants passed national examinations, a higher civil service was managed separately and posted to departments, and departments filled other positions with those who qualified through examination and probationary service. At the turn of the twentieth century, it was an elite system, strongly wedded to military values of regularity and hierarchy, privileging legal knowledge and decision making based on the accumulation of administrative law. Germany's public servants were often contemptuous of ordinary citizens, but neutral in an aggressive commitment to serve the state above politics. It was a large and decentralized public service, incorporating over a million officials by 1913.[69] It was also effective, able to adjust to the need for expertise and operating a set of welfare state policies long before these were created in other Western countries.

Effective, neutral, and aloof, Germany's civil service was potentially a formidable ally of a variety of regimes. That is, if it could be trusted. This was not an issue under the monarchy—the monarchy created it, and the well-oiled administrative apparatus and its commitment to the state was understood to mean commitment to the monarchy. But for political leaders of Weimar, the Third Reich, and the Federal Republic, this question of loyalty was of much greater concern. Each regime indicated unease about the extent to which this effective machinery of administration would follow the aims of political leaders intent on incorporating new political principles into the state.

The strong and professionalized administrative system survived the demise of the monarchy and the defeat of war in 1918. But its loyalty became an issue in the political upheavals of 1918, the 1920s, and 1930s, and the power of the civil service was clear in the attention paid to it by contending political forces. When abdicating in 1918, Kaiser Wilhelm II called upon public officials to support the new government.[70] Initial tests suggested that they would. For example, when Prussian civil servants were called upon to support a new revolutionary government, they responded that their commitment was to the state, whoever guided it, rather than to the monarch.[71]

Under the Weimar Constitution in 1922, legislation relating to the duties of public servants granted them life tenure at the same time it required their loyalty to a constitutional and republican form of government; the president would have power to appoint and dismiss public officials, although ministerial approval was also required for appointment.[72] At the same time, the upper ranks of the bureaucracy were declared to be "political," allowing the party in power to "temporarily retire" at will those holding such positions. At senior levels, governing parties would thus be able to scrutinize those appointed to higher-level positions and ensure their political loyalty. In a context in which most of those who had reached such positions had spent careers under the monarchy, this was an opportunity to colonize the upper reaches of the bureaucracy with commitment to the new regime.[73]

In the 1930s, the changes introduced under Weimar allowed the National Socialists to remove many officials who had entered the public service under the Republic; department heads became arbiters of who would remain in office and who would be retired in the early days of the new regime.[74] In 1933, an act confirmed that only those who could "at all times fully identify ... with the State of the National Revolution" could be hired into the public service. An oath of loyalty to the constitution became an oath to the "leader of the German Reich and the people" in 1934.[75] Another law in 1937 made the civil service the "executor of the will of the state based on the National Socialist German Workers' Party."[76]

As with the earlier period, the civil service, purged of those considered dangerous by the Nazis, complied with the new political principles and carried on with its duties. Yet in the aftermath of the war, the issue of loyalty was prominent again for the new regime of the Federal Republic. Could public servants who had effectively served Hitler and the Third Reich now be trusted to carry out the activities of government under a democracy? Democratization of the public service was certainly an important concern of the occupation in the immediate aftermath of the war.[77] Nevertheless, the Western allies left the civil service largely intact, focusing attention on punishing the more prominent officials for the crimes of the Nazis. The strategy was largely successful, based as it was on an assumption that the civil service would be a willing partner in allowing the public service to regain the autonomy and status that it had enjoyed prior to the Third Reich.[78] In 1949, the Basic Law of the new republic explicitly referred to the functioning of the civil service under its "traditional principles."[79]

The Federal Republic also brought a return of political parties, however, and a gradual colonization of higher-level positions with partisan sensitivity, to the extent that it was termed a party state, with a pattern of rotation in office at senior levels when new governments come to office. Command of the skills of political analysis and network management came to be viewed as important ones for making the decentralized system function effectively.[80] As partisanship infiltrated high-level recruitment, the German system was also tested for increasing commitment to European unity, which brought with it limitations on administrative autonomy. In Germany, then, a tradition of loyalty to the state was tested and at times undermined by a succession of political regimes. Clearly, those who led these regimes felt the need to ensure the commitment of those who were expected to carry out their policies.

MINISTRIES AND FRAGMENTED LOYALTIES IN FRANCE. Revolution and Napoléon left deep marks on the French civil service. Its structure—hierarchical and elitist—was still apparent two centuries later. Equally strong was the impact of elite training on the evolution of a system from patronage to a career civil service. In some ways, then, there is no *après* reform in the case of France. The development of its public service—well trained, stable, specialized, hierarchical, respected and feared by ordinary citizens—was evolutionary and largely completed by the last decade of the nineteenth century. Like the Prussian/German system, it was wedded to the notion of service to the state and ensured that administrators had considerable power over citizens.[81] Also like that in its eastern neighbor, a career in France's public service was avidly sought by the well educated and well connected.

As we have seen, after Napoléon, in the context of considerable political upheaval, control over recruitment was monopolized by ministries, where ministers defined the criteria for appointment and administered their fiefdoms and the careers of their officials.[82] Indeed, entrance examinations and recruitment processes were set at the ministerial level until after World War II. Not surprisingly, government was generally characterized by factionalism among various ministries, each of which had its own loyal corps of career officers. With intense loyalty owed to the state in general and the ministries in particular, politicians in the ongoing political upheavals of the nineteenth and twentieth centuries were often concerned about the responsiveness of the ministries to government policies and aims.

During much of the nineteenth century, tensions between politicians and administrators were accommodated through the persistence of opportunities for political patronage. Indeed, unlike the Prussian/German system, in France the patronage dispensed by ministers and elected officials in parliament continued to be a significant way to fill some government offices.[83] Personal recommendations were regularly submitted to seek ministerial preference for positions, and partisanship infused the administration of government. This system allowed ministers, prefects, and other high-level officials to develop useful political relationships and to reassure those who represented a party or coalitions in power of their commitment to the regime and the government of the day. In the early twentieth century, "Justice for all, favors to its friends" described the way the public service operated in fact.[84]

In the context of weak and changing executive leadership, the parties that formed coalition governments in parliament were thus provided with a means to influence public administration. Side-by-side with an increasingly professionalized public service, then, a patronage system that functioned at both party and personal levels provided some assurance of political loyalty. Loyalty to the state was unquestioned; within that assumption, parties sought a partisan public service by placing their people in ministerial cabinets and other sensitive positions.

In contrast to the Prussian/German system, French administrators were not "above politics"; politics was embedded in ministerial leadership and recruitment through a continuing tradition of patronage, but without unsettling the day-to-day operations of a well-trained public service. Patronage thus had little impact on the performance of the bureaucracy, but was essential in accommodating the tensions between politicians and administrators. Over a considerable period, the responsibility of the public servant to his purported political masters was twofold—the state was owed strict allegiance, but the regime and its politicians could be accommodated through patronage.

Later in the twentieth century, however, the power of the bureaucracy vis-à-vis political decision makers increased, limiting the extent to which two systems—patronage and career—accommodated each other. The bureaucracy gained greater corporate integrity and autonomy through demands related to conditions of service by emerging staff associations and through a growing body of judicial decisions in administrative law that increased the prerogatives and protections of the career public service.[85] A code of rights and obligations for the civil service emerged incrementally, and through judicial rather than legislative action.[86] The representation of corporate interest and the growing protection of the civil service in the context of continued political upheaval added to tensions about the loyalty of the civil service.

As in other countries, World War I and the Depression increased the size of the state, and provided opportunities for the public bureaucracy to grow amid considerable political upheaval and confusion. The basic principles of the system remained constant, although its coherence suffered, particularly under the demands of war. Then, under the Vichy government established in June 1940, French public administration carried on with business as usual, accommodating itself to Nazi mandates to purge Jews, women, Freemasons, and others from its ranks through laws in 1940 and 1941. Although some joined the resistance movement, the number was small, and most public officials accommodated to German demands and continued to serve the state, such as it was, and its post-republican principles of "work, family, and authority."[87]

With the demise of Vichy, reforms spearheaded by the de Gaulle government revisited the issue of loyalty. In 1945 and 1946, new policies included regulations related to the rights of public servants and a revamped process for recruitment at higher levels—henceforth to be managed by the just-established École Nationale d'Administration (ENA), whose job it was to train officials for high-level office. According to Charles de Gaulle, this new institution was necessary in order to have "a valid and homogeneous corps in all public functions."[88] On the losing end of this innovation were the various ministries and other fiefdoms that had controlled recruitment at the organizational level. At the same time, the École Libre des Sciences Politiques was nationalized and established provincial branches.[89] Thus, the ENA would be the gateway for all higher-level administrative careers, and a single national examination replaced exams at the ministry level.[90]

The issue of loyalty to the state was not far below the surface in these reforms. For the Gaullist architect of the reforms, Michel Debré, ENA was necessary in order to "teach its future civil servants 'le sens de l'État'; it must make them understand the responsibilities of the Administration, make them taste the grandeur and accept the servitudes of the *métier*."[91] For the postwar era, then, a unified national administrative elite was the objective of reformers, in part to improve efficiency, in part to encourage greater coordination, and in part to overcome the politicization of the public administration that supported the Vichy government—and to ensure loyalty to the state, whoever commanded it.

Deconstructing Max Weber

The twentieth century in the United States, Europe, and Japan witnessed a gradual but definitive consolidation of the power of a career civil service. Increasingly, the dark side of Weber's model became more salient in public opinion and politics, and civil services around the world faced a new challenge. Hierarchy, precedent, the importance of "the files," as well as the increasing size and complexity of the activities of government opened civil services to a fundamental attack on their organizing principles and structure. Efforts to improve bureaucratic efficiency and responsiveness were ubiquitous in all countries during the extensive period of civil service consolidation. For most of the twentieth century, however, efforts to increase efficiency accepted the basic idea of a career civil service.

But a new wave of reformism in the 1980s fundamentally challenged the Weberian model. In particular, ideas incorporated into "the new public management," drawing inspiration from neoclassical economics, focused on encouraging marketlike structures and incentives in the public service—contracts, pay for performance, citizens as customers of public services, results orientation—as ways of dealing with what was seen as the critical problem of public sector administration, asymmetries in the principal-agent relationship.[92] A fundamentally conservative critique of government, its popularity quickly spread among politicians responding to public dissatisfaction with bureaucracy and "big government." In addition, mission-focused public managers found the approach attractive because of its direct concern with incentives for improved performance and outcomes.

From this period on, the systems created in the nineteenth and twentieth centuries were decried as failures of efficiency and democratic governance.[93] This questioning clearly focused on the issue of performance. No country was immune to this challenge, and the "demonology of bureaucracy" was not subject to a language barrier.[94] Indeed, a full century spent consolidating rational-legal public services gave way to a fundamental questioning of their value.[95] Experiences in Britain and the United States demonstrate significant advances in efforts to undo Weber, while efforts in France, Germany, Spain, and Japan indicate that determined reformers came face to face with equally determined civil services.

Britain and the New Public Management

In Britain, Northcote and Trevelyan initiated a system that had become durable and stable, not one that was necessarily responsive or effective. For many years, the problem of the performance of government was dealt with through a series of piecemeal and opportunistic interventions, often at the behest of politicians. Indeed, most demands for patronage—in the sense of bringing in officials outside of processes set by the civil service—came from government leaders concerned about performance issues. While complaints about the civil service were frequently aired publicly, those who were engaged in reconstructing it and resisting that reconstruction came almost exclusively from within government.

Numerous commissions of inquiry and reform were of little impact until 1968, when the Fulton Committee lambasted the civil service as a holdover from the nineteenth century because of its commitment to amateurism, its constraints on the use of the knowledge of specialists, its lack of managerial capacity, and its distance from citizens.[96] Needed, the committee's report argued, was a focus on the "modern" needs of government and a significant revision in the kinds of skills sought through recruitment. It recommended that ministers should have the capacity to recruit specialists and advisers on a temporary basis to assist them. Prime Minister Harold Wilson, who commissioned the report, wanted—but was unable to secure—immediate action on many of the report's recommendations, including an end to the separation of classes that grew out of the distinction between intellectual and routine work.[97]

After the Fulton Committee Report of 1968 and its partial implementation in the 1970s, it was left to the government of Margaret Thatcher to mount a comprehensive attack on what were seen as the performance limitations of the civil service. She sought to "deprivilege the civil service," restrict the growing influence of the union organizations that represented public servants, and improve performance.[98] Initially the focus was on small-scale changes that could provide a guide to larger concerns about inefficiency, and then on the introduction of performance measures, but by 1988 a large-scale attack on hierarchy and centralization, known as "Next Steps," was in place.[99] Ministries would be reduced significantly in size and focus on policy; the civil service would be focused in these organizations, and those not in this much-leaner service would become part of a variety of executive and semiautonomous agencies, managed through performance contracts and with flexibility for executives based on competition in hiring high-level professionals. Pay and grading for all but the top civil servants would be the responsibility of agencies and departments, and these agencies and their personnel would be assessed on the basis of performance measures and annual targets.

This new emphasis on managerialism and performance encountered stiff resistance from the Treasury and from the civil servants' unions. A major public service strike of 1982 indicated the depth of the rejection of Thatcher's deprivileging, but in the end the Thatcher reforms were extensively implemented, and structures and incentives were fundamentally altered, indicating a "radical shift from a Weberian, hierarchical, bureaucracy to a minimalist state and market-centered governance."[100] Subsequent governments of the 1990s introduced citizen charters, enhanced citizen access to information, and increased incentives for good management. Then, with the advent of Labour governments, the emphasis shifted from market reforms to "networked governance and greater cooperation and coherence among government agencies," changes that also rejected fundamentals of the old civil service.[101]

The United States and the National Performance Review

The United States lagged behind Britain in the initiation of fundamental restructuring of the public service, if not in the extent of criticism of the bloat and inefficiency of the public bureaucracy. As in Britain, however, public sector performance was regularly found to be deficient. Just as the spoils system had generated continuous complaints about poor public services and corrupt officials, the system introduced in 1883 was regularly attacked for its sloth and failure to be responsive. With the victory of the civil service over the party politicians had come increasing autonomy for the departments of government and increasing difficulty of presidential management of the system. In the end, the reformers had part of what they wanted—a stable and neutral public service system, protected from parties and electoral changes—but still could not be certain of good and responsive performance. And the emergence and growth of unions and associations representing public servants continued apace, increasing resistance to system change.

As in Britain, for many decades, this problem of performance was dealt with piecemeal, on the assumption that the civil service system had become so entrenched as to be untouchable. Reforms—the introduction of incentive awards in the 1950s; increased pay in the 1960s; more centralized examinations in the same period; replacing the Civil Service Commission with an Office of Personnel Management; creating a mandarin system of Senior Executives; and the introduction of merit pay in the 1970s—did not significantly alter the civil service system. Under Ronald Regan, a more concerted attack on the bureaucracy picked up on a number of instruments of the new public management. Thus, changes involved decentralizing many federal programs to the state level, privatizing some agencies such as the post office, significantly reducing the number of employees in the system, increasing the number of political appointees at the top of various agencies, and tying performance assessments to salaries—all efforts designed to "starve the beast" that had become a major focus of attack, particularly by the Republican Party.[102]

In the 1990s, a major initiative of the Clinton administration, the National Performance Review, also sought to reinvent and reengineer government along more efficient and responsive lines, fundamentally questioning the structure of the system.[103] The effort to reform bureaucracy was turned over to departments and their civil servants to define and resolve. Performance and accountability were central to the goals of a reengineered public service, which was to be entrepreneurial and well attuned to the potential for e-government. In this and other initiatives, business models vied with decentralization and participatory management to engender the appropriate incentives for a better relationship between state and citizens, now frequently viewed as customers of government services. As in Great Britain, the problem of performance was thought to be rooted in the characteristics of the Weberian system that reformers had fought so hard to introduce and sustain.

Resisting Deconstruction in France . . .

The powerful French public administration, despite its impressive development, did not escape the kinds of criticisms that were hurled at public services in other countries. In one analysis, the system was charged with a "bureaucratic psychosis in which the major elements are a spirit of caste, unimaginativeness, secretiveness, excessive formalism, and a fair degree of officiousness. . . . Red tape often chokes the processes of administration."[104] The evolution of the French public service had brought professionalism, autonomy from political interference, and stability— but not necessarily good performance.

In the interest of improved performance, reform initiatives from the 1980s through the 2000s emphasized greater decentralization, less emphasis on secrecy and more on accountability, greater agility of process, more consultation, more concern with individual assessment of civil servants, and de-bureaucratization.[105] Reforms of the 1990s and 2000s restructured ministries away from strict hierarchy toward a role as manager of semi-independent units to be held to account for performance.

In all initiatives, the politics of change included extensive negotiation with the civil service unions, aligned generally with parties of the left and with a penchant for striking. In addition, the elite status of the higher civil service and its corporatist organization into *corps,* as well as the presence of many former civil servants in parliament, significantly impeded efforts at privatization, the introduction of semi-independent agencies, and wider introduction of the new public management.[106] Some progress was made, but in France, the power of the civil service consistently limited what could be achieved by those in pursuit of alternative models of good governance.

. . . and in Germany

The German civil service was strongly institutionalized and firmly decentralized in the postwar era. Both of these characteristics made significant reform of the system difficult. Thus, the 1949 Basic Law that set the parameters of the civil service could be altered only with a two-thirds majority in both houses of the parliament, and its institutional structures could be changed only through legislation. Moreover, decentralized management of the system at the level of the *Länder* meant that any change would have to be carried out independently in each state. The fact that many parliamentarians were former public servants only added to the difficulties of change.[107]

This does not mean that the civil service was immune from criticism. Indeed, concerns about the management of the administration and its performance came to the fore in the process of unification with the former German Democratic Republic in 1990 and 1991. This process, which increased the size of the service by about 40 percent and dramatically increased pressure on the country's budgetary system, raised significant issues about the management and cost of government.[108] Political and public opinion was attracted to the principles of the new public management in the 1990s, and proposals included the abolition or severe downsizing of the civil service.

The "traditional principles of the civil service," defended by their practitioners, were not fully effective in responding to the extensive criticism of the system's aloofness, legalism, and ponderousness.[109] In a 1997 report of the Federal Commission on the Streamlined State, for example, the legal and process-focused orientation of the German civil service was faulted and an orientation toward managerialism much preferred as a way forward.[110] A new law put into effect in 1998 altered some of the strictures on the hiring, transfer, and retirement of civil servants, and introduced some performance-based incentives for upper-level officials.[111] In the late 1990s and into the 2000s, proposals and initiatives for reform emphasized greater flexibility and better performance from the public service, but the structures of the old civil service remained largely intact.

At the end of the 2000s, the extent to which the performance demand had been met by significant reconstruction in the public service in Germany remained low by the standards of other European countries. Germany's reform initiatives were driven by an "accretion of piecemeal and gradual change . . . propelled not so much by an identifiable reformist coalition than by a complex set of actors with partly contradictory aims, priorities, and preferences," adding up to a "decline in the public bureaucratic state" but no full transformation of the concept of the public service.[112]

Little Progress in Spain . . .

The formation of a national civil service in Spain was significantly delayed and weakened by the corporatist structure of the public service as it evolved in the nineteenth and twentieth centuries. Reformers convinced of the need for coherence, for strengthening the role of political leaders in directing government, and increasing democratic protections for citizens sought, through an end run around existing structures, to weaken the hold of the *corps* and then to reconstruct the system around a radical decentralization of public authority. In this important change, the semi-autonomous civil services of Spain's seventeen autonomous communities were constructed on the national model, and many of the personnel that formerly staffed the central government were transferred to the regions.

In the late 1980s, an effort to promote "the new managerialism" was introduced under the banner of government modernization, but failed to gain traction with the civil service, which resisted efforts to impose new standards and procedures.[113] In addition, during the 1990s, the country created a number of semiautonomous agencies that were guided by management and performance principles but subordinated to specific ministries.[114] Nevertheless, in operational terms, the Spanish civil service, albeit with a weakened *corps* structure, survived mostly intact from modernization initiatives based on the new public management.

. . . and in Japan

In Japan, the great Meiji reform had produced a public service that was stable, hierarchical, predictable, elite, and practiced in law and the specialties of individual ministries. As early as the 1950s, however, it was criticized as being "antiquarian, formalistic, and heavy-handed," as well highly secretive and difficult to coordinate.[115] Its members were smart and well educated, they were respected and usually obeyed—but this did not solve the performance problem of government.

Efforts to improve efficiency were resisted by ministries and by the civil service. In the 1980s, reform initiatives were sparked by commission reports concerned about the efficiency of the public sector and about the close alliances among bureaucrats, the private sector, and the Liberal Democratic Party; downsizing and privatization figured prominently in the reforms undertaken, and public sector union strength declined in consequence of these changes.[116] By the end of the 2000s, Japan had a civil service that was more sensitive to performance issues, although its traditional characteristics remained its strongest feature.

The Beat Goes On

Clearly, the experiences of the twentieth and early twenty-first centuries confirm that passing laws and announcing change are only skirmishes along the way to full consolidation of meaningful reform. Indeed, reformers and scholars all too often focus on the legitimizing moment of change initiatives—the moment when they are formally approved in law or administrative decree—considering that victory has been achieved. The histories presented in this chapter clearly indicate that conflicts to establish career civil service regimes endured in conflicts over their durability, control, composition, loyalty, and performance. These histories also indicate that the salience of the conflicts that most engaged the civil service systems varied across countries and reflected contention about power over government decision making and the capacity of government to meet new challenges.

Throughout the period in which civil service systems were consolidated, patronage in public life demonstrated considerable staying power, particularly when governments faced major challenges or took on new responsibilities. The issue of patronage as a model for broad recruitment into the public service was certainly dead, but it lived on in debates about where to draw the line between political and nonpolitical appointments and how to ensure that governments were equipped to respond to new problems and changing demands. Wars, economic and political crises, and the rapid expansion of government responsibilities tended to favor drawing the line less rigidly. The end of crisis and expansion generally spelled the reassertion of the capacity of now institutionalized public service organizations to control recruitment and promotion.

The history of construction, deconstruction, and reconstruction in the twentieth and early twenty-first centuries also suggests a widespread pattern of reaction against the growth of civil services. In particular, a century of debate about the performance of government was married to a critique of the growing autonomy of the public service and the expansion of its capacity to withstand demands for responsiveness and efficiency. In each of the countries considered, numerous commissions, task forces, and inquiries suggested ways in which red tape could be eliminated and Weberian bureaucracies made more effective and efficient. Few had much impact until the 1980s and 1990s, when a new model of public service emerged in the guise of the new public management. This model offered a fundamental critique of the structure and incentives of the career civil service that reformers had fought so hard to bring into existence. The now embedded Weberian systems played the role of the protectors of the old system against the onslaught of politicians and academicians seeking to reconstruct the public service.

These patterns—the ongoing nature of conflict over the public service, the variety of guises in which politicians and reformers contest the further establishment of the career civil service, the addition of new protagonists as the new systems become consolidated, the reassertion of claims for patronage, and the enduring problem of performance—may also be played out in more contemporary initiatives to replace patronage with career civil services in Latin American countries. In Part Two of *Jobs for the Boys,* I test this assertion. In addition, the patterns discussed in this chapter suggest the ways in which institutions become "sticky." Control over these institutions enhances the power of particular actors and organizations, corporate identities emerge and become important in political contests over the extent to which rules of the game can be altered, processes for decision making and implementation become embedded, and those who benefit from the rules and the processes find little to gain in discussing change. At the same time, changes do occur—often in very piecemeal and uncertain ways—and from time to time in more significant efforts, attesting to the impact of strategic actors and timing in reform initiatives.

PART II

A Contemporary Record

CHAPTER 4

Latin America

Patterns of Patronage and Politics

In the nineteenth and twentieth centuries, career civil services were constructed in the now developed countries of the world. Prior to their creation, public service recruitment systems based on patronage had been of use to kings, party politicians, class elites, revolutionaries, reformers, and rascals, and had demonstrated adaptability to a wide variety of purposes. The transition from patronage to a formal career service was generally a long process, fraught with conflict between those who sought reform and those who found benefits in a continuation of the status quo. Moreover, the introduction of new systems did not end contestation about reform; conflict over the existence, control, characteristics, and loyalties of the public service continued for decades after the construction of new systems in most countries. In turn, the new systems generated their own pathologies, which then became targets for reformers in subsequent periods. For these countries, then, the transition from one system to another was far from a technical exercise in institutional engineering. It was a profoundly political process of change.

If the cases of public service reform in developed countries suggest patterns and lessons about how institutions are transformed over time and how new rules of the game are introduced, adapted, and accepted, the more recent histories of Latin American countries provide a laboratory for testing these generalizations. At the outset of the twenty-first century, nowhere in the world, except perhaps in mid-nineteenth century U.S. experience, was patronage more fully embedded in political reality than in Latin America; nowhere had it proved itself more durable and flexible; and nowhere had it been more fully decried as a hindrance

141

to development, competence, and probity—except perhaps in late nineteenth century U.S. experience.

Just as in the earlier cases, Latin America's public sector patronage systems provide evidence of considerable variety in political and administrative outcomes—often corruption, incompetence, and even violence, but also extensive policy responsiveness, the accumulation of technical expertise, focused organizational performance, and political stability. Although one scholar has commented that in Latin America, "the needs of modernizing nations are basically being served by administrative dinosaurs," the very flexibility and persistence of patronage systems were sufficient to provide a range of benefits to those who controlled them.[1] This observation certainly conforms to the lessons derived from the earlier experience of countries in Europe and elsewhere.

Also replicating the experience of other regions of the world, Latin American countries that continued to rely primarily on an extensive patronage system differed considerably in terms of standards of living and rates of industrialization and urbanization. Their party systems differed, as did the extent to which changes in personnel mirrored electoral calendars. Patronage systems were found in highly centralized and more decentralized political systems. They adjusted to democratic and authoritarian regimes and were as useful to military politicians as to civilian ones. Moreover, the overall quality of public administration and levels of competence and corruption differed across countries. Patronage systems were almost ubiquitous, but their impact was as varied as it had been in other countries in an earlier period.

Nor have Latin American countries been strangers to efforts to institute career civil service systems. Indeed, as this chapter indicates, most countries in Latin America approved constitutions and passed laws to establish and legitimize civil service systems—even though a functioning civil service became reality in only a very few of them. Thus, the conflicts of transition—or attempts at transition—are not unknown in the region. The specific uses of patronage generated a wealth of potential gains for those who controlled these systems, and the promise of neutrality and efficiency from career civil service systems was hardly compensation for what they would lose through reform. Similarly, *après* reform conflicts that were associated with system deconstruction and reconstruction in the earlier examples were also familiar in Latin America.

Moreover, Latin America's public sector reformers echoed most of the charges against patronage systems that characterized other countries. Indeed, there was virtually unanimous agreement among them that conditions of development in the region and in specific countries were significantly constrained by the quality of the public sector; key to improving the public sector was the establishment of a merit-oriented career public service.[2] Failure to have such a system meant "clientelistic practices, corruption or *amiguismo*," conditions inimical to economic, social, and political progress.[3] For many observers of Latin American reality, then, reform of the public service system was extraordinarily important to the development of the region and the establishment of good governance in the twenty-first century.

Thus, in mapping the persistence of patronage, reform initiatives, subsequent efforts to challenge them, and the governance consequences of public sector reform, Latin American countries provide a broad palette of opportunities for study. This short chapter provides an overview of public sectors in Latin America as they appeared at the outset of the twenty-first century. Subsequent chapters chronicle the experiences of the persistence of patronage, the introduction of civil service systems, the conflicts that were encountered in implementing them, and the consequences of those efforts. The stories of persistence and change show much in common with earlier histories of public sector reform recounted in prior chapters, yet they differ in one important way: in Latin America, the widespread use of patronage has not been successfully quelled.

Latin America's Public Services in Theory and Practice

In the early 2000s, Latin America's public services were characterized by important differences in size and structure. Some countries had relatively few public sector employees, given their populations; others had surprisingly large public sectors. Brazil's central government employees accounted for only 0.3 percent of the total population, and Argentina's only 0.4 percent, for example, while in Uruguay and the Dominican Republic, public sector employment accounted for 5.5 and 3.6 percent of their populations, respectively.[4] Expenditures per public employee also differed significantly across countries. Brazil's central government expenditures amounted to $85,616 per public employee, while in Uruguay it was $5,487 and in Paraguay $6,090.[5] Table 4.1 provides basic indicators of notable characteristics of the public services in eighteen countries in the region, indicating significant variation among them.

In addition to these measures, there was also considerable variance across public sectors in terms of the educational backgrounds of their employees. In Brazil, Chile, Costa Rica, Colombia, and Argentina, for example, indices of higher education were particularly high among those employed in the public sector, whereas in Central American countries, the number of those with university education was low. In Guatemala, only 6 percent of public sector employees had university educations, while the level was as high as 40 percent in other countries.[6] Salaries, and salary compression, also varied significantly from one country to another, as did the consistency of salaries across similar kinds of work.[7] Further, regulations and union protections had differential impacts on the flexibility of the public service to adapt to change.

The Theory

Most interestingly, by the 2000s, most Latin American countries had laws that mandated selection of public administrators on the basis of merit—often determined through competitive examinations—and that set up the equivalent of a civil service commission to undertake recruitment and ensure the fair treatment and political neutrality of public sector workers. Indeed, as far back as 1954, a study carried out by the Organization of American States found that seven countries—Argentina, Brazil, Colombia, Costa Rica, Ecuador, Panama, and Peru—had the legal foundations of a career civil service.[8] Some countries formally established such systems in the early twentieth century.[9] In other countries, international development assistance and reform-minded leaders in the 1950s and 1960s devoted considerable effort to putting this kind of legislation in place.[10] El Salvador, Honduras, and Guatemala all introduced civil service laws in the 1960s, and Ecuador and Peru followed suit with new legislation in the 1980s.[11] These laws included structured merit-based recruiting systems, classification of positions, and norms of compensation. Regularly, setting the legal basis for a career civil service was explained as a fundamentally important step toward greater efficiency and effectiveness in the public service.

Table 4.1. Indicators of central government public sector employment in Latin America, 2004*

	Total number of civilian public sector employees	Total public sector employees as % of total population	Total public expenditure per public employee (2004 dollars)	Total public sector wage bill as % of GNP	Av. public sector wage as % of GNP per capita
Argentina	163,096	0.41	$ 56,433	1.97	1.68
Bolivia	nd	3.16	7,638	5.41	4.96
Brazil	896,225	0.32	85,616	2.12	5.27
Chile	146,514	0.93	71,759	5.48	2.25
Colombia	569,516	1.25	23,457	10.05	2.58
Costa Rica	nd	2.53	37,156	9.36	1.78
Dom. Rep.	313,605	3.61	10,866	5.37	1.54
Ecuador	nd	1.73	21,361	5.08	2.79
El Salvador	122,085	1.84	17,016	7.80	1.47
Guatemala	nd	0.89	26.706	3.47	1.77
Honduras	113,769	1.67	14,265	10.30	1.51
Mexico	2,310,342**	2.20	51,496	5.98	2.71
Nicaragua	nd	1.61	6,360	5.62	2.86
Panama	93,912	3.00	50,153	6.18	1.97
Paraguay	38,350	2.70	6,090	8.98	2.73
Peru	616,000	2.30	11,862	7.32	1.58
Uruguay	198,215	5.89	5,487	4.68	0.93
Venezuela	457,456	1.86	38,814	13.14	3.75

Source: Iacoviello 2006:571–572 and country case study summaries.

*Dates for data vary by country, and numbers exclude teachers and health professionals.

**Includes teachers.

Indeed, in an Inter-American Development Bank (IDB) study published in 2006, all eighteen countries surveyed had a legally recognized career public service.[12] Table 4.2, with data taken from this study, indicates widespread acceptance of a civil service as a basic institution of governance; each constitution enshrines it. In addition, in all cases, subsequent laws instituted a career service. In eight cases, where initial basic laws were nullified by courts, legislatures, or executive decrees, newer legislation reinstituted the systems. In eight cases, operational regulations followed within three years of the legislation, although in Honduras there was a nine-year gap before a law was followed by enabling regulations, and in Guatemala the lag was thirty years. And in seven cases, no regulatory framework had been put in place by

Table 4.2. Career civil service legislation and regulations Latin American countries, to 2004

Country	Civil service in constitution	Basic law	Most recent basic law	Regulations for most recent law?
Argentina	1957	1980	1999	2002
Bolivia	1967	1999	1999	2000
Brazil	1988	1936	1988	NA
Chile	1980	1989	2003	No
Colombia	1992	1992	2004	No
Costa Rica	1949	1953	1953	1954
Dominican Rep.	1966	1991	1991	1994
Ecuador	1979	1978	2004	No
El Salvador	1950	1961	1961	No
Guatemala	1985	1968	1968	1998
Honduras	1957	1967	1967	1976
Mexico	1917	1963	2003	2004
Nicaragua	1987	1990	2003	2004
Panama	1972	1994	1994	1997
Paraguay	1992	1970	2000	No
Peru	1979	1984	2004	No
Uruguay	1967	1943	1943	1943
Venezuela	1961	1975	2002	No

Source: Iacoviello 2006:567–570.

2004, signaling that constitutional and legal mandates continued to be aspirational.

As in all countries, political systems in Latin America also recognized the legitimacy of political appointments to some positions. There are differences, however, in how extensively political leaders—primarily presidents and ministers—were officially granted rights to make choices based on their own criteria, as indicated in Table 4.3.[13] Yet in most cases, officially available discretionary appointments fell well under 2 percent of all positions; only in Guatemala, Brazil, and Bolivia were political executives legally entitled to greater leeway to appoint "their people."

The Practice

Taken together, Tables 4.2 and 4.3 indicate the pervasive presence in Latin America of a legally sanctioned career service. But, as is often the

Table 4.3. Percentage of public sector positions officially available for political appointment, 2004

Country	Percent of total public sector positions
Argentina	0.26
Bolivia	9.00
Brazil	9.52
Chile	1.34
Colombia	1.08
Dominican Rep.	1.32
El Salvador	0.78
Guatemala	17.76
Honduras	1.68
Mexico	0.37
Panama	0.71
Paraguay	0.83
Peru	0.46
Uruguay	0.19
Venezuela	1.60

Source: Iacoviello and Zuvanic 2006a:52.

case, de facto practices trump de jure theory. The IDB report indicates, for example, that in several countries—Guatemala, Venezuela, Brazil, Nicaragua, Mexico, and the Dominican Republic—political appointments were accepted de facto down to the level of unit or office chiefs and managers, that is, through middle ranges of the public administration.[14] In Bolivia, Honduras, Colombia, Costa Rica, and El Salvador, politicians regularly made personnel appointments down to the level of department heads and their top-level managers. Politicians in Argentina, Uruguay, Panama, and Chile were given less scope for appointments, but the reach of discretion remained considerable.

This assessment of practice no doubt underrepresents the extent to which patronage appointments continued to be the norm in many Latin American countries. In Ecuador, for example, twelve thousand employees joined the government in 1983; only three hundred of them had taken the required examination; only 10 percent of overall public sector workers had tenure.[15] In Mexico, up to thirty thousand positions changed hands when new administrations were elected. In Panama, only 18 percent of public positions were *not* available for discretionary appointment, and some twenty-five thousand employees could lose their jobs after elections.[16] In the Dominican Republic, some three thousand employees incorporated into the career system lost their jobs in 2004 as a result of a change of government administrations.[17] In Colombia, a 2004 law sought to put an end to five years of legal ambiguity in which in which as much as 38 percent of career personnel were working under provisional appointments.[18] In Venezuela, some seventy-six hundred people lost their public sector jobs after signing a referendum to recall the president in 2004.[19]

Indeed, in recognition of the gap between de jure and de facto systems, the IDB report indicated five levels of merit-based access—appointment through a process of examination or public competition—to government positions in the eighteen countries its researchers investigated. Countries ranged from complete discretion in hiring (level 0) to extensive coverage of a career public service (level 5). As indicated, only Brazil ranks high on the chart, although Chile and Costa Rica are also acknowledged to have made significant progress in implementing a career system.

At the outset of the twenty-first century, then, only three of the eighteen countries actually recruited a significant number of public sector

Table 4.4. Extent of merit-based hiring in Latin American countries, 2004

Level				
0 (low)	1	2	3	4–5 (high)
Panama El Salvador Honduras	Nicaragua Guatemala Paraguay Peru Ecuador Dominican Republic Bolivia	Venezuela Mexico Argentina Uruguay Colombia	Chile Costa Rica	Brazil
Predominance of discretion of authorities to hire, relocate, or fire employees	Largely unsuccessful efforts to limit discretion in hiring, promotion, and firing	Merit systems live side by side with clientelism in recruitment, selection, and hiring	Predominance of technical criteria for recruitment, hiring, promotion, and firing of personnel	Open recruitment based on suitability, with guarantees against arbitrariness. Hiring based on competence using valid instruments. Mechanisms for ingress, promotion, absenteeism, discipline. Non-arbitrary firing on the basis of performance.

Source: Iacoviello 2006:543. Author's translation.

workers through a structured career system. In fact, the growth of the public sector in many countries in the 1960s and 1970s generally meant rapid and partisan or personal hiring of new employees and considerable executive leadership in allocating jobs in following up on campaign promises. Thus, patronage systems in most Latin American countries demonstrated great capacity for persistence in the face of modernization and industrialization, international pressures, reform initiatives, and legislation to the contrary.

Several common practices explain the gap between Tables 4.2 and 4.3 on the one hand, and Table 4.4 on the other. A clearly important way to sustain a discretionary hiring system, of course, was simple failure to observe laws and regulations. In countries where there was greater recognition of the strictures of law, however, politicians found ways to avoid conforming to them. For example, those who held patronage positions at leadership or managerial levels had wide scope for bringing in their people through temporary appointments or as advisers to serve at the pleasure of their bosses. There were opportunities to create parallel organizations with special hiring codes and salaries; leeway to staff state-owned enterprises and agencies not subject to regular personnel rules; loopholes for hiring temporary employees, additional employees, and contract employees; the existence of special administrative islands with their own personnel regulations and codes; and the availability of executive and implementing units for special programs.

Thus, a number of avoidance mechanisms ensured that political executives continued to have considerable discretion in hiring. At times, they used these mechanisms to escape the rigidity of personnel laws and regulations, a practice that often produced elite units or groups of policy and management experts within ministries and other organizations. At other times, posts in government were carefully allocated to the party faithful, regardless of qualifications. Often, these mechanisms were fully legal and provided means for avoiding formal constraints without directly confronting or contravening the legal fiction of a merit-based system.

In many countries, the hiring of contact and other special categories of officials significantly undercut the reach of the civil service laws and regulations.[20] In Argentina and Uruguay, the use of such measures resulted in virtual "parallel bureaucracies" that political leaders relied upon rather than on established organizations of government.[21] Often, then, from middle-level administrators to top-level advisers to ministers, large numbers of those in the public service continued to be subject to hiring and firing at will, and the criteria for doing so continued to be contingent on the perspectives and priorities of those in leadership positions.

In contrast to those at middle and higher levels, employees at lower levels of the bureaucracy in many countries enjoyed job security because a tenure system evolved through the unionization of clerks and blue-collar workers such as maintenance personnel. In some countries of the region—Mexico is a good example—a large number of public sector employees were regulated under labor laws rather than civil service laws. But even with unions, the spoils system could thrive. Access to low-level positions was often controlled by union bosses and allocated as patronage for party, personal, or intra-organizational political reasons. At times, even middle-level officials who arrived through discretionary appointments were granted tenure once in office through labor and public service employment codes and contracts. Thus, although unionization and employment protections often meant extensive constraints on firing, they did not have much impact on issues related to recruitment, assignments, and promotions. Thus, stability of tenure did not necessarily mean that a politically neutral regime existed for hiring.

In summary, by the 2000s, Latin American countries were not deficient in laws mandating selection of public administrators on the basis of merit or setting up equivalents of a civil service commission to undertake recruitment and ensure fair treatment and the political neutrality of public sector workers. Yet despite the consistency of this history throughout the region, in the early years of the new century, only Costa Rica, Chile, and Brazil recruited significant numbers of public sector workers through a structured career civil service system. Indeed, the implementation of civil service legislation was extremely weak in Latin America. As concluded in the IDB study, "It is precisely the divergence between the norms and the practices that is the greatest weakness of civil service systems in their countries."[22]

Competence and Corruption

Many of the patronage systems in Latin America resembled the kind of electoral partisanship and rotation in office found in the United States in the nineteenth century. With each election, even when the same party was returned to office, jobs were lost, shifted, and allocated to party stalwarts who had been helpful in winning the election. Frequently, the first year of a new administration was one in which little was accomplished other than recruiting personnel and making plans for new initiatives. Similarly, the final year of an administration, taking place in an election year, was often a time of poor performance as officials engaged widely in electoral mobilization or worked to establish alliances to ensure they could find jobs after the election.

As will be seen in a later chapter, Mexico perfected this system within a hegemonic one-party system in which each new administration of the same party witnessed massive changes in personnel. This system of rotation in office helped cement loyalty to the dominant party for seven decades and created a form of political stability based in part on the anticipation of future gains by the politically and administratively ambitious. Bolivia, Colombia, Ecuador, Guatemala, Honduras, El Salvador, Panama, and Peru were much less able to find stability in the operation of such a system, even though it was deeply embedded in all these countries.

It should not be surprising, then, that public sectors in Latin American countries did not inspire great confidence at the outset of the twenty-first century. In the late 2000s, most countries of the region scored relatively low on Transparency International's governance index linked to perceived corruption, as indicated in Table 4.5. For each country, this table reports its ranking in terms of private sector perceptions of corruption in the public sector, with a score of 10 signaling the highest level of probity perceived. Only two countries, Chile and Uruguay, scored above 5 in 2008. Politicized public sectors were certainly fodder for such perceptions.

Yet party identities as a criterion for appointment to office generally coexisted with more specific uses of patronage. Presidents, ministers, and other high-level officials had the capacity to use this power to attract highly qualified staffs to carry out specific policy initiatives of their own or of the president.[23] More generally, the ability of Latin American countries to pursue policy changes could also be significantly attributed to the use of patronage. Thus, for example, the neoliberal reforms so widely adopted in the 1980s and 1990s in many Latin American countries were often put in place and supported by ministries of finance and

Table 4.5. Transparency International Corruption Perception Index, 2008

World rank	Country	IDB merit hiring score (0–5)	Index	Number of surveys
23	Chile	3	6.9	7
23	Uruguay	2	6.9	5
47	Costa Rica	3	5.1	5
67	El Salvador	0	3.9	5
70	Colombia	2	3.8	7
72	Peru	1	3.6	6
72	Mexico	2	3.6	7
80	Brazil	4–5	3.5	7
85	Panama	0	3.4	5
96	Guatemala	1	3.1	5
102	Dominican Republic	1	3.0	5
102	Bolivia	1	3.0	6
109	Argentina	2	2.9	7
126	Honduras	0	2.6	6
134	Nicaragua	1	2.5	6
138	Paraguay	1	2.4	5
151	Ecuador	1	2.0	5
158	Venezuela	2	1.9	7

Source: www.transparency.org/regional_pages/americas/corrupcion_en_america
_latina/americas_cpi. August 17, 2009. Column 3 from Table 4.4.

planning whose hiring policies were discretionary but focused on the recruitment of technocratic talent into government. Mexico, Chile, Bolivia, and Argentina are good examples of this pattern.

Similarly, in the 1990s and 2000s, when ministers and presidents sought to implement extensive new policies for urban development, social protection, or poverty reduction, they also tended to rely extensively on personally selected subordinates who in turn recruited through patronage with an eye toward policy impact. In this way, for example, innovative cash transfer programs were rapidly—and expertly—put in place in Mexico, Brazil, and Chile in the 1990s and 2000s by ministries and specialized agencies whose mission was clarified and focused through the use of "smart" patronage.[24]

Thus, in some cases, the patronage system encouraged the responsiveness of bureaucratic actors to executive policy leadership and the rapid implementation of new policy initiatives. In Bolivia, noted for having an extremely politicized public sector despite numerous efforts at reform, the system was consistently used in the 1980s and 1990s to facilitate a wide range of policy changes. It allowed political leaders to attract a new generation of well-trained young people into government, where they were often given significant responsibilities. In addition, the allocation of positions for partisan purposes—providing incentives to form winning legislative coalitions—made it possible for several governments to act boldly to introduce a range of new economic policies.[25] By parceling out patronage to parties as an inducement for favorable congressional votes on economic restructuring, privatization, and decentralization, governments were able to advance important policy changes, even though at the same time they were extremely constrained in how far they could pursue public service reform. In essence, they used their control of patronage to advance significant policy change in other sectors.

It would, of course, be disingenuous to argue that incompetence and corruption did not find comfortable homes in a very large number of Latin American governments. Moreover, some part of these characteristics can certainly be laid at the door of the ongoing presence of extensive patronage systems, although it is perhaps impossible to know how much. At the most general level, most countries of the region had weak institutions, lax regulatory systems, and arcane legal processes that also encouraged poor performance and corrupt practices. Nevertheless, patronage systems can make impunity an ongoing condition when public officials fail to perform their duties or do so in ways that are illegal, unjust, or improper. Thus, initiatives to alter this reality continued to inspire reformers in the 1990s and 2000s.

Conclusion

Latin American countries were successful in establishing career civil service systems in law. Yet politicians found a variety of ways to bring their people into government through special contractual arrangements or the creation of units and organizations outside the regulatory standards for the civil service. Thus, despite a plethora of laws and formal

strictures, partisan and personal appointments continued to predomi-
nate in the region. Some political leaders used patronage to achieve
clearly defined goals, while others adopted it in ways that only contributed to low performance and poor management of the public sector.
Thus, an important lesson of this chapter is that patronage systems demonstrate the same diversity and flexibility in Latin American countries as
was historically the case in a number of now developed countries.

The story now shifts to four case studies of the persistence of patronage, efforts to construct Weberian bureaucracies, and the challenges
that such initiatives faced. In the next chapter, the histories of Brazil,
Argentina, Mexico, and Argentina provide examples of strong legacies
of patronage. In Chapter 6, efforts to introduce reform in these countries demonstrate the importance of elite projects and reform moments
in making change happen. Chapter 7 indicates that efforts to consolidate new systems are as difficult for later as for earlier adopters. In distinction to the experiences of the countries discussed in Part One, however, Latin American reformers continued to face major constraints in
consolidating career civil service systems.

CHAPTER **5**

Roots and Branches

Traditions of public service in Latin America owe much to the patronage system inherited from colonial empires. Kings and viceroys, nineteenth- and twentieth-century presidents, cabinet ministers, party leaders, agency and department heads, among many others, personally appointed the officials who carried out the work of government. As elsewhere, positions in government were awarded for a variety of purposes, and appointments were often the result of pulling strings and pleading for the attention of potential patrons.[1] Across broad expanses of time, this system of personal appointments remained a fundamental aspect of politics and administration. Yet its use had distinct consequences for the creation of national states and the dynamics of national politics.

Through a general overview and then a focus on four countries in the region, this chapter complements the histories presented in Chapter 1 in three ways. First, it demonstrates the ways in which patronage systems in Spain and Portugal were transferred to their colonial empires, providing insight into how traditional institutions can be embedded in new soil. Second, it considers the ways in which patronage was used, abused, and constrained in the management of power relationships across time and space. Third, it shows how common institutional legacies were translated into distinct histories of nation building, party development, electoral competition, regime consolidation, and policy innovation. These roots and branches created characteristics of public sectors that twentieth- and twenty-first-century reformers sought to alter.

Roots

In the Spanish New World, metropolitan methods of state building— religious orthodoxy, royal patronage for civil and church positions, and the sale of offices—set standards for public sector recruitment from the late fifteenth to the early nineteenth centuries. Many positions were at stake; in addition to the range of necessary civil administrators, non-salaried positions with rights to the collection of fees were also distributed through royal favor. Overall, when transferred to the Americas, a patronage system based on royal favor was used explicitly to advance the fortunes of those born in Spain and of "pure blood." Race and place of birth were thus important criteria for the distribution of positions; whether or not competence was sought varied by time and place. Characteristically, the allocation of even low-level positions involved appeals to the royal court in Spain, a process entailing long periods of waiting for responses to correspondence sent across the Atlantic and not infrequent voyages by petitioners for the same purpose.[2]

Despite these wide powers of appointment, the Spanish crown faced constraints in the use of patronage in its colonies. Tenure, for example, was often long once an appointment had been made, and at times positions were passed along to the next generation. This was particularly true at middle and lower ranks of the colonial administration, where officials were generally appointed for life. Moreover, royal grants of *encomienda* ensured that those who were favored with authority over land, peoples, and resources had some independence from the king. Certainly distance curtailed the ability of the crown to ensure that public decisions were always taken in the interests of the monarchy. All these factors limited the capacity of the New World patronage system to be fully responsive to the court in Spain.

In addition, the practice of selling positions in government and the church grew steadily from the mid-sixteenth century, further constraining the reach and flexibility of the patronage system.[3] Established as a royal monopoly by Philip II, selling offices was an important source of income for Spain, providing over a million pesos to state coffers and accounting for about a quarter of all official positions in the colonies between 1700–1750.[4] So dependent did the crown become on this mode of allocating positions and status that public auctions for positions were common in the governance of the colonies. For the purchasers of many such positions, resale or inheritance of the office was a possibility.[5] In other cases, the office remained property of the crown and the appointment reverted to the monarch at the end of tenure.

There was a lively market for these sales. The purchase of a position, popular with colonial military and commercial elites, meant improvement in social status. The purchase of office provided at least one way for those born in the Americas to penetrate the monopoly of the Spanish-born over public office.[6] And venal practice clearly undercut the capacity of the crown to mold its administration, particularly when offices were sold at auction.[7] Despite their dependence on these sales, kings were not unmindful of this loss; available data indicate that more offices were for sale in areas relatively insulated from war and piracy; in areas at risk, fewer offices were put up for sale.[8] Nevertheless, at moments when such sales were most widely practiced, the loss of monarchical and metropolitan control was significant, and the quality of administration is thought to have declined considerably.[9]

Beginning in the 1770s, the overseas impact of the reforms of the Bourbon kings became apparent, as they sought to reassert central control over the colonial administration.[10] Based on principles of stability and competence, reforms fixed salaries according to official position and instituted procedures for promotion and retirement. The possibility of rising in the ranks through an incipient career system thus became more possible.[11] And, at the same time, full-time, salaried officials of the crown filled a larger number of public positions, and education became a more important qualification for service. Military and legal training were preferred for those appointed to higher office, and primary education was expected of those in lower-level positions. Even the sale of office was gradually infused with a greater calling for professional qualifications. While the laws and reforms of the Bourbon kings did not set out methods of recruitment distinct from those of the patronage system, and while the sale of public office continued, albeit on a reduced scale, the reforms did seek to improve the effectiveness of government and its responsiveness to the center.[12]

The Bourbons wished to alter the way the patronage system worked with a clear eye toward improved efficiency. What did not change, however, was the preference for those born in Spain *(peninsulares)* over those born in the colonies *(criollos)* and the ultimate discretion of the crown to make appointments based on whatever criteria were most useful to it. Thus, more emphasis on greater efficiency and effectiveness was sought through the patronage system, though the system remained intact. Moreover, "the decision to forgo sale of office in the hope of eventually realizing greater profits through improved bureaucratic efficiency and honesty was an expensive transition," and in some sense self-limiting, given short-term exigencies of the treasury in Spain.[13] In addition, claims on appointments by place of birth increased the level of contention between *peninsulares* and *criollos,* and the end of the Bourbon kings in 1808 in the face of Napoléon's invasion introduced an opportunity for the colonies to strike for independence.

As in the Spanish colonies, royal patronage in the Portuguese colony of Brazil extended to the military and the church.[14] But, here, centralization of power and control from the peninsula was never as well instituted as in Spain. Local notables early on captured considerable capacity to make decisions, and the *os grandes do lugar (*local elites) became known as those who held the power to distribute what few public offices there were.[15] However, when the Portuguese royal court fled to Brazil in 1808, the number of available positions grew substantially, and the crown asserted more control over their allocation. Even in the hinterlands, royal patronage became more important, and all appointments—regardless of level—required royal approval.[16]

With the establishment of a Brazilian monarchy in 1822, expertise and education were important to Emperor Pedro I and thus became more critical in the appointments he made. Examinations for some positions were introduced early in the nineteenth century.[17] Education in law was increasingly expected, even of local officials.[18] Yet, an underlying tension between *os grandes do lugar* and the central government remained an important aspect in determining claims to public position, and the hand of regional elites was also strengthened in the 1830s. As a consequence, a low-quality patronage system based in the regions contrasted with a much higher-quality patronage system based in the central government at this time.[19] Throughout the remainder of the nineteenth century and well into the twentieth, this bifurcated patronage system was apparent in Brazil, as was a distinction between greater competence in the center and lesser quality at the regional level. It was, throughout, a patrimonial state, in which public sector jobs had become "the 'noble profession' and the vocation of all."[20]

Patterns of appointments set in Europe continued to influence public service in the newly independent states of Latin America in the nineteenth century and much of the twentieth. In Spanish America, independence brought those born in the colonies into public office in significant numbers, but other discretionary standards for recruitment remained largely the same. And, despite a variety of efforts to set up professional public services, public administration in Latin American countries continued to be based on patronage, with the orientations and strategic needs of presidents and cliques (and later parties) the most important factors determining who would hold appointive office and who would be left standing in line.

These strategic needs were extraordinarily important to the politics of the nineteenth century. Overall, the period was characterized by ongoing conflict among oligarchic cliques, liberals and conservatives, secularists and clericalists, federalists and unitarists, regionalists and centralists, republicans and authoritarians. Those in temporary control of state offices incorporated these conflicts in government by drawing their partisans into public service—until ousted by other factions. *Caudillos* frequently reigned regionally and nationally, and dominated politics through their militias and appointments. Internal war was frequent, interstate wars were destructive, and neither led to stronger states. Nor were wars definitive of winners and losers, as they had been in many European countries.[21] For most countries, this period was marked by weak incipient states, ongoing violence, and factional control of government. By the 1830s, only Chile had been able to consolidate a relatively coherent state, and by the 1890s, the same could be said only of Mexico, Argentina, and Costa Rica. None established a career civil service.[22] Predemocratic initiatives to do so through authoritarian imposition were doomed by the weakness of the state itself.

And, as middle-class and then mass-based political parties developed in the twentieth century, patronage became more closely aligned with partisanship and loyalty to the party or to the personages who led the party. As governments took on important tasks in industrial and social development, parties increasingly functioned through brokers who mediated claims among local, regional, and national levels of parties and distributed benefits to particular clienteles.[23] Thus, depending on the country, patronage could be focused on partisan loyalties or loyalties to individuals—*caudillos,* party bosses, military leaders, or *caciques.*[24] At the same time, many countries were able to incorporate numerous technocrats into policy-making positions in government, to the point that scholars began to note their dominance in policy decisions, eclipsing the roles of legislatures, parties, or their leaders.[25] Often, this kind of recruitment and policy development process led to the creation of some effective administrative organizations, even when this characteristic was not shared widely among state agencies.

As regular elections became more often observed in twentieth-century Latin America, tenure in nonelected office increasingly came to reflect electoral cycles. The eventual institutionalization of strong executives generally gave presidents extraordinary powers of patronage, even when the state itself remained weak. Control over patronage was a major ingredient motivating political campaigns and the expectations of party workers and voters. In contexts of poverty and limited employment opportunities and an expanding state, elections could be hotly contested; their payoffs were eagerly sought by potential winners and their losses feared by those in power. Electoral violence and coercion were common. In Colombia, the patronage payoff of electoral politics was a major source of the internecine warfare that characterized the period known as *La Violencia* in the 1940s and 1950s.[26] Military regimes followed civilian precedent in reserving patronage powers for high-level officials and colonizing the public service with their supporters and brother officers.

And Branches

By the mid-twentieth century, however, the consequences of similar recruitment processes were varied in terms of the strength and coherence of central states. For example, Mexico, Chile, Uruguay, Brazil, and Argentina eventually built relatively strong states that had the capacity to generate development strategies for industrialization, to provide for relatively broad social provisioning in public health and education, and to create effective national identities. Colombia, Ecuador, Peru, Paraguay, Bolivia, and most of the Central American countries, on the other hand, continued to be characterized by weak states that had neither a monopoly of force nor widespread presence outside of large cities.

Other differences were clear. Elites in some countries shared a common "national project," while elsewhere conflict surrounded its definition.[27] Formally, federalism was strong and enduring in Brazil, while Chile developed a highly centralized government. Informally, regionalism continued to play a strong role in the politics of most countries. Integrative national parties became significant in Mexico, Peru, Venezuela, Argentina, Colombia, Costa Rica, and Uruguay, while party identities shifted and proliferated in Brazil and Central America. Across differences and similarities, patronage helped consolidate relatively strong political systems and fracture others. In sum, the system embedded in the colonial period endured, even while the identity of those who managed it changed, and the stakes in the appointments process were defined by the needs of elites, parties, and political regimes. This was clear in the particular experiences of Brazil, Argentina, Mexico, and Chile.

Brazil and the Politics of O Sistema

For centuries, patronage was the cement that held a large and centrifugal political system together, that eased the relationship between central and regional elites, and that laid the basis for the formation of political parties in Brazil.[28] It was a durable system that survived empire, independence, republic, dictatorship, depression, war, and economic growth— not to mention repeated cycles of centralization and diffusion of political power.[29] The system was important for individuals and families and was a standard mechanism for knitting together loyalties and obligations across wide expanses of territory. For politicians and administrators, patronage was a rational means to achieve objectives; for evolving state structures of authority, it helped create and maintain an important degree of political stability. Long known as *"o sistema,"* the network of personal and informal relationships amounting to "the system" endured across centuries and regimes.

The construction of the patronage system began with land, loyalty, and order. Land grants in far-flung areas of Brazil were central to Portugal's early colonial policy, and were more heavily used than in Spanish America.[30] Following a feudal and prebendal pattern in the sixteenth century, the territory was divided into twelve regions, each region then assigned on a hereditary basis to a captain-major *(capitão-mor)* who could distribute land in *sesmarías,* with the king reserving ultimate title. Civil and military administration of each region was the responsibility of the captain-major, soon replaced by governors, who were the linchpins in an ongoing struggle between center and periphery of the empire. Within each region, elites who were given hereditary land grants became local lords and militia heads and, ultimately, political bosses, known throughout this period as the *coronéis,* in recognition of the role they played in maintaining order in their bailiwicks and backwaters.[31]

In Lisbon and its coastal outposts in Brazil, the monarchy established an educated and hierarchical cadre of competent officials, who at the same time were dependent on the administrative and military loyalty of semi-independent governors and *coronéis.* Indeed, colonial Brazil was akin to Tokugawa Japan, with its "combination of . . . a highly centralized authority at the head of which stood the Portuguese monarch and the upper bureaucratized layers of the royal administration, and . . . a highly decentralized power monopolized by delegatory landlords in their capacities as patrimonial officials."[32] In this context, personal relationships and the distribution of honors and posts were extraordinarily important in maintaining loyalty to the center and some stability of government.

When the court fled Portugal and reestablished the empire in Rio de Janeiro in 1808, a royal household and a state administration suitable for that empire were soon established and began to grow apace.[33] During the empire, the centralizing, hierarchical, and bureaucratic features of colonial government were strengthened, but never enough to break the importance of the informal relationships that brought the royal government into touch with the *coronéis* and others who sustained local and provincial authority. Nevertheless, the court in exile—which fled with a massive administrative apparatus—expanded opportunities for the distribution of posts and honors that emphasized the authority of the monarchy.

The emperor had absolute control over all appointments, his signature essential for even the lowest-level clerk until 1834. Actual appointments involved long processes of petitioning and documentation, closely vetted by ministers and other officials. Yet provincial officials and others found ways around the royal signature, primarily through the appointment of temporary officials; as in more contemporary times, temporary officials of this earlier period had a habit of enduring in office with tenure.[34] Sons of landlords entered the public service, as well as the church, and helped knit power relations across empire and republic. At the same time, efforts to introduce competitive examinations for technical posts in the military and treasury date to the first twenty years of the nineteenth century; historians are agreed that relatively high standards of administration existed in Rio and coastal cities.[35]

Outside of Rio, the power of local elites, the vulnerability of the poor, slavery, and military conscription all reinforced the importance of cultivating patrons with local power. Elite families rose and fell on their success in working local, regional, and national patronage networks.[36] For elite families, a son with a legal degree and an appointment to a local or regional post was instrumental in protecting links to the center, providing opportunities for a political and national career, and building a modern façade for the *coronéis*.[37] For the humble, the need for protection from conscription and subordination to the "execrable conditions prevalent within the Brazilian armed forces," as well as the need for access to land and other resources, ensured local boss control in elections.[38] The judiciary, and the powers delegated to local magistrates, were central to this system that became adept at managing partisan rivalries and electoral outcomes.[39] Efforts to strengthen the judiciary, to build a centralized army, to collect taxes, to establish constitutions based on liberal principles—all activities reflected a social order based on patronage, protection, and loyalty. The declaration of independence in 1822 had little impact on this system at either national or local levels.

The nineteenth century, which brought first empire, then an independent monarchy, and then a republic, was notable for the halting spread of central authority more deeply into the hinterlands without breaking the importance of patronage relationships in the accommodation of local, regional, and central interests. This trajectory toward greater central authority was a difficult one, however, replete with occasional setbacks. In 1834, for example, an act amended the 1824 constitution and provided for much greater responsibilities and authority for provincial governments; legislative assemblies were established at this level.[40] Yet local elites tended to thrive most fully when they worked in consort with officials in Rio, and "it was through the skillful use of patronage that the capital truly emerged as center."[41]

Elections demonstrated the capacity of ministers, governors, and local bosses to exchange loyalty for positions and pork. "Personal loyalty, personal connection, made every Deputy in Parliament beholden to two masters: the village chief whose friends and relatives were electors, and the Cabinet member who named that chief to the coveted position of delegado, National Guard commandant, or substitute country judge."[42] Moreover, "party labels were put on and taken off almost as easily as a set of clothes," mirroring efforts to create coalitions of disparate clientelist networks, and "the essential question . . . revolved around who would get the official posts."[43]

When the monarchy was replaced by a republic in 1889, the trend toward centralization was again checked by centrifugal forces. Eventually, central administrators were left with functions—carried out with relative competence—only in the "conduct of the national finances . . . the conduct of foreign policy, and the maintenance of the services of the federal district (Rio de Janeiro)."[44] Yet the complex of local, regional, and federal networks continued to pull the country into some semblance of unity and order, enough for some to quip that "patronage begot Brazil."[45] The bureaucracy cemented in place a personalist state, owed loyalty by its beneficiaries and control over which was contested among rival political parties. For David Maybury-Lewis, the local ramifications of patronage remained a characteristic of Brazilian politics well into the modern period. "Politics everywhere entails patronage but in the Brazilian interior it involves little else" he wrote in 1968.[46] Frances Hagopian demonstrated that the networks of elite dominance of government at the state level altered little even with regime change.[47]

Despite the strength of this system, some officials in central ministries in the nineteenth century were able to develop relatively stable careers and a reputation for competence. In this fashion, an administrative apparatus grew slowly into a relatively modern bureaucracy, actively engaged in a network of bargains that made it possible to ensure order, move from a monarchy to a republic, facilitate the creation of political parties, and implement a range of not-insignificant policies, such as the abolition of slavery in 1888. With the growth of political parties and the emergence of mass politics in the twentieth century, however, the public service became an even more important focus for patronage politics. Elections of presidents whose support was anchored in state and local political machines meant that jobs for the boys were an extremely important benefit of winning elections.

Indeed, the vulnerability of a patronage system to the demands of politics and the priorities of leaders of political parties was very apparent during the first decades of the twentieth century, when the reputation of the public service declined significantly. From time to time, the public service was the focus of congressional attention; in 1907, 1911, 1913, 1914, and 1929, reform bills were introduced into the congress, none with success, however.[48] By the end of the 1920s, the federal government was "poor and enfeebled."[49]

In 1930, a public sector increasingly viewed as incompetent was only one of a number of problems Brazil faced, however. The worldwide depression hit the country's export economy hard, and political factionalism among traditional party machines threatened stability. Getúlio Vargas, at the head of a military coup, assumed power in a "revolution" against the traditional oligarchs and quickly proclaimed the rights of labor and urban populations more generally. A major focus of his efforts was to increase the central authority of the state and to engage it in a more proactive way in economic development.[50] This led him to a serious concern with the administration of government.

Argentina and the Politics of Instability

Nineteenth-century Argentina was a cauldron of political instability and ongoing and often violent conflict about the political hegemony of Buenos Aires over the country's provinces. Consolidation of national power was regularly contested by regional *caudillos*, "access to power came to depend on the control of militias, and 'parties' emerged as simple fronts to legitimize—not always successfully—changing leadership. Exile, political assassination, venality, nepotism and coercion were incorporated as instruments of domination."[51] In midcentury, it was difficult to ascertain if a national government even existed, as efforts to collect taxes and duties, issue a national currency, and deliver the mail all ended in failure.[52] The creation of a national military, begun in the 1860s, was consolidated only gradually, and it was not until the 1880s that a national state took coherent form, a consequence of activities begun two decades earlier.

The foundations for this national state first relied on a delicate balance of personal relations between presidents and regional *caudillos*. Its eventual consolidation owed much to the increasing ability to co-opt regional interests through the distribution of subsidies to provincial governments and the allocation of public posts to larger numbers of people, particularly in the military and the expanding corps of teachers in national schools.[53] By the mid-1870s, 85 percent of nearly thirteen thousand federal officials were carrying out their activities in the provinces, and finally providing the administrative capacity to knit together a state.[54] With expanding opportunities for awarding public positions, an electoral spoils system gradually emerged. "Nepotism and the development of a spoils system, the inevitable consequence of pre- and post-electoral bargaining, exacerbated the instrumental use of public jobs, as the election of a governor or a president entailed changes in public administration, from municipal to ministerial levels."[55]

This incipient system was eventually consolidated in an oligarchic era of "order and progress," amounting to a "pact for domination" of Buenos Aires over the rest of the country.[56] At the same time, an economic boom fueled by massive immigration and high prices and new technologies for agricultural exports provided resources for significant investments in development. This condition was taken full advantage of by President Julio Argentino Roca (1880–1886, 1898–1904), who wrested public responsibilities away from the Catholic Church, set up a national registration system, established free public education, and spurred investment in railroads, ports, roads, bridges, and other infrastructure.

From the 1880s until World War I, oligarchic governments followed policies that enhanced urbanization and rapid economic growth, elections served to circulate power within a small elite, and greater state engagement in the economy allowed for significant growth in appointive positions in government. During this era of government expansion and increasing executive control over politics and policy, Argentina became one of the richest countries in the world.[57]

Late in the century, this prosperity encouraged the mobilization of middle and working classes in reaction to elite control over power. The middle-class Unión Cívica Radical (UCR) and the Socialist Party were both formed in the last decade of the old century. The UCR finally won an election in 1916 after establishing a nationwide machine for electoral mobilization. Radicals in political positions rapidly brought their people into the administration of the state and accommodated numerous networks of patronage and spoils managed by regional and local strongmen.[58]

A military coup in 1930 turned power over to a conservative elected regime in 1932, and subsequent military interventions, in 1943 and 1945, were instrumental in bringing Juan Domingo Perón to power. The populist Peronist regime incorporated the working class and its unions into a solid base of support for the Justicialist (Peronist) Party and introduced significant advances in the political and economic position of labor. During the decade in which he was in power, Perón's control over patronage and the distribution of policy benefits was extensive and personal, and was both an instrument and a consequence of centralized power.

Over the same time period, Perón and his working-class party and union supporters became an enduring challenge to the military. Ousting Perón in 1955, the military intervened in subsequent governments in 1962, 1966, and 1976.[59] Throughout this long period of political instability and military activism, political mobilization was high, political violence often endemic, and policy change frequently dramatic. As in the nineteenth century, winners populated government with their supporters—military and civilian—and losers lived to contest control over the public sector and its administrative apparatus another day. Conflicts over policies and the incorporation of unions and workers into the political arena drove these politics, but the distribution of patronage contributed both to political instability and the potential for frequent policy change.

Throughout much of the twentieth century, then, patronage was used to diverse ends by a variety of regimes. Thus, Perón was able to use the system of personal appointments to strengthen his control of labor and the government and to bring about significant change in the beneficiaries of state policies. Military regimes used patronage to recolonize the public administration. Under the dictatorship installed in 1976, for example, public administration at the level of ministries and agencies was farmed out to various branches of the military—"the Navy got this, the Army got that, and so on," as an academic observer of the process phrased it.[60] As in Brazil, the military regime in power between 1976 and 1983 rapidly increased the number of state-owned enterprises and expanded the public sector, creating more jobs for its supporters, civilian and military alike. With a return to democracy in 1983, public positions again became means to reward the party faithful and pursue new policy agendas.

Mexico and the Politics of Stability

Mexico had a nineteenth-century history that was almost as violent and unstable as that of Argentina. The consolidation of national power was a significant project during much of the second half of the century. Eventually, the dictatorship of Porfirio Díaz (1876–1880, 1884–1911) brought central control and stability to the country, as well as a set of significant development-oriented policies, including a strong focus on political order, stimulating investment in infrastructure, opening the country to foreign investment, and putting the state's fiscal affairs in order. To pursue his agenda, Díaz used his patronage power to employ many political supporters, among them a group of early technocrats known as the *científicos,* followers of positivist political philosophy and the application of science to government, society, and economy.

But the regime that brought order to Mexico was destined to dissolve into chaos in reaction to the Porfirian use of the military to suppress dissent, the unbridled concentration of wealth, the constriction of opportunities for mobility and political rights, and a variety of other grievances. The first of the twentieth century's great social revolutions brought this regime to an end in 1910.

The revolution was long and violent, but the consolidation of power that occurred in its wake laid the basis for an authoritarian political regime that endured for seventy-one years. This regime, dominated by the Partido de la Revolución Institutional (PRI) and a strong and centralized presidency, built loyalty to the state and co-opted numerous potential opponents through skill and the clarity of the informal rules of the game. It developed an efficient clientelist system that originated in an extraordinarily powerful presidential office and spread throughout the public sector and the party, down to the most remote village in the country. In this system, public sector investments, land, electoral opportunities, and public sector jobs were all currencies that made the system work and ensured decades of stability in the political system, even while it created and systematized extensive inequalities and injustices.

As it consolidated power in the 1920s and 1930s, the PRI regime developed clear rules of the game: new presidents appointed ministers, heads of state-owned enterprises, and the mayor of Mexico City. Presidents were central in selecting nominees to run for election as governors, mayors of large cities, deputies and senators for the national congress, and could even indicate favored candidates for state-level legislative elections; those nominated almost always won election, given the evolving hegemony of the PRI. Presidents also selected the leadership of the PRI. Official and friendly unions were headed by political appointees often selected by the president. In turn, the various ministers, governors, mayors, PRI leaders, heads of state-owned enterprises, and union leaders selected their own people, who in turn selected their people, and so on, until the whole system could be envisioned as a classic pyramid of patronage.

This system was legitimized through an important public sector labor law of 1938, which made a distinction between "base" personnel—blue-collar and many clerical workers—who would have the protection of labor laws and rights to unionize, and "confidence" personnel, who could be freely selected for public service by those holding positions of authority. "Base" personnel were usually appointed through patronage networks, but then joined strong public sector unions that had collective bargaining agreements with the government ensuring job stability.[61] Traditionally, some 50 percent of the public sector held such positions, while "confidence" appointments characterized about 40 percent of the public service, incorporating almost all middle- and higher-level officials.[62] Another 10 percent were found in specialized agencies such as the foreign service, the statistics agency, the attorney general's office, and the tax office, where it was possible to develop relatively stable careers and to move upward within the same bureaucracy.[63]

In the aftermath of elections—for which there was a strict rule of no reelection—massive numbers of political and bureaucratic positions changed hands, even while the same party won. In part, the movement in the first year of a new administration might resemble a game of musical chairs, as those who were in public positions found other appointments. Generally, job seekers spent the last year of an old administration establishing contacts for future job possibilities and the first year of a new administration trying to benefit from the actions of the prior year. Often, when higher-level people moved from one position to another, or in or out of government, they brought along their people. This system was particularly important in welding the dominant party, the PRI, to the government of the day. Often, in fact, "the administrative apparatus has been a flexible and manipulable appendix of the political system that was born after the revolution."[64]

As indicated, the system worked extremely well for a long time. Those in public sector jobs knew the rules and what they had to do to ensure their employment in the next presidential administration; those who lost jobs knew they would have other chances in the future, when a new president came into power; and those who were new to the job market knew there were good opportunities for gaining employment if one had the right connections.[65] Throughout the system, there were patrons who had jobs to dispense and promises of jobs to come.

In the absence of effective political competition, those uncomfortable with the system had few options. "Given that electoral competition was *de forma,* the hallways of the administrative apparatus were witnesses to the real competition for power, in the distribution of positions, electoral and administrative ones. And given the extremely wide legal and extralegal power of the president in office, the apparatus was the real instrument through which the hegemonic group activated political agendas, the real budgets, and the rest of the instruments of power."[66]

Because the system was pyramidal and carefully managed from the top down, patronage could be extremely useful to presidents and party. Certainly it ensured active engagement in political campaigns as citizens throughout the country—even in remote rural areas—knew that jobs and spoils would be distributed in the aftermath of elections to those who worked hard and gained the attention of political bosses at various levels. Public positions were helpful in managing conflicts and signaling the limits of dissent. In addition, presidents could act relatively effectively on their policy agendas because they could select like-minded individuals to occupy leadership positions in key ministries, and key ministers were clearly aware that they needed to select subordinates who could deliver on the shared agenda or they risked losing their jobs.[67] There was also room in this system for awarding loyal union leaders, co-opting dissenters, and undermining the appeals of opposition parties. Expertise could be recruited along with loyalty, and professionalism at the top of organizations could be ensured.

Perhaps nowhere were political officials more conscious that maintaining the political basis of the administrative system was essential to the functioning of the political system—the public service was a spoils system with a purpose, "a functional unit of the PRI."[68] And yet, the increasing presence of technocrats in public positions suggested the sensitivity of the system to the need for expertise and modernization in the public service.[69] Clearly, "being able to count on a reliable and flexible system that could be manipulated through the orders of the political group in power was a strategic factor of the system."[70]

Chile and the Politics of Professionalism and Regime Change

With a highly centralized and coherent state dating to the 1830s, the public service system in Chile became strongly oriented to political parties in the twentieth century. A multiparty system emerged early in the history of the country, and presidents, although given wide constitutional powers, often needed to create support coalitions in the congress, and these were generally cemented through the sharing of ministerial and administrative appointments among parties.[71] Thus, patronage was a strong component of the parliamentary and oligarchical system that held power between 1891 and 1924, and party competition underscored the importance of the distribution of jobs, particularly to the middle classes, as incentives and rewards for voting.

Yet, like Mexico, this patronage system was able to meld elements of technical and administrative merit into its operation. An identifiable "technocracy" was evident in Chile by the 1920s, when the role of the state in the economy began to grow.[72] And as the size of the state increased, and as administrations sought to replace representatives of the nineteenth-century oligarchy in public positions, officials from the rising middle class flooded into government in the 1920s and 1930s.[73] A fascination with the prospect of planning and apolitical public policies encouraged a trend toward appointing more technically qualified public officials. Between 1927 and 1931, under the dictatorship of Carlos Ibañez, a new generation of public officials was recruited into government, and "an increasing number of state institutions were gradually to achieve a sort of 'relative autonomy' by which managers, technicians, and professionals in general acquired a large amount of room for maneuver in the formulation and application of developmental policies."[74] Engineers were especially sought after for recruitment into this new cadre of public officials.[75]

From this period on, the patronage system combined political and professional values, and notions of the autonomy of public organizations gained traction. Equally important, from this period on, public officials began to identify and promote issues of concern related to their pay, benefits, and stature, and they served as important proponents of the growth of the state.[76] When public sector growth did occur, it was often at the margins of the ministries of government, through the creation of numerous agencies and state-owned enterprises whose responsibilities were linked to development but whose benefits often had extensive electoral significance.[77] Through party and bureaucratic networks, clientelism reached from party headquarters to local voters.

The patronage system remained vibrant through the 1960s, with "politicians acting as employment agents in many cases."[78] Its character was shaped, however, by legally imposed educational requirements for positions at different levels of government and by legislation that granted tenure to those appointed to public office. A dual promotion standard of merit and seniority also helped curb the impact of partisan, family, and personal relationships, although promotion rules still allowed for considerable favoritism in bureaucratic careers. Informal and formal rules tended to be observed simultaneously, and according to one observer, "It was a clientelist system, but it was selective clientelism, a kind of career system for those who performed well."[79] And, with greater guarantees of job stability, those benefitting from tenure—even though selected on the basis of patronage—grew over time.

One response of new presidents feeling constrained by the rules and the expanding tenure system was to create new positions and new organizations, sometimes paralleling already existing units, thus increasing the size of the bureaucracy to accommodate the need for political appointments.[80] "They couldn't get rid of anyone, so they had to create new organizations," according to one observer.[81] Relatively efficient and professionalized, subject to frequent reviews and efforts at reform, the system remained closely linked to the political system and to the electoral calendar. "In a highly competitive multiparty system like the Chilean, patronage politics are rational, given that no political party will renounce them if they favor the opposition. Clientelism, expressed through patronage, is an *all-win-game* for the parties."[82]

Patronage also suited the generals who took over power by force through a violent coup in 1973. Throughout the highly centralized Pinochet regime (1973–1990), military officials took over at least half the cabinet, "served as subsecretaries, university rectors, diplomats, administrators of state corporations, regional intendants, mayors, governors, and members of the junta's four legislative commissions. . . . 35 percent of the army generals on active duty in 1985 held some sort of government post . . . reaching 44 percent by May 1988."[83] Although the overall size of the public sector shrank during the dictatorship, the use of public positions was central to its consolidation. In introducing very significant policy changes, the patronage system gave the military—with a "sultanistic" General Pinochet at its head—wide discretion in staffing government positions with military and civilian officials, some of whom were drawn from among right-wing party activists.[84] The extensive capacity to make appointments was clearly important in the early ascendance of the "Chicago Boys," whose conservative brand of economics deeply shaped the policies of the Pinochet regime.

With the return to democracy in 1990, and with the success of the *Concertación* coalition of parties of the center and left, the patronage system aided in recolonizing the government with those committed to a social democratic market economy and democratic elections. Particularly in terms of economic policy, the selection of ministers of finance, with their capacity to select their teams of advisers and subordinates, was enhanced by the continuation of a centralized and presidentialist system and by networks among policy makers that had been forged during the years of dictatorship.[85]

As in the case of Mexico, the patronage system in Chile had informal but clear rules of the game. It generally worked through a quota system. "There is clear understanding in Chile of the need for political balance," commented one observer. "That is why in the past there has always been an effort to bring in people across the political spectrum, at least

Table 5.1. Patronage systems in Latin America: diversity, limitations, and achievements

Country	Ends sought through patronage system	Constraints on use of patronage	Important system limitations	Important system accomplishments
Brazil	State building; accommodation of local elites; centralization of authority; expertise in government; party loyalty	Independence of local elites; shifting loyalties; intense competition for office	Dispersion of patronage networks and power; corruption; variable competence at distinct levels of government; competition among localities for spoils	Long-term management of claims for regional and local autonomy; development of some competent organizations; clear rules of the game for political advancement
Argentina	Centralization of authority; party development; regime consolidation; incorporation of new groups into political system	Independence of regional strongmen; shifting loyalties; intense competition for office	Dispersion of patronage networks and power; corruption; intense competition for public positions; instability	Consolidation of political parties and regimes

Table 5.1. (continued)

Country	Ends sought through patronage system	Constraints on use of patronage	Important system limitations	Important system accomplishments
Mexico	State building; consolidation of central power; expertise in government; party consolidation; co-optation of dissent; accommodation of elite demands	Initial dispersion of power	Corruption; policy and personnel changes with each administration	Centralization of power; extensive presidential power; dominant party consolidation; stability over long periods; high levels of voter participation; clear rules of the game; technical and professional expertise; smooth transitions of administrations; capacity for policy change
Chile	State building; centralization; consolidation of political parties; expertise in government; regime consolidation	Limitations on rotation in office; Gradual development of administrative autonomy; Intense competition for office	Creation of additional positions; Growth in size of government	Clear rules of the game; technical and professional expertise; management of party competition; capacity for policy change

within the *Concertación*. For example, if a minister is a Christian Demo-
crat, then it is tradition to have a Socialist as the vice minister. If there
are four directors of services below them, then one would come from
each of the coalition parties. From 1990 on there has been a strong tradition of political parity. At the same time, there has been an emphasis
on getting really well-qualified people in government."[86]

Conclusion

Brazil, Argentina, Mexico, and Chile each had deeply embedded patronage systems for staffing their public administrations. Yet these patronage
systems were implicated in very different political histories, at times
encouraging political instability, at other times political order; at times
stimulating corruption and incompetence, at other times expertise and
professionalism. As was the case in other countries in earlier periods,
patronage was used to manage—or try to manage—political power, but
it did not define the quality or the ends of government. The summary of
these systems in Table 5.1 reflects distinctions in the diversity, limitations, and achievements of patronage in these four countries, echoing
findings presented in Table 1.1.

Diverse outcomes of patronage are clear in the brief histories of four
countries. In Brazil, it helped knit local and national, regional and central into a semblance of political order. In Argentina, patronage was part
and parcel of a turbulent history of ongoing political instability and
civil-military relations. This history stands in strong contrast to the case
of Mexico, in which the concerted use of patronage was a critical ele-
ment in establishing and maintaining long-standing political stability.
In Chile, competitive elections generated clear rules of the game about
selecting personnel for administrative roles, a military regime was able
to use patronage to colonize the public service and to alter policies in fundamental ways, and a return to democracy was characterized by careful
distribution of patronage to manage party competition and policy development. The following chapter indicates how reformers attacked the persistence of the patronage systems implicated in these distinct histories.

CHAPTER 6

Crafting Reform

Elite Projects and Political Moments

Brazil is a useful starting point for a closer assessment of the politics of civil service reform in Latin America because it has the oldest system in the region and thus provides a longer lens of history for exploration. Established by President Getúlio Vargas, the country's career civil service was entrusted to a newly formed and powerful Administrative Department of the Public Service (DASP) in 1938. At the time of its creation, the DASP was given responsibility for the public service, along with extensive authority over government functions, legislation, and budgets. It was designed to be a superministry responding directly to the president. Its leadership was fully committed to professionalism, expertise, and the application of rational science to the problems of administration; the career system it put in place was to mirror these characteristics.

Given a long history plagued by patronage and spoils, from this time the professionalism of the public service became something of a national "project." Brazil's constitutions—five since 1934—all included commitments to a public sector selected by merit.[1] Thus, a career civil service was introduced under a development-oriented authoritarian regime in a pattern similar to that of the early experiences of Prussia and Japan. Its design and initial activities were the work of a small group of public officials, much of whose inspiration came from ideas about scientific management current in academic circles of the time. As in the earlier cases of authoritarian imposition, the initiation of a new public service system raised little public controversy.

This pattern—a political moment seized opportunistically and a new institution crafted as an elite project—characterized three other experiences of civil service creation in Latin America. In the 1990s in Argentina, and in Mexico and Chile in the 2000s, small groups of reforming intellectuals and public officials were able to put their ideas into practice largely through serendipitous political events that opened up room for change. These groups generated plans through networks, research projects, think tanks, and conferences and then found themselves in positions to advance their reformist agendas when unanticipated—and often unrelated—events opened up room for them to move ahead with their plans. Surprisingly, given the depth of traditions of patronage, new public service systems were introduced with little debate. This chapter explores these experiences and suggests why the political moment of transition raised so few political eyebrows.

Brazil: Constructing DASP without Deconstructing Patronage

After the coup in 1930, President Vargas's agenda was extensive, calling for a much-increased presence of the state in the economy and the empowerment of the working class. The crisis of the depression of the 1930s provided space for significant changes in the public policies most relevant to the country's economic development. The administrative apparatus was a principal beneficiary of this expansionism; the ministry of labor, industry, and commerce, as well as a new ministry of education and health were created, given new responsibilities, and provided many new positions in government. Ministries in the areas of agriculture, justice, and finance were reorganized, strengthened, and enlarged. At the same time, Vargas and his close advisers became more sensitive to the importance of an efficient and responsive state apparatus to the achievement of his economic and social goals. His early interest in administrative reform was thus largely instrumental, a means to an end of a more centralized government focused on industrializing the country and providing services to an expanding electorate.

By the mid-1930s, the central public service had increased significantly in size and responsibilities; its performance—and the continued crisis of state fiscal conditions—had not noticeably improved, however. The congress, newly established through the constitution of 1934, was deeply concerned about the sorry state of the economy; it thus set up a commission to consider a wide range of economic and financial reforms and, as part of these tasks, created a subcommittee to consider the financial drain of the public service. In a process that echoed early days of public sector reform in Britain, then, fiscal concerns led to an elite project pursued with little public engagement. A small number of people considered to be experts in public administration were selected to prepare a plan. Mauricio Nabuco, the father of an improved career system in the foreign service, was chosen to chair the administrative subcommittee in 1935. The resulting report, which recommended the creation of a central personnel agency for both national and regional public services, focused attention on the need for a uniform career system across the government.

Nabuco, who was sensitive to the important political role of patronage in cementing Brazil's political and administrative system together, believed that this system needed to be preserved in some form. At the same time, he was drawn to the importance of merit and competence in public life.[2] His solution provided for a qualified patronage system. The report thus recommended that appointments be screened for competence even while politicians would continue to be in charge of appointments.[3] Once chosen through this political selection process, public servants would then become part of a regular career system. The report, referred to President Vargas, came to grief through the opposition of the finance ministry, whose minister and staff believed it was too expensive a proposition. On the minister's order, the report was suppressed, and Nabuco's work died without action.[4]

A new commission, under the direction of Luís Simões Lopes, a presidential adviser on matters of administration who had traveled and read widely in the subject, was more successful. In what has been referred to as "the Brazilian equivalent of the Northcote-Trevelyan Report," he recommended the creation of a Federal Civil Service Council with the task of overseeing examinations and recruitment to a career system.[5] Ministries would continue to manage careers, but entry into them through an open competitive examination was to be overseen by the new agency. It would be an activist organization and report directly to the president. Nabuco's idea of combining patronage with examinations for fitness was set aside, dismissed by Simões Lopes as counter to ideas of modern public administration.[6] Indeed, the new civil service plan was strongly influenced by discussions of public administration in the United States at the time, which focused centrally on professionalism, administrative science, and technical competence.

The law was passed in 1936, and the civil service council was established, with competitive examinations for entry into the public service at the center of its responsibilities, through personnel units in each of the ministries. Yet, in an echo of the problems facing the Nabuco report, resistance from the ministry of finance for fiscal reasons significantly limited the impact of the new council. Moreover, despite legislation and a new agency, the bureaucracy was not easily turned from past patterns of patronage. Brazil continued to be, in the words of one minister, "the land of electoral clientelism, of incompetence, of favors, of bureaucratic waste."[7]

This early fate of the career system was not unique in the Vargas government from 1930 to 1937, however. The period was replete with laws and decrees about a wide variety of policies and programs that foretold significant changes but that then lapsed for lack of implementation. Moreover, although public and elite criticism of government was widespread, reformers did little to cultivate broad support. Like the Northcote-Trevelyan Report, Brazil's initial career civil service remained the work of a few members of government and intellectuals; it was not the result of publicly demanded reform.

Then, a coup in 1937 established Getúlio Vargas as head of the *Estado Novo*, an activist and authoritarian regime committed to the rapid transformation of the Brazilian economy and society. An effective public sector was to be instrumental in accomplishing his goals. Indeed, the constitution of the regime established a new department—a superministry, in effect—the Departamento Administrativo do Serviço Público, or DASP, with powers far outflanking other government agencies. Mandated by the constitution, DASP was subsequently created through a presidential decree law, Vargas's preferred method for announcing most public policy.[8]

The design of DASP, once again by a small group of specialists, conformed to the authoritarian desire to centralize control. Its intellectual origins owed much to the contributions of U.S. administrative reform experts such as W. F. Willoughby, Louis Brownlow, Charles Merriam, and Luther Gulick, all advocates of a central staff agency and principles of scientific management.[9] Nevertheless, the powers accorded the new agency far surpassed any previous reform models, domestic or foreign.[10]

DASP, reporting to the president, was based on a distinction made prominent by the academic literature of the times between the "ends" and "means" of administration; DASP was to be in charge of the means.[11] It was to review legislation, draw up the budget, assume responsibility for government purchases, and oversee public administration and public buildings. It would supervise all government personnel and was to implement and supervise an examination system for entrance into the public service. At the state level, *Daspinhos* (little DASPs) were set up to replicate the activities of the federal department. Nationally, DASP would deploy teams of consultants to assist in the reformulation of state-level public administrations. Eventually, this process helped create a network of administrative reformers that linked a number of states. Further strengthening the agency, its direct link to the president helped insulate it from the resistance of ministries, including the ministry of finance, which sought to maintain its own, more decentralized control over positions.

A central purpose of DASP was to put a definitive end to the practice of patronage by establishing a new, modern, and technically competent career public service. Initially, its examination system was applicable to about a quarter of all federal administrative positions.[12] Positions at middle and high levels of the government continued to be categorized as "confidence" posts, available for appointment outside the examination system. The expectation was that the promotion of those entering the service by examination would eventually mean that many mid-level "confidence" posts would be taken over by those moving up through the ranks in the career system.[13]

The *Estado Novo*, committed not only to securing central presidential power but also to a rapid advance in state-supported industrialization, was generous in the creation of new organizations and the expansion of existing ones. Between 1937 and 1945, a series of semiautonomous state agencies—to produce steel, iron ore, petroleum, and power, and to promote foreign trade and collect data, for example—was set up, initially tied directly to the presidency, with funding insulated from regular budget processes. These new agencies provided wide scope for presidentially sponsored appointments. In addition, many ministries acquired new activities—vocational schools in education and much new regulatory activity for labor and justice, for example.

Committed to a development strategy of rapid industrialization, Vargas's appointments generally privileged those with technical expertise in the semiautonomous agencies. Vargas then encouraged agency leadership to follow his lead and appoint sectoral experts and other highly qualified people to middle- and high-level positions. From this time, these agencies began to develop strong reputations for high performance of their functions. In some cases, the increased autonomy was used by agency leaders to set up competitive entrance examinations for positions requiring specific kinds of expertise. In later years, these agencies would be referred to as "pockets of efficiency," set on a path toward technical decision-making and good performance through presidential patronage.[14]

Thus, DASP was to create a career public service, but this service was to coexist with a significant range of patronage appointments available to presidents, ministers, and other high-level officials for pursuing the presidential agenda of rapid economic and social development. At the same time, Vargas was skilled in using the agency as a hedge against extensive pressures for patronage positions; he could not be responsive, he would reply, because of the strictures of DASP.[15] Patronage and career systems together supported the *Estado Novo.* Indeed, given the strong legacy of patronage in Brazil, it was not always easy to keep a clear distinction between the two systems. Qualifying for a position in government, as indicated in a letter written to Vargas in 1944, might have been a result of both examination and personal intervention. "I am a poor girl, my widowed mother's only support," wrote one supplicant. "I worked hard to prepare for the DASP typist examination and I passed it. I received my certificate, but have not been offered a position yet. I ask for your intervention so I can care for my poor mother."[16]

Despite the persistence of the patronage system, the years between 1938 and 1945 were golden ones for DASP. Its influence grew steadily as it proved a useful mechanism for Vargas to centralize control and to limit the bureaucratic autonomy of ministries and agencies. It focused much of its attention on professionalizing the lower and middle ranks of the public service, where the attraction of distributing jobs for the boys was most seductive. In addition, DASP became a center for disseminating ideas on proper public administrative structures and processes. It sponsored seminars, courses, and publications that enhanced the reputation of its generally high-quality and technically oriented staff. Its influence extended to the private sector, as it "provided a large part of the trained managerial personnel for Brazil's growing industry, which hired them away from the staff agency as quickly as they attained journeyman competence."[17]

As part of its mission, DASP focused on inculcating values of efficiency, professionalism, and technical problem solving; it focused blame for the absence of these values on politicians and *o systema*.[18] DASP's president, Simões Lopes, established the Fundação Getúlio Vargas in 1944 to train public officials and to carry on the intellectual work of administrative reform heretofore focused within DASP. Indeed, the intellectual reputation of DASP endured in the more troubled times ahead in part because those appointed to the Fundação had strong technical orientations and many were "graduates" of DASP itself. Yet the department's golden years were numbered, as will be seen in Chapter 7.

Argentina: Crisis and Change

Argentina's 1991 experience of creating a Weberian career civil service was a function of a massive economic and fiscal crisis that generated a political moment in which major new initiatives could be undertaken and carried out in short order. In addition, however, the creation of a new public service career system owes much to a few political leaders finding negotiating partners in those who wanted to salvage something from the chaos of crisis and a massive downsizing of the public sector. In relatively short order, a new public career system was created to provide stable, career-trajectory jobs for a significant number of Argentine public officials.

This 1991 episode was not the first time that efforts had been made in Argentina to create a civil service system. The constitution of 1957 limited one aspect of patronage—high levels of rotation in office—by guaranteeing job stability to public employees, at the same time denying them the right to collective bargaining. In 1973, a civil service system was established, but soon recruitment by examination was suspended, and a variety of economic measures severely reduced its impact. This initial effort left its mark on the personnel system, however. Unable to increase salaries due to austerity measures, supervisors regularly reclassified personnel to higher levels so they could be better remunerated; gradually, any relationship between job classification and responsibility was fully obscured.[19] Subsequent laws and decrees established job classifications, which by the 1980s had multiplied into numerous specialized categories that made the management of the public service difficult if not impossible.[20]

Reformers of the 1980s focused attention on training and improved work conditions rather than trying to untangle the complex system of classifications in place.[21] An initiative of 1987, modeled on the French experience of an elite service, created a Government Administrators Corps to allow "master managers" to serve across government, assigned where they were needed most. Although this service eventually incorporated about two hundred well-qualified people, its implementation gradually lapsed, with those in this category diminishing over time.[22] Nevertheless, during the economic crisis of 1989–1991, this corps provided a professional base for planning a number of government responses, including the creation of a career civil service.[23]

Despite these and other reform initiatives, at the outset of the 1990s, the largest number of public officials in Argentina belonged to the category of *personal convencionado*. These were people who were appointed by discretion and who continued to have careers that could be advanced or constrained through the discretion of their superiors or patrons, yet who had tenure rights after one year of service and expectations that seniority was important in job assignments. They were protected by workers' rights legislation that also applied to the private sector. In this system, then, there was a degree of job stability for many public servants; they could be brought into the system through patronage, but remained on the public payroll through a system of tenure. This limited the extent of personnel turnover when administrations changed, by restricting the number of discretionary positions available to politicians—unless, of course, they could expand the overall number of officials, create new organizations, or create new job titles and responsibilities. They frequently took advantage of these possibilities.

In 1991, the government of Carlos Menem, deeply enmeshed in an economic and financial crisis that was the most severe of all countries in Latin America, including a hyperinflation that reached over 20,000 percent between 1989 and 1990, undertook to introduce a new civil service career system. Much of the ability to introduce it, in fact, was a consequence of the crisis. In the context of a gathering hyperinflation, Menem and the Justicialist (Peronist) Party easily won presidential elections in 1989 and moved quickly to implement a series of neoliberal economic reforms. The depth of the crisis was an important stimulus to action, but Menem's rapid response to it was also facilitated by the ability to staff the public service with his people and to use public goods to reward supporters.[24] Within twenty days of taking office, he had in hand economic and administrative emergency laws that gave extensive powers to the executive to decree policy changes without the need for legislative approval. This provided the political foundation for the promulgation of a broad set of laws and decrees to deal with the economic emergency and the fiscal crisis of the state.

To lead the economic and government reform initiative, Domingo Cavallo was appointed minister of the economy in January 1991, a month in which the Argentine currency lost almost 27 percent of its value.[25] Taking the reins quickly, the minister engineered the absorption of the ministry of public works, in charge of privatizing the country's extensive state enterprise sector, into his own ministry. Almost immediately, he recruited a cadre of three hundred "Cavallo boys" to fill the expanded ministry and provide loyalty and advice that made coherent policy making possible.

The focus of the efforts of Cavallo and his personal team was not, of course, a career public service. It was to stabilize the national economy and to reduce the extensive public sector deficit that threatened that stability. Pressure from the International Monetary Fund and the World Bank certainly influenced the policies selected to deal with the crisis, as did models from other reforming countries such as Chile, but the footprint of domestic actors—Menem, Cavallo, technocrats in government, the unions—was definitive in the shape of these policies.[26]

As indicated, their capacity to introduce policy changes was aided by comprehensive laws put in place in 1989 and 1990 to give government extensive powers to pursue privatization, decentralization, deregulation, and contracting out of services.[27] The policies introduced were indeed draconian. One hundred eleven state-owned enterprises were privatized in four years, health and education responsibilities were decentralized to the provincial level, and deregulation lessened the activities of the government in economic management.[28]

In two years, these activities reduced the size of the national public sector dramatically, from 347,000 in 1989 to about 200,000 in 1991.[29] The losers of what one official called a "savage downsizing," and another called a "violent reform of the state," of course, were the large number of employees who were part of the national union structure of public officials. The unions normally would have strongly resisted these changes. But given the extent of the economic crisis that had been building in the 1980s, and the extraordinary powers given to the president to deal with it, the highly organized and influential unions, always important in Argentine politics, were on the defensive.

Menem used his patronage of key government positions—in labor and health ministries and in regulatory and oversight boards—to encourage labor leaders to negotiate difficult reforms, many of which were unpopular with their members.[30] Party leadership positions were also assigned to those close to Menem.[31] In addition, he could count on the backing of a number of governors, deputies, and senators who were tied to him through clientelistic networks. And while there was no direct citizen participation in the development of new policies, public opinion supported Menem in pursuit of change because of the hyperinflation and the depth of the crisis.

These actions presented party and union leaders with a difficult political dilemma: if they accepted their limited bargaining role they could remain "in the room" when important decisions were made, with some potential to influence outcomes and with some capacity to reap patronage benefits for the leadership. The alternative was to break with the Menem government and risk even more draconian measures. Most unions chose to negotiate.

This was true of the most important union of public sector employees, the Unión del Personal Civil de la Nación (UPCN). Because it was in a weak position—the crisis had undermined the power of all unions, and this particular union was closely allied to the governing party—UPCN leadership wanted to provide as much protection to its membership as possible, and a regularized career system with tenure was one possible way to achieve this. The union wanted to ensure job stability for at least some of its members. Those remaining in the public sector were also eager to establish some semblance of job security.[32] At the same time, in the ministry of economy reformers were eager to find a way to generate support from—or at least neutralize—the UPCN. As a Peronist or "officialist" union, it was capable of at least slowing down reform processes that affected public sector workers, if not actually halting them.

Within the ministry, a team began working on a plan for a career service to discuss with the union's leadership. The result was the Sistema Nacional de la Profesión Administrativa (SINAPA), which was to create a simpler public service career system, provide for the meritocratic recruitment of officials, and bring stability and better working conditions to the profession of government in the country. According to one observer, "SINAPA was the candy given to the union for allowing downsizing to take place."[33] In addition, in an important concession to the UPCN, the government promised to institute collective bargaining for public sector salaries.

A new Permanent Career Commission, with representation in each ministry, would oversee SINAPA. For recruitment, the new system called for public announcement of job openings, with a description of the job and the qualifications for it, and selection based on qualifications determined through either an examination or interviews. In addition, seniority would cease to be the measure used for advancement from one job classification to another; and all promotions would be the result of competitive processes. Within classifications, advancement would be through a combination of time in position, annual performance reviews, and the accumulation of credits received by training activities through the National Institute of Public Administration (INAP). The name of the new system signaled the expectation of its creators that its ultimate impact would be to professionalize Argentina's government. Its focus was on the national government, but its goals and processes were expected to trickle down eventually to provincial and municipal levels of government.

Returning to the earlier model of the Government Administrative Service, SINAPA also established a special category of executive officials, whose responsibilities included important administrative and advisory responsibilities. Candidates for these positions entered through a competitive process, but employers could select among the top candidates, allowing some room for discretion. In addition, managers could hire provisional employees who could then compete with other candidates for a particular position.[34]

SINAPA was thus to constitute a Weberian public service in Argentina and was designed to incorporate some thirty thousand positions that would be distinct in recruitment and career mobility from the extensive system of personal appointment and tenure that characterized the public sector prior to the reform. The system got off to a very good start. Initially, twenty-two thousand positions were eligible to be classified into the new system, and about half of those occupying these positions asked to be incorporated into it. Moreover, between 1993 and 1999, over eight thousand jobs were filled through this system, over a quarter of all positions that became available. In 1992, a law granted rights for collective bargaining to public sector employees, and in 1998–1999, the first collective agreement was signed and approved, including within it those who were part of the new civil service.[35]

In Argentina, then, the creation of a merit-based public service was intended to establish a unified system of public service as part of a broader reform of the state that was itself a response to a major economic crisis.[36] It was to include positions in the central ministries of government and also a range of semiautonomous agencies. Its introduction was the work of a small group of public officials who had been granted significant authority to deal with the crisis. They acted rapidly, and while they were deeply engaged in negotiations with the political interests represented by unions and parties, the reform was not publicly discussed. The scope of the crisis hindered those who should have been most opposed to the initiative from being able to resist it. And, initially, the new civil service system generated promising results in terms of the numbers of positions incorporated into it.

Mexico: Parties in Competition

Success does not last forever, even in well-oiled machine politics. Thus, in the 1980s in Mexico, the traditional system of presidential and PRI hegemony began to fray. First at the local level and then at the state level, parties other than the PRI began winning elections. In 1983, opposition candidates were the victors in important cities, and the first non-PRI governor since 1929 was elected in Baja California in 1989. In the 1990s, numerous opposition candidates won elections for mayors, governors, deputies, and senators, and in 1997, for the first time in its history, the PRI lost control of the national congress. Then in 2000, the PRI lost the presidency to the Partido Acción Nacional (PAN), which won the presidency again in 2006. In the early 2000s, then, Mexico was well on its way to having competitive democratic elections at all levels of government. Even in areas in which the PRI machine continued to control local and state political events, margins of victory declined, and the PRI and its candidates for office were increasingly aware of competition for government positions.[37]

Interestingly, the system of public sector employment that had characterized the PRI regime for decades did not change with the arrival of increased electoral competition—at least not immediately. When mayors, governors, and presidents from opposition parties were elected, they took advantage of opportunities to select their people for positions down to middle levels of the public service, just as their predecessors in the PRI had done. And, just like their predecessors, they made their appointments with a variety of purposes in mind—to reward eager campaign workers, build party loyalty, recruit expertise, buy off potential troublemakers or rivals, and pursue an agenda of policy change.

But a new political calculus rooted in party competition did eventually open up an opportunity to bring together a set of academic researchers keenly committed to public sector reform, opposition party leaders, and presidential advisers for an unexpected introduction of a career civil service in 2003. Prior to this, public sector reform had occasionally been considered as part of presidential agendas. For example, in the context of an economic crisis in 1982, advisers to President Miguel de la Madrid (1982–1988) assessed the possibility of creating a career civil service, but concluded that such a reform would have the adverse effect of strengthening union control of the public sector.[38] In another initiative, a general auditing secretariat (SECOGEF) was established in 1982 with a mandate to audit public sector activities. The following year, a general bureau for the civil service was established within the ministry of finance with a remit to increase the efficiency of the public sector and particularly to control the costs of public services.

None of these initiatives flourished. De la Madrid's successor, Carlos Salinas de Gortari (1988–1994), demonstrated again why the patronage system could be such a valuable resource to Mexican presidents. He used it masterfully to empower a large group of technocrats in the area of economic policy; in a few short years, these professionals fundamentally

transformed the basis of the Mexican economy and the relationship between the state and the economy. At the same time, between 1992 and
1993, over a million federal employees were reassigned to the states,
primarily through an education reform that made states the principal
employers of teachers.[39]

In turn, Salinas's successor, Ernesto Zedillo, returned to the proposition of a career civil service, turning SECOGEF into a secretariat for
auditing and administrative development (SECODAM), and calling for a
program for the modernization of the public administration. Yet his
administration was unable to forge an agreement between the ministry
of finance, which favored a centralized and carefully structured system,
and the general accounting secretariat, which favored a less rigid system.[40] And when Vicente Fox, the first opposition party leader to be
elected president in seven decades, took office in 2000, he was skeptical
of the idea of a career service, making a connection between a Weberian public sector and the potential for rigidity and unresponsiveness.
Fox was much more inclined to favor public sector reforms patterned
after private sector management principles.

Despite the failure of many initiatives, in the 1990s a small group of
academics began to coalesce around the idea of a professional career
civil service. Academics from the Autonomous University of Mexico, the
National Public Administration Institute, the Centro de Investigación y
Docencia Económicas (CIDE), and El Colegio de México, with José Luis
Méndez and Mauricio Merino as two of their prime movers, became
convinced that issues of corruption and incompetence could only be addressed in the public sector if the patronage system were severely curtailed and replaced by a career system. Joined by reform-oriented public
officials, they published numerous articles, consulted with government
officials, and disseminated among academic, government, and other elite
audiences a strong message about the importance of reform.[41] In particular, these reformers were impressed by the professional service created
within the Federal Electoral Institute in 1992, which incorporated over
two thousand people.[42]

Throughout this decade, their reform project remained primarily an
academic discussion. In 2000, however, a PRI senator, Carlos Rojas, introduced legislation to establish a professional service. His motivations
were largely political, focused on helping ensure that those who had

been placed in public positions through the patronage of the PRI would have opportunities to remain in government through a system of tenure. The legislation gained little notice, however, as the PRI was in a minority position in the congress as a result of the 2000 elections.[43] But in the spring of 2002, a senator of the PAN, César Jáuregui, concerned about the future of his party's officials in government, also presented a bill proposing a career civil service. Six months later, in an effort to be part of any negotiations that might occur around the idea, a representative of the Partido de la Revolución Democrática (PRD) introduced a proposal in the chamber of deputies.

Activities occurring in Mexico's legislature, long relegated to the periphery of decision making in the country, had to be taken more seriously by the executive in a context in which the PRI could no longer ensure fast approval for just about any presidential initiative. The proposals of 2000 and 2002 encouraged the Presidential Office for Governmental Innovation, a unit set up to introduce reforms drawn from private sector management experience, to begin thinking about how to engage legislators in civil service reform discussions while at the same time putting the imprimatur of the executive on any resulting legislation.[44]

The presidential office turned to the recently created Mexican Network for Professional Service, an association of the academics and government reformers who had begun to study and discuss the issue in the 1990s. According to one participant in these early discussions, the network was a "group of academics, public servants, but above all friends; we decided to pursue an integrated strategy to achieve what for many generations had been an aspiration. . . . Fora, debates, publications, and discussions with legislators were among actions undertaken."[45]

Mexican universities and international bilateral organizations joined them in organizing a major conference on civil service reform in 2003, drawing on international experts to popularize, among opinion leaders and legislators, the idea of a career service.[46] Academics at the conference argued, among other things, that introducing mechanisms drawing on the new public management—the approach favored by Fox—without first installing a career service would lead nowhere.[47] They were also able to point to some organization-specific cases of career services in Mexico that had demonstrated efficiency and professionalism in carrying out their responsibilities.[48]

Now in a position to influence the government's strategy, the reformers decided to keep a low profile. As a consequence, they worked in concert with the Office of Governmental Innovation and the members of the three parties who had introduced reform initiatives.[49] They benefited from support from the ministry of finance, which was concerned about the rising costs of government. What emerged from this process was a carefully negotiated agreement that tried to avoid great resistance from parties or officials within government.

Indeed, the political consensus in favor of the new system was significant and unusual. This characteristic owes much to its design. First, it was not intended to be relevant to base workers. By focusing on a professional civil service, the authors of the new system avoided any need to confront the power and political control of the Federación de los Sindicatos de Trabajadores al Servicio del Estado, FSTSE, the public sector union federation. According to those concerned about the new system, "You just can't mess with labor legislation [put in place in 1938]. This is a path reformers can't go down."[50] The reform would focus on confidence employees only.

Others were also left out of the new system. When it became clear that governors, increasingly important in the Mexican political system because of competitive elections and greater decentralization, were generally opposed to a new federal service, in particular not wanting to see the federal officials assigned to coordinate with state agencies *(delegados)* as part of the system, their concerns led to the exclusion of these positions from the civil service. Moreover, the new career service would apply only to ministries of the central government and not to the state enterprise sector. And organizations that already had a career service—doctors, teachers, foreign service and public security officers—would also remain outside the new system. The presidential office was also excluded from it.[51]

The political moment responsible for the introduction of a career service in Mexico corresponds in many ways to an important incentive identified by Geddes (1994). She predicts that a civil service system will be introduced when the balance among political parties represented in a legislature suggests that alternation in political power is likely and that the jobs of partisans in government positions will be in jeopardy if they are not encapsulated within a career service. This condition clearly existed in 2003, when the congress was composed of 208 PRI and 207 PAN legislators, along with smaller numbers in several other parties that could be encouraged to join voting coalitions.

Yet the reform was by no means inevitable. Reformers worked hard to establish the issue of the public service on the agenda, lobbied the congress, and worked very closely with the office of public sector reform in the presidency. Power relations between the legislature and the executive also played an important part in the outcome by encouraging presidential backing for change. According to a principal architect of the new reform, for example, "Fox made the decision to introduce the legislation because the PRI and the PRD [with fifty-three votes] would pass legislation about a civil service anyway, and this gave his administration an opportunity to make sure they did not become losers in the [design of the] legislation."[52] In addition, the parties were under some pressure to produce in the legislature because many proposed laws had not been approved during the congressional period then drawing to a close.[53]

In relatively short order, a new Servicio Professional de Carerra (SPC) was negotiated among the three parties and the president's office and then introduced and approved by both houses of the congress without contrary votes. A new ministry of public service was created from the existing ministry of auditing and administrative development and took over functions from the civil service unit of the ministry of finance. Its activities were to be coordinated with committees in each ministry responsible for the actual operation of the system. The public service ministry was to set norms and standards and oversee processes in the other ministries. It would have an advisory board of government ministries.

The new service was directed toward about forty-three thousand middle- and higher-level positions in the central government—officials designated as liaison officers, chiefs of department, subdirectors, area directors, adjunct directors, and directors general. These positions corresponded to those at the third level of importance and below, a level that the reformers believed marked a difference between the responsibilities of political decision making and professional administration. Those currently serving in these positions would have a choice of whether to opt into the new system or not.

The new professional career service for the Mexican government sought to wed elements of a classical career system with elements of the new public management.[54] It mandated open competitive processes for filling government vacancies and opportunities for a career ladder within the public service based on merit and performance reviews. The performance reviews, in particular, were promoted by the PAN, whose ideas on the public sector had always been shaped by extensive private sector experience.

The job facing the new ministry and its collaborators was enormous; job and qualification descriptions were practically nonexistent, and there were no mechanisms in place to assess candidates competitively. Implementation of the new plan was to be gradual, with a three-year timeline, and much of the responsibility for getting the new system working well was to rest with individual ministries. Yet the initial leadership of the new ministry of public service—committed reformers—sought a more centralized and rapid implementation of the plan. Within two years, the goals set for three had been reached, and the ministry of public service had taken over a considerable amount of the hiring responsibility that was to be under the control of the ministries. But decisions made in the design of the law, its regulations, and its initial operation would come back to haunt the new system as it was being implemented, a topic to be considered in Chapter 7.

Chile: Scandal and a New Administrative Elite

In Chile, the traditional patronage system functioned through a carefully balanced ballet among parties in the aftermath of elections. Positions in regional governments as well as a large parastatal sector that emerged in the 1930s provided a range of posts for distribution among parties and interests. Efforts to change this situation had been undertaken prior to the 2000s. For example, in 1930, civil service regulations protected employees from some of the ups and downs of national politics. In the 1950s, a newer set of regulations provided for greater job security. In 1960, a reform provided public servants with tenure rights once they had been appointed (generally through patronage) and established a promotion system based on merit and seniority.[55]

Public sector reform was back on the agenda in the mid-1990s. In 1994, the government introduced total quality management, process simplification, citizen-rights charters, awards for innovation, information offices, and a variety of programs for improving management.[56] Recruitment processes were devised that gave presidents, ministers, and other high-level officials ultimate control over appointments, but which mandated processes of review of candidates as a way of "rationalizing" patronage appointments at middle and upper levels.[57]

Then, in the late 1990s, academics in universities and think tanks became more concerned about aspects of government that left many public officials without clear guidelines about their performance and career expectations and resulted in the politicization of higher levels in the bureaucracy. In contrast to reformers in most other countries, those in Chile were less concerned by low-quality public services or even particularly corrupt public administration. In general, the public service in Chile worked relatively well. In fact, the IDB report of 2006 ranked Chile as having the second most professional public service in Latin America, just behind Brazil. Meanwhile, a World Bank official declared that "Chile's public administration may be the most professional and capable in Latin America."[58] Internationally, it was ranked twentieth among 133 countries in a corruption index developed by Transparency International.

Instead, the reformers sought greater separation between political and administrative positions, believing that this was a way to promote more transparency and improved performance. And they believed that a better career service needed to be devised for those in government. At the time, the bulk of the country's public sector had grown into a stable and entrenched service, provided with tenure but an uncertain career system and capped by an extensive high-level patronage-based leadership cadre. The reformers faced a dilemma—should they focus on providing a broad career system for the public service, such as in Argentina, or try to bring greater stability to the higher ranks of the public service, more along the lines of Mexico? They selected a third strategy by designing a system to provide more transparently qualified people to serve in the highest levels of government.

A think tank representing the views of the business sector in Chile, the Comisión de Estudios Públicos (CEP), convened a committee of twenty-seven publicly respected figures broadly representative of the political spectrum and began to generate a plan of reform. They organized a large conference on public sector reform and published a two-volume study, one volume of which focused on the modernization of the state. Within this plan was a proposal for focusing on higher-level managers in government. The experience of New Zealand, a country visited by a core group of reformers to assess the workings of the first adopter of the new public management, was used as a model for considering how to fashion a professionalized government elite.

According to one member of this group, "We put a lot of effort and thinking into what kind of civil service we wanted. We were clear that what was needed was a top-level service, somewhat on the model of the U.S. Senior Executive Service or the U.K. senior executive model. So we developed this kind of a system, but adapted to a presidential system. We wanted the president/minister to be able to remove people so there would be accountability, but the bottom line was that you couldn't just bring in your friends. . . . We didn't want an autonomous bureaucracy that would not be accountable."[59] Their plan was presented to President Ricardo Lagos in mid-2000, and while no action was taken at that time, the group continued to talk about the reform publicly and to make more people aware of their concerns.

The plan focused on the existing 3,100 positions in government recognized to be political. A new Senior Public Management System (Sistema de Alta Dirección Pública–ADP) would focus on 2,450 of these positions, reducing the number of fully discretionary political positions to 650. Seven hundred and fifty of the remaining positions at the top level of the administration of the government and 1,700 jobs at the next level would be part of a system of career officials, scrapping the coalition party and quota system for them. Under the plan, the high-level positions would be filled through an open competitive process, and the second level would be filled through an internal competitive process focusing on merit and fit for the office. The reformers were convinced that "if you have excellent people at the top, their leadership will filter down to better performance below. The top levels—directors of services—are powerful people and it's good to have these positions filled with really good people. Then, the idea is, you can have vertical penetration."[60]

An autonomous Commission for High Level Public Management (Consejo de Alta Dirección Pública) would oversee competitive processes of recruitment and the development of clear job descriptions and skill criteria for available positions. The commission would have five members selected by the president for six-year terms and would be composed of the presidentially appointed director of the Civil Service Office and four others who were to represent political parties; the senate would confirm the nominees. This commission, then, continued the prevailing practice of incorporating party and ideological quotas, but now one step removed from the appointment of more public servants. "In naming the people for the commission, there has been a real effort to represent the whole spectrum of political parties—the opposition has selected one from the right and one from the center right parties, the government one from the left and one from the center left. There has been no effort to make this into a commission of highly regarded elites; it is an explicitly political board."[61] The civil service office would be located within the ministry of finance so that appointments and budgets could be more easily aligned.

The new career system particularly targeted the chiefs of services, who held positions just below vice-ministers and who were the principal operational officers in the Chilean bureaucracy, and their immediate subordinates. The commission would ensure competitive processes that would lead to the selection of three to five qualified individuals for each post that became vacant. This list of candidates would then be recommended, and political officials would be able to select among them. To be selected to be part of a list of acceptable candidates, a candidate would have to receive a favorable vote from four of five commissioners.

The candidates who were selected to take on positions would be hired for three years on the basis of a contract that spelled out responsibilities and expectations for performance—the influence of the New Zealand model was clear. If their performance during the first three years was judged satisfactory, they could expect to be contracted for an additional three years. To provide incentives to give incumbents longer periods to remain in these important positions, it was to be expensive to dismiss them. The purpose, explained one of the plan's proponents, was "to give to the central government competent and suitable high level public managers who would optimize the management of institutions and head up the tasks of modernizing the public services."[62]

In addition to allowing political officials room for some discretion in hiring, the reform plan incorporated other measures to make it politically palatable. It focused on central ministries of government, and was to be expanded only later to other parts of government. It was also to be a decentralized system, functioning through the ministries, and its reach was limited to the most important positions in government just below ministers, vice-ministers, and regional secretaries of the ministries, considered to be confidence posts. Moreover, new appointments would only be made when incumbents retired, resigned, or were removed from office. This was an eminently political plan, which reserved considerable discretion in the appointments process for political and personal criteria to be recognized.

Despite these important accommodations, there was little interest among political leaders for such a system. Then, a political scandal erupting around the ministry of public works and transport (MOP) in 2002 opened up space for the reformers' plan. "MOPgate" involved a practice of paying public sector employees additional salaries in cash. As public sector wages had lagged behind those of the private sector, ministries had begun offering *sobresueldos* (top-up salaries, but *sobre* also means envelope) to high-level officials, in a system of incentives that helped attract well-qualified people but remunerated them in a way that was clearly not lawful.[63] The funds were channeled through a private contractor, GATE, and other consultancies.

This practice came to light when the minister of public works was asked publicly how he paid his people; he responded that he paid them in envelopes, referring to how the cash payments were regularly delivered. The comment was widely reported. Other improprieties also came to light in the same period—the use of presidential funds for electoral purposes, "honoraria" provided to other high-level officials, illegal transfer of financial instruments by an important state-owned industry, revelations of influence peddling by deputies in the congress. The president of the country was implicated in some of the stories of corruption.

Chileans were mortified that their "clean" country was hiding so much corruption. The president's approval ratings in public opinion polls declined precipitously almost immediately. A study found that 57 percent of those interviewed believed that many or practically all public officials were corrupt and received bribes.[64] Seventy-five percent agreed that corruption was caused by the distribution of public positions through party connections and not through competitive processes of merit.[65] In response to these concerns, the government sought the support of the opposition parties in an agreement about the management of the public sector. The government was in a weak position, and the opposition was interested in finding new opportunities in government. "The opposition was convinced that it would win the 2006 elections. The Lagos government was at its lowest point, and many thought it would not last out its term. The opposition saw the development of a civil service as a saving grace, a lifesaver, so that it would not have to take over a government in crisis. Government had incentives, because of crisis, to show it was doing something."[66] Indeed, confirmed one of the reformers, "Without the scandal, there would have been no reform."[67]

The small group that had been discussing public sector reform took this as a window of opportunity to reintroduce the plan it had ready and had introduced to government two years before the scandal. "If you have a project of reform, you have to take advantage of the spaces that become available. Those spaces are defined by the weakness of the opposition— that is, all those who don't want change to happen, like most politicians."[68] The law that emerged was defined quickly. Three people took the lead in the discussion: President Lagos; Pablo Longueira, of the opposition Unión Democrática Independiente (UDI) party in the chamber of deputies; and José Miguel Insulza, who was minister of the interior and a leader of the Socialist Party. In developing a major agreement about the reform of the state, the "Political-Legislative Pact for the Modernization of the State, Transparency, and Promotion of Growth," these three followed a custom of legislation worked out within and among parties with the assurance that once a proposal was presented to the congress, party discipline would ensure voting for and against.

The legislation was passed in January 2003. There was no public discussion of the forty-nine initiatives included in the new law, and the congress was presented with a final package to vote on, under the assumption that the traditional form of generating legislation through party leadership deals would be followed. "The law was designed, it was agreed to by the heads of the party, it was simply presented to parliament for vote, with the assurance that a vote would be quick and favorable."[69] The new Sistema de Alta Dirección Pública became Law 19,882 of 2003 and came into effect in January 2004.

Conclusions

In the cases of Brazil, Argentina, Mexico, and Chile, the introduction of civil service systems was largely unnoticed by public opinion or media attention. In none of these cases was there any mobilized public action to promote reform. Although public opinion was inevitably critical of government, the reforms that occurred were not the result of campaign promises by politicians or parties seeking electoral support. Interestingly, there is no evidence that public sector employees were important actors in the reform initiatives. Instead, the plans for reform were the work of small groups of people who had identified a common concern over the politicization of the public service. These concerns led them to generate models for new systems of government employment that they hoped would be adopted and implemented.

But they would not have gotten far had it not been for a political moment in which normal resistance to altering a patronage system was at low ebb and decision-making structures were in disequilibrium. In Brazil, the initiation of a centralizing authoritarian regime pushed clientelistic political parties to the margin of political relevance and allowed a president to move rapidly on many fronts, including that of public sector reform. In Argentina, an extraordinarily deep economic crisis allowed government-based reformers considerable room to introduce a wide range of policy changes. Under normal conditions of much more disaggregated decision-making power, legislators, governors, and public sector unions would have had much greater capacity to prevent or stall reform. In Mexico, unilateral action by recently empowered party leaders in the congress created a situation that the executive could ignore only at the peril of a more aggressive reform than desired. This situation stood in significant contrast to the earlier context in which hegemonic party control of the patronage system had given presidents extensive power. And in Chile, a corruption scandal brought public sector reform to the policy agenda when an administration had few resources to fight it and when party leaders had powerful motives to come to an agreement. Largely because of these particular moments, the introduction of change was much less conflictful than might have been expected, given the extent to which patronage systems were institutionalized.

The newly designed systems reflected some characteristics that had evolved in the prior patronage system. In Brazil, a patronage system that had a history of engaging relatively competent people in higher-level positions in government encouraged reformers to find ways to replicate it at lower levels. In Argentina, middle and lower levels of appointments had become less important to parties as those within government had increasingly been anchored in place through tenure and as the system became ever more complex. Reformers generated a government-wide plan for change and a means to simplify and rationalize the preexisting system. In Mexico and Chile, the prior centralization of the patronage system was reflected in reformers' concerns with higher levels within the public sector. Moreover, while the prior patronage systems may have emphasized increasing levels of education among political appointees, there was little tradition of elite corps, rigid social class barriers, or educational "reserves," found in Europe and Japan.

There were, then, significant similarities in the process of reform, even while the reforms themselves differed. In the aftermath of reform, however, process and content came closer together as those who resisted reform adopted similar strategies to slow it down or defeat it. And the contention that was largely absent from the crafting and approval of reform was more than apparent as reform was being implemented. These topics are taken up in the following chapter.

CHAPTER 7

Ambiguous Futures

The Politics of Implementation

Introducing career civil services in Brazil, Argentina, Mexico, and Chile was surprisingly easy. Small groups of reformers generated ideas, little public and intra-governmental discussion accompanied the planning process, and negotiations and approval processes took place under conditions that eased acceptance of the new systems. A new and centralizing regime in Brazil, an economic crisis in Argentina, an electoral standoff among parties in Mexico, a corruption scandal in Chile—the story for each is distinct, but in all, unusual circumstances surrounded how the well-institutionalized patronage process was challenged and replaced in law.

These unusual circumstances limited the extent to which opposition to reform could be organized and mobilized while plans were made and votes counted. Moreover, in all cases, reformers made important compromises in the scope and intent of their civil service projects in order to encourage their adoption. Despite these concessions, however, unresolved issues, tensions, and open questioning of the life chances of the new systems emerged in the aftermath of formal approval and threatened the longer-term survival of new institutions. In fact, implementation, not law or decree, determined the extent to which patronage would persist as an important aspect of recruitment into government service in Brazil, Argentina, Mexico, and Chile.

Implementation, and the conflicts that surrounded it, also shaped important characteristics of the emergent career services in these four countries, such as their coverage and management. In these cases, then, efforts to introduce neutral and stable public services encountered ongoing pressures in which the construction of a new system was confronted by repeated efforts to alter and undermine it. Brazil's public service system was eventually consolidated in ways not anticipated when the DASP was first created in 1938. And twenty years after the introduction of a new system of public sector employment in Argentina, and almost a decade after this event in Mexico and Chile, the fate of their career services was not yet resolved.

In the end, it seemed that reformers in Latin America had unique moments to move ahead with their projects; the opponents of reform had significantly longer windows of opportunity to undermine them. Clearly, public sector reform does not come to an end with the approval of a new system, however emphatic the legislation or regulatory regimes and however persuasive the arguments of the reformers. The story of reform in four Latin American countries thus parallels the experiences of early adopters of civil service systems reviewed in Part One of this book. In particular, Chapter 3 focused on conflicts about the existence and control of new civil service systems, as well as the criteria that would characterize recruitment and the loyalties of public servants. In all cases, also, the performance of civil services, once consolidated, raised new concerns and conflicts.

This chapter also indicates the vulnerability of new career civil service systems to post-reform pressures by showing how reform initiatives in Brazil, Argentina, Mexico, and Chile confirm that implementation is fraught with opportunities for distorting the content and intent of law. Conflicts related to existence, control, criteria, loyalty, and performance were as present in these cases as in earlier cases from other regions of the world. In addition, this chapter explores a variety of mechanisms that reform opponents employed to defeat, limit, or alter the new systems. Despite differences in their design, and equally diverse conditions under which they were introduced, strategies adopted by those who sought to resist change were remarkably similar.

Resisting Civil Service Reform: Deconstruction and Reconstruction

Many scholars, of course, have pointed to the importance of the implementation process for determining policy and institutional outcomes.[1] Putting new rules of the game into practice is always fraught with problems—designs are never perfect when they are transformed into operation; the wisdom of initial activities and decisions is called into question; capacity limits become evident; assumptions about logistics prove unrealistic; red tape limits initiative; and accomplishing goals can often take longer than anticipated, even in supportive environments. These kinds of implementation problems are likely to be unavoidable and can be credited to human and organizational error and inabilities to predict future events and the consequences of action. But implementation processes also reveal that after-the-fact challenges to reform can be deliberate strategies of opponents of change to truncate, alter, or undermine the new initiatives before they are fully consolidated and institutionalized.

Deconstructing the DASP, Finding Purpose in Patronage

Events occurring after the creation of the DASP and its new career system are a critical part of the history of public sector reform in Brazil. This history is a long one among Latin American countries, and indicates that career civil services can be constructed, deconstructed, and reconstructed numerous times without fully losing the capacity to incorporate patronage. Indeed, seventy years after the creation of the civil service considered to be the region's most extensive and professional, Brazilian presidents had access to more than eighty-one thousand personal appointments in 2009.[2] These presidential appointments included all high-level officials, of course, such as ministers and vice-ministers, but also the occupants of all positions that involved policy decision making, including the leadership and management cadres of Brazil's extensive parastatal sector. In the early 2000s, then, Brazil's civil service glass was simultaneously half full and half empty.

As indicated in the previous chapter, between 1938 and 1945, DASP experienced a heyday of power and prestige. Yet its wide-ranging responsibilities and extensive authority placed it on a collision course with the ministry of finance, which never effectively relinquished control over the budget to the new agency. Moreover, because DASP was "deliberately used by Vargas as an instrument of personal rule," it was immediately the subject of hostility by politicians and administrators who resisted the centralization of power under his dictatorship and who identified DASP with the authoritarian regime.[3] Its technocratic bias, its negative framing of politicians, and its strong endorsement of centralization and control as means to improve administration did little to win it friends outside the president's core of supporters.[4]

It is not surprising, then, that DASP faced a hostile reaction in 1945, when Vargas's *Estado Novo* was overthrown by the military and elections for a new government were called.[5] Almost immediately, many of its powers were taken away, ministries regained control over numerous personnel decisions, and DASP's influence over the civil service waned as political parties actively sought votes through the use of pork and patronage. In a decree law of 1945, DASP was stripped of most of its responsibilities other than setting standards, training, and research. Its budget was reduced by 10 percent.[6] An important part of the constitution of 1938, DASP was not mentioned in that of 1946.

In 1947, in a move reminiscent of actions that followed the Pendleton Act in the United States, legislation drafted by the ministry of finance was introduced to disestablish DASP in favor of expanded responsibilities for the ministry and special commissions that would organize and manage competitive examinations. Although this initiative failed and DASP survived, the then president declared that budgetary constraints precluded holding examinations, and officials made extensive use of temporary appointments to circumvent entrance through the DASP system.[7] DASPistas resigned in protest against their diminished status and power, a move that was interpreted by new political leaders as evidence of the authoritarian preferences of the departments' personnel.[8] Clearly, the close relationship between the chief executive and DASP as "his" agency had been broken.

As presidents reverted to the older legacy of appointing virtually all central public officials, the pay grades and classifications of personnel that DASP had worked hard to establish were weakened so that appointments could be made more easily. Many were brought into the public service through temporary appointments and hiring outside the provisions of the civil service. In rural areas, the *coronéis* regained significant power over local politics as they were courted for the votes of their clienteles; legislators and parties needed jobs to distribute to their supporters. And patronage at all levels was justified in part as a feature of democratic systems, in distinction to the authoritarian origins of DASP. The 1947 constitution granted tenure to many of those with interim or irregular appointments. Moreover, in the aftermath of the *Estado Novo,* public service unions grew stronger as government employment increased. Maintaining and expanding benefits rather than supporting merit were their principal concerns. In subsequent years, legislation was regularly introduced in the congress to eliminate or further diminish the activities of the agency.[9]

DASP continued to exist, but survival was its only claim to fame through much of the 1950s. Succeeding heads of the agency—no longer dignified as presidents but downgraded to general directors—became skilled at trading budgetary support for the continued survival of the agency, albeit in disempowered ways.[10] They took cover in claiming that the department was a purely technical agency of government. Simultaneously, the ministry of finance regained much of its influence in the management of government affairs and became adept at using budgetary constraints to curb the growth of both the career and the appointive civil service. The budget of DASP declined from 2.2 percent of the national budget in 1945 to 0.3 percent in 1962.[11]

These post-1945 years of darkness for DASP were temporarily interrupted between 1951 and 1954, when Getúlio Vargas was elected president of the democratic regime. DASP resurfaced, and examinations were reintroduced; the agency was again assigned responsibility for the overall civil service, reversing the claim of ministries over internal appointments.[12] At the same time, the president extended the use of patronage, especially drawing in working-class supporters of his political party. Earlier expectations that DASP would be a superagency with control functions over much of government were not revisited.

With the brief exception of these few years, the return to a competitive electoral regime after the *Estado Novo* gave a new lease on life to the politics of patronage in Brazil. In this political system, with pervasively clientelist political parties, the use of patronage was highly valued and well practiced. Thus, even while presidents—following the earlier pattern established by presidents in the United States—consistently committed themselves publicly to a merit system, their actions belied their words just as consistently. In pursuit of patronage, examinations were regularly suspended and efforts were made to "blanket in" temporary employees.[13] Only Jânio Quadros (1961) acted in support of entry by examination, and began to provide support for reassembling DASP and expanding its training mission, but his resignation after seven months in office put an end to this initiative.

Juscelino Kubitschek (1956–1961) found patronage to be an extraordinarily useful way of pursuing his policy agenda of rapid industrialization and political support building, reportedly distributing seven thousand jobs in the year after his election.[14] Quadros's successor, João Goulart (1961–1964), brought patronage to new heights as he appointed party members, cronies, and political bosses to public posts.[15] Goulart's period in office was a rocky one, and he used appointments to government office liberally to reward partisans of his political party and to shore up his legislative agenda by providing jobs in exchange for congressional votes. Many of his choices lacked competence, and his use of powers over appointments to state agencies created widespread dismay and scandal among economic and social elites in the country, not to mention the leadership of the military. In his case, the restraining hand of the ministry of finance, controlling appointments through its rein on the budget, was unable to provide much defense against his highly politicized selections. By the mid-1960s, the introduction of the career civil service in Brazil was declared a failure, and Gilbert Siegel announced that "the DASP is dead, or dying."[16]

When Goulart was overthrown in 1964, Brazil's new military presidents demonstrated a clear disdain for the politics of patronage. They blamed parties and the practices of patronage and clientelism for the inefficiencies and corruption that they saw as emblematic of Brazil's style of mass politics. Their intention was to centralize and depoliticize the government, and particularly the executive, so that it could play a stronger role in stimulating and guiding economic development.[17] The national interest could best be served, they believed, through the technocratic management of government and the expansion of the role of the state in the country's development. The traditional political elites who managed local, state, and national networks of pork and patronage could not be trusted to lead the country anywhere but in their own narrow self-interest—or so believed the leaders of a regime that was labeled a leading example of "bureaucratic authoritarianism," albeit one that preserved elections and legislatures.[18]

But patronage, it turned out, was a good way to pursue the military regime's goals. Military presidents took charge of appointment powers and used them extensively to put military officials and technocrats in key positions of authority, policy making, and implementation, conscious as all leaders are of the importance of loyalty among those they rely on to carry out their agendas. "The new rulers centralized economic policy making in the national ministries, strengthened the executive in firm military hands, and purged key federal state posts of traditional as well as populist politicians and replaced these with uniformed military officers and civilian economists, engineers, educators, and professional administrators—the core of a new technocratic elite."[19] Similar efforts to build a new bureaucracy committed to rapid economic development and an end to politics were replicated in some state-level governments. At times, those chosen to leadership positions of ministries and parastatal agencies were administrators who had long toiled within those organizations and whose responsibilities were primarily technical.[20]

Early military governments were particularly interested in high-level public officials, seeking a solution to concerns about bureaucratic inertia and inefficiency.[21] Nevertheless, as Hagopian has documented, traditional politicians accommodated to the military regime and, after initial purges of "old style" politicians, gradually began to reoccupy high-level positions, but without tarnishing the technocratic bent of the new state administration.[22] Equally important, military rulers accommodated their style to an increasing need to establish political support for their development agenda. By the mid 1970s, an expanded state had fully embraced the use of patronage not only for its technocratic aims, but also for its political ones.[23]

Several years after the negotiated withdrawal of the military from politics in 1985, observers of Brazil were hard pressed to find that it had made much impact on *o systema*. In 1988, Fernando Henrique Cardoso indicated parallels between the newly restored democracy, the dynamics of the military regime, and pervious democratic governments. "Up to a certain point, trading posts and favors is a normal fact of any political system. What has become abnormal in our current political situation is that favor is traded for favor, post for post. . . . The result is that we are witnessing a restoration of oligarchical power, the same type of power that was utilized in 1964 to contain popular pressure."[24] Patronage politics served a purpose for the military, and its potential for political and policy use did not need to be reintroduced to the democratic regime that was installed in 1985.

Yet all the while that the patronage system persisted and reasserted itself, the ranks of the career civil service also continued to expand across administrations and regimes. Those appointed through patronage for temporary, irregular, or noncareer posts were gradually granted permanent tenure and incorporated into a structure that protected them from arbitrary firing or replacement, once they had demonstrated that they had relevant skills for the jobs they were assigned. Thus, and as in the United States, a patronage system lived side by side with an expanding career system when government itself was expanding—as it was consistently doing in Brazil from the 1940s through the 1980s.

With the return of civilian government and democratic elections in 1985, the government assessed its public sector, discovering that it had amassed many more than 20,000 agencies, including 553 focused on health, 339 on education, and 282 on industry and commerce. Officials discovered 897 agencies whose purpose was to coordinate agencies.[25] Moreover, and perhaps reflecting dissatisfaction with the extent to which dismay over extensive clientelism had contributed to the coup in 1964, the constitution of 1988 gave tenure to all public officials, increased complex hiring procedures, and made decreasing the size of the public service extremely difficult. The constitution and a new labor law of 1991 granted equal pay for officials at different levels of government and improved pension levels.

The constitution also promoted the retirement, on generous terms, of a significant number of civil servants. The overall number fell by almost 20 percent between 1991 and 2001 through these retirements and other downsizing measures.[26] At the same time, replacements consistently privileged those with university degrees: in 1995, 39.2 percent of newly hired civil servants had such credentials; in 2001, 94.1 percent did.[27] Thus, newer members of the civil service were highly qualified by educational standards.

Yet these reforms were quickly criticized for their failure to combine better conditions with incentives for bureaucrats to be more responsive and accountable to citizens.[28] The constitution, according to many, was looking backward at the "old public administration," one anchored in a set of protections for public sector workers with little attention to the problems of management and performance.[29] And, as the constitution specified in extensive detail the organization and procedures of the public service in Brazil after 1988, changes that would affect its operations and performance had to be put in place through an amendment process.

This problem was attacked in 1995, under the presidency of Fernando Henrique Cardoso (1995–2003). In that year, a Plan for the Reform of the State Apparatus was announced, with the cautious support of Cardoso and strong backing from his minister of federal administration and reform of the state (MARE), Luiz Carlos Bresser-Pereira.[30] Strongly influenced by the influential *Reinventing Government* of David Osborne and Ted Gaebler, and by the progress of the new public management in Britain, Bresser-Pereira set out to reinvigorate the public sector of Brazil.

His initiative focused on reducing the size of the public administration, creating more accountability among public officials, and increasing the autonomy of many organizations and organizational units. He planned to do this by decentralizing many line ministries, privatizing public agencies, and generating a series of mechanisms in which public services would be produced or coproduced with the private sector or the not-for-profit sector.[31] He and his team wanted public officials and agencies to have clear objectives and to be regularly assessed in terms of their performance of these objectives.[32] At the same time, the policy-making, objective-setting, and performance-monitoring roles of central ministries and agencies were to be strengthened. Thus, "Rather than attempting—one more time—to build a classic career system, Brazil could learn from the experience of others, avoid the pitfalls [of] the weberian [*sic*] civil service model, and move forward in the construction of a truly modern, efficient and professional bureaucracy."[33]

The amendment that put this reform initiative into place also made incursions into the career system by placing certain limits on tenure and capping salaries of high-level officials in many agencies. It also reduced some of the privileges of those who had positions in the career civil service and sought to incorporate organizations into a total quality management program. Management contracts and performance indicators became part and parcel of the language of bureaucratic reformism in Brazil in the 1990s.[34]

The announcement of the reform initiative brought considerable resistance. Objections were strongly voiced by the National Workers' Union, the Union of Federal Civil Servants, and the Workers' Party (PT). These organizations were important in ensuring that the range of benefits enjoyed by public servants—including access to housing, transportation and meal subsidies, and other benefits—would continue. In addition, opposition came from the president's office and the ministers of planning and education—not because they were against reform in the public sector, but because they did not share Bresser-Pereira's approach to the problem or did not believe it was the most important priority for the government.[35] The judiciary was also opposed, largely because of concerns about the tenure of public officials, and the staff of the legislative branch was similarly worried about job security.[36] The president kept clear of the controversies surrounding the initiative, and many of his party supporters were strongly opposed, fearing the reaction of public servants deprived of tenure.[37]

Nevertheless, the fact that much of the career system incorporated lower-level officials, leaving middle- and higher-level officials to be appointed by the president and ministers, provided an opportunity to garner support from upper-level public servants. These managers and bureaucratic leaders, in fact, had little stake in maintaining many of the privileges of the career system—it was not, after all, their system—and they were brought on board by Bresser-Pereira and others in discussions about performance and responsiveness, especially in the context of a newly established democratic system.[38] He framed the reform initiative as one to enable "managers to manage" and to have the flexibility to respond to problems and the needs of citizens.[39] Private contracts were to be the principal mechanism for attracting well-qualified middle- and upper-level managers, not an expansion of the civil service system.

In addition, Bresser-Pereira, no doubt aware that bureaucracy is a popular whipping boy, ensured that the proposal was widely discussed in the media, and often framed as changes that would ensure greater responsiveness, accountability, and democracy. He also found support among progressive governors and mayors who were eager to gain more room for maneuver in their dealings with the federal government and in the management of their own political and bureaucratic households. He sought selective salary increases as a further incentive for support. As he wrote about his experience, "It was time to criticize the existing situation, denounce privileges, and demand change."[40] Against his advocacy were those who argued that he was undermining the state and the civil service through his commitment to neoliberal principles.[41]

Progress on the approval of reform was slow. The amendment to the constitution was discussed for two and a half years in the congress, and unions and parties were influential actors in lobbying deputies about their concerns over security and benefits. One issue of contention, for example, was that of when it was possible to dismiss a public servant; the reform team found it expedient to compromise on this issue, making dismissals dependent on costs of personnel rather than number of personnel.[42] Moreover, judicial and legislative agencies were able to opt out of the reform. The effort to reverse the constitutional guarantee of civil service tenure was eventually approved, but other parts of the reform faced stiff resistance.[43] The combination of the resistance of career civil servants and politicians who wished to maintain their discretion in hiring proved extraordinarily difficult to overcome.

The reform was eventually approved in 1997, largely as a result of the mobilization of citizen and upper-level bureaucratic support. Almost immediately, difficulties of putting the new system in place surfaced. The reform, close fought through the congress, proved to be extremely complex in implementation, taxing a large number of organizations to establish plans, objectives, indicators, training programs, evaluation methods, and other aspects of administration needed to make the new public administration work. Noticeably, results differed across agencies and ministries.[44]

Then, at a critical point of its implementation, the reform lost its most visible advocate, Bresser-Pereira, who was asked to take over as minister of science and technology. The ministry of state reform that he had headed was merged with planning and became a ministry of budget and management in Cardoso's second term. A secretariat of management was established to take on many of the policy-relevant personnel functions, and a human resource secretariat was formed to carry out operational activities—these units, constricted in focus, were the descendants of the once-powerful DASP. Shortly, they were disbanded and their responsibilities reassigned to other units. Gradually, the reform team Bresser-Pereira had assembled became engaged in other activities.[45]

In Cardoso's second administration, reform attention also shifted to the creation of an "entrepreneurial [emprendidora] public administration," whose goals were to bring personnel management into closer relationship with the budget and to focus on core careers in the civil service as mechanisms for resuscitating a permanent career service. And, as with previous administrations, a number of less comprehensive initiatives were introduced, such as total quality management, e-government, training initiatives, and other efforts to make the bureaucracy more responsive and agile.[46]

In a continuing conundrum, the reputation for professionalism and technical expertise of Brazil's middle- and high-level officials grew stronger, even as criticism of the leaden impact of the bureaucracy overall continued to be voiced in the face of new initiatives. In addition, where civil service entrance requirements were firmly implemented, government agencies found ways to hire staff "on loan" from international organizations, universities, or foundations, expanding opportunities for adding to the number of employees, but often strengthening their reputations for expertise and professionalism at the same time. Thus, in 2001, 10,597 people were hired on short-term contracts, while 660 were recruited through the examination system.[47]

Issues of fiscal control of the public wage budget continued to head the agenda for public sector reform during the subsequent administration of Luiz Inácio Lula da Silva (Lula) (2003–2011). Management training, as well as greater emphasis on policy-making (as opposed to implementation) skills, characterized the modest forays of the administration into public sector reform. And civil service unions were more central to discussions of salaries and benefits under Lula than they were in preceding administrations.[48] Overall, however, the administration of government was not a high priority for this president. Nevertheless, a basis for performance-oriented pay and evaluation of individual performance, two mechanisms that most public services resist strongly, were left in place. Moreover, overall pay improved during the Cardoso and Lula administrations, ensuring that public positions would remain attractive to well-qualified people, whether entering through the examination system or by personal appointment.

Thus was Brazil's public service constructed and reconstructed on numerous occasions. The civil service eventually gained considerable stability, although its autonomy may never have reached the levels anticipated for a Weberian career service. Its performance certainly never matched the expectations of its creators and early supporters. In the end, public sector reformers sought to address issues of performance by integrating alternative approaches to public management—most notably the new public management and close fiscal monitoring—in the public service.

In the 2000s, the Brazilian bureaucracy continued to face significant challenges and criticisms related to its efficiency and capacity to deal effectively with ongoing public problems. In attacks that sounded familiar across the world, the Brazilian bureaucracy was painted as immobilist and unresponsive. Neither the career system nor patronage had been able to solve this ongoing problem. Yet Brazil of the 2000s offered some opportunity for change in the staffing of the public sector. A booming private sector helped diminish to some extent the pressure for jobs, and curtailing some of the state's role in the economy made "pork" less available. In this context, evidence began to surface that parties were becoming less dependent on the traditional uses of patronage and pork and more focused on promising programmatic initiatives to a large and diverse voting population.[49] The transformation of the public sector, then, may eventually owe something to the lessening of the importance of jobs for the boys.

Argentina: Pushing Reform to the Margins

Twenty years after the creation of Argentina's SINAPA, the number of officials incorporated into the system was in decline, the size of the public sector had increased, and most public functionaries in a position to hire subordinates did so through a system of temporary contracts and project management positions that fell outside the career system. By the end of the 2000s, the career public service system had been largely pushed to the margin by a resurgence of political appointments introduced through a variety of mechanisms.

Numerous actions helped eviscerate SINAPA. During the 1990s, the number of regulatory agencies overseeing newly privatized industries increased, thus expanding opportunities for opting out of the system and creating large numbers of positions available for direct appointment. In addition, in 1995, an executive decree by President Menem opened the door for a return to widespread use of patronage appointments. "Product and service" contracts allowed for hiring services, and the personnel to carry them out, that were not counted in the budget as salaries. As such, significant numbers of people could be hired outside the government system.[50]

Moreover, through Decree 92 of that same year, high-level officials were allowed to expand the use of temporary contracts for personnel they wished to hire. Such temporary appointments were expected to be filled primarily by public officials at middle levels, by advisers to higher-level officials, and by those with technical skills thought needed for particular activities. Often, renewal of these 180-day temporary positions was automatic, at least while hiring officials continued to hold public positions of confidence.[51] In 2002, there were almost 17,000 such appointments, in addition to another 1,200 in projects funded internationally, about 16 percent of 116,000 employees.[52]

Other mechanisms were used to marginalize the new system. New job titles, such as "program manager," were introduced outside the SINAPA system.[53] This title reflected efforts of numerous ministries to call new initiatives "programs," allowing for a politically appointed program manager.[54] Similarly, observers of the official hiring process complained that job descriptions were tailored to specific candidates, a situation criticized as having a correct methodology but an implementation system that left room for patronage and clientelism.[55]

In addition, a major economic crisis in 2001 encouraged those with hiring rights in the public service to provide additional jobs for family and friends who lost employment in other sectors. This left considerable space for the continued practice of patronage appointments. It also provided opportunities for politicians and their appointees to marginalize career public servants from decision making on sensitive issues, and to avoid their activities as implementers.[56] Moreover, a hiring freeze in 1999 contributed to the aging of the SINAPA corps; recruitment into the system was suspended in 2000.

In addition to the weakening of SINAPA, most high-level officials in Argentina continued to have the capacity to hire personal advisers, to constitute, in effect, their own cabinets.[57] About 125 high-level officials, designated by the president, were recognized as political appointments in 2002, along with over 350 "off schedule" officials and another 600 advisers whom high-level officials could name as part of their personal cabinets.[58] In addition, they were able to hire a significant number of managers, directors, and executive assistants (known as supernumeraries), as well as additional people through short-term contracts.

Almost two decades after the introduction of the career system that was expected to incorporate thirty thousand positions initially and then to grow, SINAPA managed a portfolio of fewer than twenty-five thousand jobs. In 1999, the year characterized by its largest cadre, the career service it incorporated amounted to 24.9 percent of the public service, declining thereafter to about 22 percent and then to just over 20 percent. In the IDB report on public services in Latin America, Argentina was characterized as a country with "very developed processes that are only partially used."[59] The credibility of the system was also undermined because of concern that high-level officials under SINAPA were, in fact, political appointees.[60]

Moreover, throughout the first twenty years of SINAPA's existence, its management did not find a stable home. Continued competition among agencies meant that the responsibility for reform passed from the vice presidency to the chief of the cabinet, then to the ministry of economy, and then back to the chief of the cabinet, with the creation of a subsecretariat for the modernization of the state, and then to a subsecretariat for public management.[61] A longtime observer of Argentine public management and state building, Oscar Ozlack, characterized SINAPA as a "cemetery of projects" of reform.[62]

Although SINAPA was systematically marginalized through these strategies, the organization did create an important legacy—the annual collective bargaining taking place between the government and the two largest unions of public sector employees, the UPCN and the Asociación de Trabajadores del Estado (ATE).[63] These negotiations focused on salaries, benefits, and professionalism, but their payoff for the unions, the bureaucrats, and to some degree the politicians was to ensure job stability. "The bureaucrats and the unions get what they want from this system, something they value—labor stability. But when you have this kind of arrangement, it is difficult to have a strategic vision" of the reform of the state, said one official in charge of developing such a vision.[64] Thus, although SINAPA itself was far from stable and institutionalized, it brought a measure of predictability to careers and salaries for a significant part of the public administration.

Overall, however, the weakening of SINAPA left behind growing spaces for political appointments. Subverting, scuttling, or eluding the regulations imposing a career public service was widely practiced by public officials who sought flexibility and wide scope for recruitment based on their own criteria. Lack of consistency was the cost. By the end of the 2000s, Argentina had in place a complex system of tenured public officials outside a career system, a broad career system, a corps of government administrators, a massive number of temporary and contracted employees, and a plethora of special categories of appointments.

Yet the use of a variety of mechanisms for undermining SINAPA's effort to establish a system-wide civil service did not necessarily undermine the performance or capacity of the Argentine public sector. Indeed, some observers of Argentina's return to patronage saw in this resurgence a new kind of political appointment, particularly at middle and high levels. They saw less influence of party and the importance of paying electoral debts through appointments to public positions than under the previous party-based patronage system, and renewed emphasis on trust and loyalty, flexibility and performance. One indicator of this trend was that those selected through discretion for posts in the country's state-owned industries demonstrated the highest levels of education in the public service.[65] The career civil service had become largely irrelevant to much of the public sector, but the basis for patronage had shifted somewhat from party loyalty to greater attention to personal, policy, and professional loyalty.[66] In effect, the Argentine public administration might have allowed for some professionalization through this reinvigoration of the patronage system, at the same time that the career system was marginalized.

Defenders of the reenergized system of political appointees justified this trend by citing the need for flexibility in bringing new ideas and initiatives into government. A public service could be highly politicized, but not necessarily always incompetent, according to one knowledgeable observer:

> For some, the contracts were for political payoffs, but also for some to overcome deficiencies left by downsizing and voluntary retirements, when the best people left government. . . . Politicians use appointments . . . to bring in good professionals to ensure they can do their jobs well and serve their political masters. And then they bring in technical people. It really is important to have friends around you when you are in government, it allows you to trust that your priorities will be pursued, that there won't be sabotage or unfriendly leaks of information.[67]

Indeed, while electoral patronage as a reason for appointment might have been in decline in the 2000s, the importance of having "your own people around you" continued to be important to many officials.[68]

Despite the resurgence of patronage, for many in the public service, tenure was eventually likely, given public sector labor legislation and the annual negotiations over salaries and benefits with the unions. Temporary and other "off schedule" officers were regularly eligible for tenure after some time in service. Careers, however, continued to be determined by the organization for which they worked, and their relationships to their superiors continued to be important for assignments and promotion. In this patchwork system, some officials, such as those in the foreign service, the Administrative Corps, as well as those serving in institutions such as internal revenue and social security, reached high levels of expertise and professionalism, with a regularized—but specific—career system.

The initial intent of SINAPA was a creditable effort at reform, and its early implementation was approached with considerable energy. Nevertheless, it was then largely ignored and limited in its impact, particularly during the 2000s.[69] Most ministries and agencies continued to use—or ignore—discrete mechanisms to imbue their organizations with professionalism. As a consequence, a variety of personnel management systems continued to operate, outside the norms of the formal system established in the 1990s, and created a "parallel bureaucracy" of temporary employees and specialized appointments.[70] Thus, "many names for the same jobs and many different salaries paid for the same work" characterized the day-to-day workings of the public service of Argentina.[71]

By the end of the 2000s, SINAPA was considered a failed initiative by many, an experiment with a highly uncertain future. Even those who submitted to the system's regular processes for recruitment and hiring could become disenchanted with their experience, as one official concluded. "The problem with a regular process is that if you get the job, it was because it was the best process ever; if you don't get the job, the process was unfair and the system corrupt."[72] Argentina had yet to make a clear transition to a Weberian system.

Nevertheless, SINAPA lived on, as did plans for its future. The national director of the office of public employment was clear about this. "We want to make a reform of SINAPA that should have been done long ago. We want to increase salaries, and do more with developing job descriptions and the profiles of people who are appropriate for filling these jobs. We want to work more on horizontal promotion and focus more on training. We also need to do more with evaluating performance."[73] This was a tall order for a system that continued to find itself at the margins of decisions about public sector jobs.

Mexico: Reform and Retreat

The reformers who took advantage of an opportune political moment to introduce a career civil service in Mexico acted rapidly to implement the reform. Indeed, as indicated in the previous chapter, goals meant to be achieved in three years were accomplished in two. For the acceptability of the Professional Career Service (SPC), however, this approach proved counterproductive.[74] As in the initiation of most new systems, a variety of start-up problems plagued it, and little time was allowed for ironing out difficulties before its application was generalized. These issues helped open up space for counterattacks on the reform and the organization that was responsible for it.

Overly rapid implementation of the system was evident in poor organization, considerable confusion over how it would work, and undue complexity in the procedures to put it in place. As a consequence, months could pass before all procedures had been accomplished for filling a position, a factor that did little to win friends among officials who were complying with the regulations when they were in need of new employees. In the first year of the new program, over 50 percent of listed positions were vacant; in 2005, 27 percent were vacant.[75] While this trajectory showed considerable progress, it was no doubt of little solace to managers who continued to want to fill positions more quickly. Performance reviews also proved complicated and ineffective.

None of these problems was insuperable, but time was needed to correct them. However, the cumbersome early years of the SPC created skepticism among many that the system was either viable or useful. Perhaps more important, implementing the reform rapidly meant that the new ministry of the public service centralized control over hiring processes and decisions, quickly running afoul of the interests of other ministries and departments that were expecting a larger degree of control over appointments.

In the initial years of its operation, then, reformers helped place the new career system in jeopardy. The first chief of the Public Service Department, a lead reformer during the planning process, reflected on these early activities in a 2008 publication. "We could say that from 2004 to 2006 a grave tactical error was committed, demonstrating the lack of understanding of even the most basic aspects of policy implementation, and that consisted of trying to implement all the subsystems rapidly, simultaneously and in a centralized and digitized way."[76]

Another of the reformers argued that implementation problems could be traced back to the process of policy making. "The strictly technocratic focus that has been adopted and implemented in this public policy, emphasized issues of rationality and content, but has avoided the steps of debate, negotiation, and approval characteristic of the political world"."[77] Another reformer was equally harsh about the origins of the system. "There was absolutely no engagement of society in this law—none at all."[78]

Whatever the sources of the problems—and they were numerous—in the absence of widespread commitment to the new system and considerable criticism of its start-up activities, ministries in search of new recruits found ways to avoid or subvert civil service processes and to maintain their autonomy from the public service ministry. Temporary appointments and extensive use of appointments to advisory roles, permitted under the new law, helped executives bring in their people. When they rejected candidates vetted through the official system, managers also had greater recourse to discretionary hiring.[79]

In addition, the political parties that now shared more equally in power in the legislature were in a stronger position to negotiate and bid on jobs. Indeed, negotiation among parties threatened the survival of the new system, as "parties would prefer to negotiate positions than have to give over their power to a civil service system."[80] Thus, the stability and predictability of the patronage system under the PRI regime became more competitive and contentious under a more democratic system of shared power. This increased difficulties of establishing a professional career services, as available positions were avidly sought by the parties.

These issues of the SPC were serious enough that in 2005 reformers in the new ministry of public service reassembled the academic team that had been so important in the development of the civil service law. After a discussion within this team, the ministry decided to contract researchers at the Centro de Investigación y Docencia Económicas (CIDE), who had been instrumental in the design of the program, to carry out an analysis of its initial progress.[81] In a report issued in 2007, these researchers concluded that the new system had established modest but important objectives, made progress in its first three years, but confronted a series of challenges that were cultural and political as well as administrative in nature.[82] The cultural problem was the long tradition of discretion in appointments. The new system created a "strait-jacket" that constrained the ability of high-level managers to build their own teams once they were themselves appointed to be part of a larger team.[83] Researchers further pointed to a number of ways in which the initial implementation of the SPC had been in error.

The report argued that the problems were not caused by the original law, but by the efforts that had been made to put it into effect.[84] Through a new set of regulations, they argued, the original intent of the law could be recovered and the system put right. They recommended new operational guidelines that would put the ministry of public service in the position of norm-setter and overseer of the processes that would be carried out largely by the ministries. Each ministry would design its own system of recruitment and hiring within this larger framework. In addition, the report recommended that there be greater transparency in how the system was operating, clearer guidelines for the operation of all aspects of the new system, and more attention to the development of careers once people became part of the SPC.

Coincidentally, at the time the report was issued, a new administration had just assumed power. This new government was less supportive of the SPC than its predecessor had been, and so high-level encouragement of the reform weakened. From the beginning, the new president, Felipe Calderón (2006–2012), placed high priority on issues of public security, drug trafficking, and reforms in fiscal, energy, and social security areas. Public sector reform was much less visible on his public policy agenda.[85] Moreover, the president, who had a more conventional political profile than his predecessor, was ambivalent about the reform measure itself, recognizing more fully the importance of jobs for the boys.

Predictably, newly appointed ministers complained to the president that they were unable to bring in their own people for important positions. One high-level official reflected the concern that those recruited through the SPC were not as responsive to his leadership as his own people would be. He questioned not only the competence of the newly recruited officials, but even the utility of the system in increasing competence. "I hate the new system. My department is full of incompetent people I can't get rid of. They got into the system because the ministries sometimes developed tests for specific people, to make sure their person got in."[86] The credibility of the SPC was called into question. "You hear of selling exams, of bribes and other ways of getting around the system—people taking exams for others, for example."[87]

A new minister of the public service confronted even more problems, discovering that in the context of a system that had yet to be consolidated in practice, newly incorporated civil servants became very concerned that they were going to lose their jobs.[88] In addition, a congressional audit demonstrated important limitations and problems with the new system.[89] According to this study, almost 40 percent of hiring within the SPC had not ended with the selection of the most appropriate candidate.[90]

In this context, the report of the CIDE researchers provided guidance for revisions in how the system could work more effectively. Under regulations adopted in 2007, ministries were given greater autonomy to implement the new system.[91] The SPC would establish norms and frameworks for operation, but each ministry would design its own system of recruitment within the general norms set up by the overall system. This change was widely viewed as administratively and politically wise. Administratively, it would increase the efficiency of the recruitment process. Politically, "ministers accepted this because they were relieved to have power back after such a centralized system [under President Fox]."[92]

In the new administration, politicians and higher-level administrators in search of greater autonomy also found additional space for a counterattack on the public service law. In particular, they argued that the 2003 law had been mistaken in identifying positions that were inherently political as subject to the new system. Thus, they argued that the positions of general director and deputy general director were political posts and should be available for discretionary appointment by political leaders. In 2006 and again in 2007, they sought to alter the bar that distinguished political appointees from those who could be incorporated into the neutral public service career, and they lobbied hard for a revision of the law to include general directors and their deputies as positions for "free designation" by political leaders.[93]

In addition, the ministry of finance, having lost control of its civil service unit when the new ministry of public service was created, lobbied for a return transfer of its activities to finance. Flagging high-level support for the new system was clear in 2009, when the president sided with the finance ministry in introducing a government reorganization plan to the legislature that would abolish the new agency. In this plan, the ministry of public service's responsibilities would be turned over to finance. The congress, then strongly in the hands of the PRI, resisted this initiative, concerned about the potential for the executive to return to a full-blown patronage system in benefit of the PAN.

Opposition to the SPC, in addition to unanticipated start-up problems, meant that by the end of 2007, only eighty-three hundred public servants were part of the new system. It had been expected to grow to incorporate some forty-three thousand officials when the law was passed in 2003. Of those who had become part of the SPC, two thousand were employees who had opted into the system, and the rest had joined it as a result of a competitive process of recruitment.[94] According to reports from the ministry of public service, seven thousand newly appointed officials during eighteen months in 2007 and 2008 were appointed through the old discretionary system.[95]

The ministry of the public service continued to survive, however, and the professional career service was alive, if not well, at the end of the 2000s. Yet at this juncture, the patronage system that had existed for so long in Mexico continued in the ascendance. In short, the future of the country's civil service was not at all assured, in large part because, as in other settings, "politicians want flexibility."[96]

Chile: Complaints and Acceptance

Chile's new recruiting system for high-level public officials was carefully designed with its political acceptability in mind. As indicated in the previous chapter, the operation of the new system was to be overseen by a political commission, with commissioners appointed by the president in accordance with a traditional, if informal, party quota system. It would mandate a process for assessing the competence of candidates for high-level office that left considerable room for discretion by hiring officials. The new commission was set within the ministry of finance to avoid potential conflict between appointments and budgetary concerns. Moreover, the system was to focus on a small and discrete set of officials in central ministries initially and be implemented gradually as positions became vacant.

These characteristics of the reform helped ensure it a more promising early life than the reforms in Argentina and Mexico. Overall, signs for the future of the new system were positive at the end of the 2000s. From an initial 16 positions filled through it in 2004, the number had grown annually to 704 positions by 2010.[97] Some 100 services (of a total of 141) were headed by those selected through it.[98] One analyst described the Sistema de Alta Dirección Pública as "one of the most institutionally vigorous and consolidated in the region."[99]

Yet, like the Mexican reform, Chile's also experienced start-up problems. At the outset, for example, among the least enthusiastic about the reform was the Lagos government, which initially tried to resist the approval of the law; when that did not seem to be a winnable strategy, it sought to include many transitional elements in the system to allow for the continuation of political appointments and to exclude services from the reach of the new system.[100] Once the law was passed, the government delayed for a year in appointing commissioners to the new *consejo* that would implement the plan. Indeed, after six years as part of this board, one commissioner reflected on early implementation difficulties. "At the beginning," he wrote, "I received more than a few calls from high-level leaders recommending some person for a position. They were annoyed when I refused to listen to their petitions. One minister even refused to open competitive processes for recruitment."[101]

Although the design of the process allowed for "mutual gains for the parties—keeping confidence positions but being assured of competence," it was not a first choice for many politicians.[102] As in other countries, "The government people would rather select their own people and the opposition would like to see a good program fail."[103] Politicians at times rejected all the candidates put forward for open positions and resorted to selecting temporary employees to replace the confidence workers they believed they had lost.[104] Moreover, as most of the activities that were related to job descriptions, candidate profiles, and hiring decisions were carried out at the ministry level, the commission in charge of the recruitment process had limited capacity to ensure that neutral standards were being followed.[105]

Ministers and vice-ministers, along with service directors who sought new people, were vocal in complaining that it often took as much as six months to fill a position. Along with academic assessors of the new system, they also found fault with a market model for filling public positions that was unable to pay market-rate salaries. Thus, explained one observer, "There is a competitive process for a position and, if the salary is good, you'll get the best people applying. But what happens if the salary is not competitive? You can end up with no applicants or with applicants who are not the best."[106] This fueled some concern that the recruitment process was discouraging well-qualified people from applying for positions.

Then, when an opposition coalition assumed power in 2010, attacks on the validity of the system escalated, given that the new system was "countercultural" to Chilean political tradition.[107] The new administration worked to reclaim positions that were filled through the new high-level appointment system so that they could be assigned to political appointees. Moreover, reformers were alarmed at the possibility that the *consejo* overseeing the ADP would lose its autonomy from the government in power and become more politicized.[108] In terms of its institutionalization, the ADP was still fragile, and after significant public debate over the practice and limitations on politicians bringing in their people, the 2000s closed with a series of proposals and studies for altering the system of appointments.[109] The ADP's future was brighter than the outlook for the new systems in Argentina and Mexico, however, because it required politicians to give up much less discretion over recruitment than was the case in the other countries. Moreover, its six years of operation had given it the legitimacy of a formal institution of government, an important characteristic in Chile's politics.

Methods of Attack: A Catalogue

Opposition to efforts to consolidate career civil service systems took a variety of forms in Brazil, Argentina, Mexico, and Chile. Indeed, opponents of these systems had a quiver full of mechanisms that could be used to undermine the legislation or decree of new systems. Combined with evidence from the countries considered in Part One, these cases make clear that the activities of anti-reformers, wherever they live, have much in common. In fact, as suggested below, their strategies to limit or end a civil service innovation followed a clear template of options for resistance.

A common feature of these strategies is that they could be applied during the implementation of new civil service systems. They could be used in various combinations and at times were interdependent, as, for example, when efforts to weaken the implementing agency through budgetary constraints, questioning its reputation, or delay in providing it with leadership or regulatory powers were followed by efforts of other organizations to reclaim authority over hiring decisions or by politicians to alter the levels of officialdom subject to the new system. In addition, many of these strategies could be deployed repeatedly or over long periods of time to undermine civil service regimes.

Opt Out of the System

The first strategy that proved useful to many opposed to change was that of opting out of the new system. In most cases, resisting incorporation into a new civil service system was a feature of policy planning and negotiation that truncated reform prior to its approval. Characteristically, government organizations and agencies that boasted their own career system argued against their incorporation into a new law, as happened in Britain, the United States, Spain, Brazil, Argentina, Mexico, and Chile. In each country, organizations claimed that their own system was incompatible with the proposed system or that the kinds of expertise and skills needed in the operation of the organization were so specialized that recruitment of appropriate people would be hindered by the regulations of the new system. They also argued that the kinds of people needed for the organization or agency to do its work required salary schedules that were above what would be allowed under the new system.

Opting out was also a strategy that could be useful to opponents of reform during implementation. Frequently, the creation of a new agency in the post-reform context provided an opportunity for avoiding incorporation into an already established system. This was clearly the case in

Argentina when many agencies created after SINAPA was established were able to evade incorporation in it.

Most typically, ministries of foreign affairs, tax agencies, central banks, security organizations, state-owned enterprises, and more technically-oriented departments made principled stands against inclusion in a new system. In addition, frankly political organizations, such as presidential offices or cabinet secretariats—units acknowledged to work on executive agendas and to undertake sensitive political negotiations—were also often excluded from the new systems. At times, ministries of the interior argued that their responsibilities were "too political" for their officials to be incorporated into a civil service.

Opting out was a useful strategy for some organizations. In part, the arguments were credible—there may, in fact, be very good reasons for excluding some organizations, departments, or units from a civil service system. In part, however, reformers often recognized that their chances for introducing new legislation would be enhanced if they agreed to such exclusions, whether the official rationale for doing so was strong or not. In particular, they might calculate that the opposition of often well-connected agencies such as the foreign service or security organizations could scuttle their plans. To ease their way forward, they would be only too ready to negotiate the exclusion of some parts of government. Once this had occurred during the planning process, it was no doubt easier for other organizations to make similar arguments during implementation.

Disestablish the Organization

A much more aggressive strategy, and one that was clearly part of the contention over implementation, was a direct attack on the agency responsible for overseeing a new civil service system. Chapter 3, for example, indicated repeated efforts in the United States to do away with the Civil Service Commission after it had been established, and this chapter provided evidence of a similar effort in Brazil after the fall of Vargas's *Estado Novo*. Those who questioned the utility of the new professional career service in Mexico, including the president, sought to end the life of the ministry of public service in the late 2000s.

Arguments against the implementing agency were likely to be couched in protests against centralization of recruitment and career advancement decisions, the lack of flexibility appropriate for many positions, the aloofness of commissioners and other officials to the real needs of particular jobs, the potential capture of the commissioners by the president, and the inability of such an agency to properly understand the many and complex requirements for filling offices in modern government. Again, these arguments could be defended as basic principles for good public management, but their proponents regularly included political parties and legislators who were affected if a new system were to take hold. Presidents could certainly initiate or support new legislation to this effect, and could also use their powers to restructure the executive branch, at times in concert with legislative action. Interestingly, this strategy could be coupled with rhetoric in which the principles of a neutral and career-oriented civil service are extolled.

In none of the clear cases of this strategy—the United States, Brazil, Mexico, and Chile—was this approach successful in eliminating the responsible agency. However, in these cases, initiatives to disestablish the organization responsible for managing the new civil service system were evident signals that the very existence of these agencies was at stake and that contention over reform was being carried to new arenas during implementation. Whether or not the strategy was successful, it weakened the credibility and political stature of the implementing agency.

Starve the Beast

A related but less public strategy was that of starving the agency responsible for implementing the new system by restricting its budget and thus undermining its capacity to carry out its work. As we saw in the case of the United States, the early funding of the Civil Service Commission was so limited that it was unable to pursue much of its agenda. In Britain, budget strictures were regularly used by the Treasury to limit the power and conduct of the civil service. Similarly, in the post-Vargas era in Brazil, DASP was first relieved of 10 percent of its budget and then lost successively greater amounts until its incapacity to operate caused some to declare that the agency was effectively dead. In Argentina, hiring freezes were part of budget constraints that limited the scope of SINAPA.

Starvation can be put into effect with little public discussion of the importance or advisability of a career civil service. It is thus a strategy that can be undertaken without joining a debate about the civil service or the specter of patronage. Instead, a coalition of legislators opposed to the reduction in political appointments or a ministry of finance wishing to gain or reclaim control over personnel costs can effectively undermine an agency though close oversight of the budget without much public or political notice. And, in contrast to the failure of disestablishment, starvation as a strategy can be quite effective in truncating a reform and moving the responsible agency to the periphery of political power and effectiveness. This was certainly the experience of DASP in Brazil and SINAPA in Argentina. It also was quite effective for a considerable period in the United States when the Civil Service Commission was kept chronically short of resources.

Delay the Process

If those opposed to reform were presidents or powerful executives, or even those heading the agency responsible for the implementation of the reform, they had considerable capacity to cancel or delay opportunities for examinations or other competitive processes of recruitment. In the case of the United States, this was a strategy used by presidents, including those rhetorically committed to a civil service system, in the first two decades after the Pendleton Act. In France, control over the examination process provided significant opportunities to keep the patronage system alive. In Brazil and Argentina, budget constraints were used by presidents and others to interrupt the processes that would be essential to bringing public officials under the umbrella of the new service.

Implementation could also be delayed by the failure of executives to nominate or appoint commissioners or others to take charge of a new system. Similarly, issuing regulations to put the system in operation could be delayed indefinitely, as was the case in seven of the eighteen Latin American reforms surveyed in Table 4.2, or overlooked for long periods, as was the case in two additional reforms in the same table. Even in Chile, where political compromise was strong in the approval of the new ADP, a reluctant president delayed the appointment of commissioners.

Again, like the starvation strategy, a direct attack on the principles of a neutral career civil service was not necessary to pursue this approach.

It could be done quietly, even in concert with rhetorical commitment to the new system, simply by invoking budget constraints or a freeze on regular hiring activities of government. Thus, delaying was often a partner strategy of starvation, when in fact it might become impossible to carry out regular recruitment processes.

Question the Credibility of the New System

Attacking the credibility of a new system was a further strategy of resistance that opponents of reform found useful. Quite regularly, in fact, the legitimacy of a career service could be undermined through implications that the agency responsible for its implementation was incompetent or politicized. Certainly the case of Brazil demonstrated efforts by enemies of DASP to link it clearly to the authoritarian and centralized practices of the Vargas administration; it was considered to be a tool of his personal leadership. In Argentina, opponents claimed that the processes for hiring through SINAPA were often "cooked" to the advantage of particular candidates, a charge that was echoed more strongly in Mexico. In addition, efforts to shake the credibility of a new system could take the form of questioning its utility. In Mexico and Chile, for example, opponents questioned whether the new system was in fact producing better public servants than the traditional system.

As we saw in the case of Mexico and Chile, reformers could contribute to the ability of opponents to make such charges when their initial implementation efforts were confusing or very time-consuming. Even supporters of reform could question the legitimacy of the new system when it could take several months to fill a position. In the case of Mexico, the initial problems of the SPC were great enough that the ministry of public service chose to invest in a thorough review of its activities.

Attempting to undermine a civil service reform by attacking its credibility required anti-reformers to take a public stance against an agency or a process. However, they could do so without at the same time having to go public with an attack on the concept of a civil service. What they called into question was not the idea of a neutral and stable career system, but how the new system was working. Indeed, as the case of Mexico indicates, reformers and those opposed to change could even find common ground in calling for revisions in the operation of a new system.

Reclaim Authority over Recruitment

In all civil service systems, there is a clear tension between system-wide rules and procedures and individual agencies of government that want control over recruitment. In the context of a new system that is intended to impose common criteria and processes across a broad swath of government, ministries that strongly prefer to control hiring into their own organizations lose their capacity to do so. In addition, and across the experience of many countries, as indicated in previous chapters, ministries of finance tended to be in the opposition to new recruitment systems that were not primarily controlled by them. While autonomy was important to all ministries and agencies, finance ministries were particularly concerned about new systems that threatened their control over the public payroll. Moreover, many ministries of finance considered that it was their appropriate role, as government watchdogs, to claim a special concern for who was hired into public service.

Once a career civil service system was in place, therefore, ministries sought to reclaim their authority over hiring decisions. Reclaiming was generally done in combination with other kinds of attacks on the organization in charge of managing the new system—a civil service commission or a ministry of public service. In cases in which these organizations were successfully weakened through direct political attacks or through quieter means of starvation or delay, ministries had opportunities to reassert their control over recruitment. At times, this could mean informal redesign of the system, but it was also a strategy that could be carried out through a process of system restructuring after a civil service had been operative for some time. The ongoing tension over control, and the strategy of ministries to reclaim turf, tended to be ubiquitous in the introduction of civil service systems and was apparent in the cases of Germany, Japan, France, Britain, Spain, the United States, Brazil, and Mexico.

Recapture Positions for Patronage

The design of career civil service systems depended significantly on decisions about where to draw the line between politics and administration, and between decision making and operations. In the design process, reformers made calculated decisions about which upper levels of government officialdom should be included or excluded from coverage. Often, part of the process of promoting reform was negotiation over where this line should be drawn, and was undertaken before change was approved, as was also the case of organizations that sought to opt out of the new system. The development of plans for civil service reform in all of the cases considered in this book demonstrates that decisions about what positions were to be included in the new system were contestable and important to reformers and opponents alike.

But recapture could also be a strategy for altering a career civil service during its implementation. Anti-reformers, often political parties in the legislature, but most frequently executives such as presidents, ministers, and agency heads, generally argued that the designers were mistaken in categorizing the kinds of activities that higher-level officials were engaged in. Frequently, for example, third- and fourth-level officials were considered decision makers by those who would redefine the system, and as administrators or operative officials by the reformers. In addition, the categorizations of general directors and service heads were often in dispute.

In the United States and Brazil, conflicts over where the line was to be drawn were played out in legislative battles long after a civil service system was put in place. In the United States, the Reagan administration sought to redraw the line a full century after the Pendleton Act. In Mexico, major initiatives to redraw the line emerged in the post-reform era, encouraging ongoing discussion of what positions were primarily for decision making and which were primarily for operational activities.

Engineer the Job to the Candidate

Civil service legislation generally incorporated processes for developing job descriptions and examinations to ensure that properly qualified individuals were selected for appointment. In some cases, those who wished to maintain their control over recruitment decisions had opportunities to fashion job descriptions and examinations to fit the profiles of particular candidates for office. This strategy was time-consuming and usually applied in individual cases of hiring. Yet it could have system-wide impacts, such as when job descriptions regularly embodied expertise or experience that was primarily available only to those who have held the job in the past, or when examinations set very low bars for qualification.

In the early reform history of the United States, for example, examinations designed at the agency level often required little more than basic literacy, providing significant opportunities for selecting those with other qualifications, such as party affiliation or personal loyalty, from among many who were considered qualified for the job. Charges about the neutrality of job descriptions and examinations were in clear evidence in Mexico and Chile. Similarly, job descriptions often required special expertise or skills that only those who had long held the job could demonstrate. Restricting the recruitment pool through particular requirements that were tested in examinations was also apparent in France, Britain, Japan, and elsewhere, where knowledge of law or the classics played an important gatekeeping role for those who sought positions in the higher civil service.

In particular, where civil service recruitment had been evaded through the use of temporary appointments or other such measures, engineering the job to the candidate could be used to bring those with nonstandard or short-term positions into the system without directly attacking it formally. All requisites were complied with—they were simply altered to fit particular goals of the hiring official or ministry by bringing their people under the civil service umbrella.

Create New Categories

Histories of civil service systems in many different countries were rife with evidence of ingenuity in creating new categories for hiring outside of this system. Characteristically, those wishing to use patronage to hire "their people"—usually ministers, presidents, and other high-level officials—brought in outsiders as special advisers or as temporary or provisional hires. Special advisers and those on specific contracts could be hired and remunerated in a wide variety of ways, often at the discretion of the hiring agent or agency.

So pervasive was this strategy that a public service could end up being significantly staffed with special or temporary employees, as was the case of Colombia cited earlier, where after a five-year moratorium on civil service hiring, provisional appointments constituted 38 percent of the public service. The case of Brazil indicated a long history of this kind of activity. In Argentina, the extent of temporary, contract, and other special categories of hiring was so extensive that the government was charged with having a parallel bureaucracy. In Mexico, hiring of temporary personnel and special advisers far outpaced the rate of incorporation into the SPC. Generally, temporary hires could be easily renewed in their positions and were sometimes blanketed into the civil service system and given tenure when administrations changed.

This strategy was fully legal and did not require coordinated action among opponents of reform. It was also an extremely flexible mechanism to undermine a new civil service system because positions could be created or made to disappear depending on circumstances. It was a strategy that was extremely useful on an individual level for those who were hired and those doing the hiring. At times, however, these officials faced difficulties with finance ministries that attempted to control the extent to which temporary or special appointments could be made by controlling personnel budgets.

Resisting and Reshaping Reform

The catalogue of mechanisms that were employed to constrain civil service reform during its implementation is extensive, and it is clear that strategies of obstruction could be undertaken in a variety of combinations and sequences. In practice, these mechanisms required different means to put in practice, several were sensitive to issues of timing, and they were often carried out by distinct actors. In addition, some opposition strategies were relatively apparent in that they involved the articulation of a series of arguments about why the career system was inappropriate or wanting in some regard. Publicly expressed attacks generally required some coordinated action among opponents—a legislative coalition to disestablish or starve a civil service commission or ministry, for example. But there was also a variety of means to work quietly to undermine the advances of a civil service system—engineering job descriptions and creating new categories of employment as means to work around the new system, for example. The ubiquity of these strategies is apparent in Table 7.1. The table adds descriptions of the forms various strategies took, their timing, and the actors most likely to employ them.

Table 7.1. Mechanisms for resisting implementation of civil service systems

Mechanism of resistance	Definition	How put in practice	When likely to be attempted	Who carries out	Examples of use
Opt out of the system	Resisting incorporation into a new civil service regime at agency or service level	Often a result of bargaining over the scope of reform in design phase; can be used in implementation when new agencies are created	Prior to approval; sporadically when new agencies created after reform	Reformers and ministry and agency heads	Britain, U.S., Spain, Brazil, Argentina, Mexico, Chile
Disestablish the organization	Legislating out of existence an agency or commission charged with managing a civil service system	Through the design of new legislation	In the aftermath of regime or administration change	Usually parties and legislators in legislatures; can be in coalition with presidents or through executive reorganizations	U.S., Brazil, Mexico, Chile, possibly Argentina
Starve the beast	Reducing the budget of the implementing agency to impede its function; canceling	Control over funds needed to support a CS reform agency and its activities	In the aftermath of regime or administration change, in response to executive/	Legislators and parties in legislature, ministry of finance, presidents	Britain, U.S., Brazil, Argentina, Mexico

	opportunities for examinations or public competitions		ministry of finance opposition		
Delay the process	Failing to appoint commissioners/ministers in timely fashion; failing to develop operational regulations to put legislation in action	Failure to act, usually by president; can also involve failure to provide legislative approval	In initial months/years of a new CS system; when terms expire; in aftermath of regime change	Usually presidents, but also legislators	U.S., France, Brazil, Mexico, Argentina, Chile
Question the system's credibility	Calling attention to the failures of the implementing agency or the process undertaken in recruitment; questioning the quality of the results	Reviews; complaints to legislators, political leaders; media attacks	In initial months of a new CS system, particularly as it experiences start-up problems; in the aftermath of administration change	Often high-level administrators and political appointees, ministers, vice-ministers, and others constrained by a new system; academics and reformers join in critical assessments	U.S., Britain, France, Spain, Argentina, Mexico, Chile

Table 7.1. (continued)

Mechanism of resistance	Definition	How put in practice	When likely to be attempted	Who carries out	Examples of use
Reclaim authority over recruitment	Decentralizing personnel decisions to ministry or agency level to thwart system-wide rules	Through new legislation or restructured operational procedures	Periodically in response to pressure from ministries, especially ministry of finance	Ministry of finance, ministries and agencies in general	Germany, Japan, France, Britain, U.S., Brazil, Mexico
Recapture positions	Legislating reduced coverage of the civil service system	Through new legislation or formal executive action	Periodically in response to dissatisfaction with existing system	Parties and legislators, often in coalition with ministries	U.S., Brazil, Mexico, Chile
Engineer the job to the candidate	Using loopholes in law or procedures to craft job descriptions or examinations to fit the candidate	Creation of job descriptions and input into examination contents	Periodically to fit convenience of those seeking more autonomy in recruitment	Hiring officials, ministries, agencies, political executives	U.S., Britain, France, Japan, Spain, Brazil, Argentina, Mexico, Chile
Create new categories	Inventing means to hire public officials outside the regulations of a civil service system	Creation of new categories, new contract systems, agencies	Periodically to fit convenience of those seeking more autonomy in recruitment	Hiring officials, ministries, agencies, political executives	Britain, U.S., Spain, Brazil, Argentina, Mexico, Chile

Indeed, the path toward civil service reform was a rugged one as it wound through the politics of construction and then the perils of implementation. In Latin America, patronage was tenacious, and, as a consequence, many Latin American public services continued to be heavily politicized long after initiatives to make them less so were undertaken. As indicated throughout this book, the resilience of this form of recruitment owed much to the utility of patronage in achieving a wide variety of purposes and to the common interest of those who controlled such systems in maintaining their discretion in filling positions in the public service. It also owed a considerable debt to the strategies that opponents of reform employed to undermine, alter, or truncate change initiative.

The Politics of Institutional Creation and Re-creation

Positions in the public service provide valuable benefits to those who control them. Skillfully employed, the distribution of jobs through patronage can help create empires, regimes, systems of class dominance, political parties, policy coalitions, high-performing organizations, personal fiefdoms, dynasties, and mafias. Loyalty and commonality of purpose, centrally important to accumulating and deploying power, travel comfortably with the ability to accumulate and deploy positions in government. Little wonder, then, that across history and countries, politicians have sought to use institutions of patronage to manage political power and achieve a diversity of goals. Patronage persists, not because of historical anomalies or perversity, but because it continues to be a valuable instrument of power.

Patronage is also an eminently flexible way to manage government; its ends can be adjusted as time, purpose, and circumstance suggest. Clearly, the case histories in this book attest to its strategic importance for leaders seeking diverse objectives. They also indicate that patronage can be mismanaged as well as managed and that it is regularly challenged by alternative claims for employment in the public sector and by a variety of factors that limit its effectiveness. Perhaps most important, as a mechanism that is deployed through political and organizational hierarchies, it is dependent on the skills and purposes of those who manage it. As an institution, then, patronage is inherently capricious.

Despite this fundamental flaw, how and why a patronage system falls victim to efforts to replace it with a career civil service is not obvious. Most politicians and many managers who would have to adopt new approaches to recruitment and career development if a civil service were

241

put in place can be expected to question if it will be as useful to them in achieving their goals. Indeed, throughout history, they have found ways to oppose the introduction of new systems of employment in public office. *Jobs for the Boys* provides clear evidence of ongoing political, personal, and even policy resistance to the demise of patronage systems.

Yet opponents of civil service reform in many countries ultimately lost the battle to preserve broad discretion in assigning positions in the public sector. Those who struggled to maintain this discretion and flexibility were almost always bested by those who sought neutrality and stability. Overall, the cases indicate that this end was achieved through the strategic action of reformers, including the ability to survive numerous challenges over long periods of time in order to consolidate institutional change. Those who advocated for predictability and an end to politicized public services generated reformist projects and then took advantage of unusual circumstances—a crisis, a change in leadership, an electoral draw, a scandal—to push their plans forward through legislation or decree. These moments were often when practitioners of patronage were weakened, distracted, divided, or publicly unable to resist the incursion of a new system. Nevertheless, the greatest challenges to civil service reforms often came after they had been adopted and introduced. Indeed, new rules of the game were sometimes subjected to long struggles for survival, and a broad variety of strategies assisted their opponents in undermining or curtailing their effective consolidation. In brief, the persistence of patronage is explained by its utility and flexibility; its demise, on the other hand, must be politically constructed.

Three of the histories recounted in this book were still in the process of construction, and numerous others were facing challenges of reconstruction as it went to press. In the reform initiatives introduced in the late twentieth and early twenty-first centuries in Argentina, Mexico, and Chile, opponents of reform initiatives continued to work to undo or alter them in the interest of discretion and flexibility. It is reasonable to anticipate that the struggle for bureaucratic stability, predictability, and neutrality will continue in these countries, whether or not the initiatives considered here are consolidated or will become artifacts of failure. In countries that had successfully consolidated civil service regimes in prior decades or centuries, new theories about efficiency, effectiveness, and responsiveness confronted established systems, and reformers were eager to introduce new changes.

This array of experiences indicates a set of similar conflicts and trajectories across diverse cases in time and geography. Of course, each case is
a unique story, with its own cast of characters, plot, and dénouement.
Yet, across them, generalizations emerge with regard to how change happens and how it is forestalled. In this chapter, I consider the interplay of
historical contexts and the impact of agency in constructing, deconstruct-
ing, and reconstructing the public service.

First, I return to the discussion of history and its legacies to draw
some conclusions about the factors that constrained choices for new institutional designs. Indeed, a growing literature considering European
and U.S. experience has tackled the important question of how legacies
of the past shape the emergence of new rules of the game for managing
economic, social, and political systems and how those rules in turn
shape subsequent change.[1]

In contrast, in discussions about the importance of a reformed public
service in today's developing countries, these issues have been much less
fully addressed. Instead, in such countries, the starting point for designing change has generally been to deplore the state of the public services
and the evident dysfunctions of public organizations. In this perspective,
the past—held responsible for the sorry state of governance—must be
overcome, even obliterated, if economic, social, or political progress is to
be achieved. In contrast to the evidence of the ongoing importance of
embedded practices, best practices and idealized models of "what ought
to be," not historical legacies, are expected to shape new institutions.
Indeed, the metaphor of "getting to Denmark," that is, acquiring a wide
range of effective institutions, has been used to describe development
plans that ignore the process by which institutions—in Denmark and
elsewhere—evolved and changed through unique processes of conflict
and consolidation.[2] One purpose of this book is to bring together experiences that are not often compared—those in which history is taken seriously as a factor that explains not only continuity but also change, and
those in which many have assumed that history must be shed like the
skin of a snake.[3]

Second, I explore the process of policy and institutional reform to help
explain the timing and dynamics of efforts to bring about change. A bur-
geoning literature on reformist initiatives helps us to understand the
extent to which there may be room for contingency, innovation, and
even institutional engineering in developing new rules of the game,

even in the context of institutional "stickiness."[4] Drawing on the stories of reform considered in this book, I assess how institutions are shaped and reshaped through the actions of agents of change, the projects they devise, the moments that allow them to move forward, and the conflicts and mechanisms that undermine the consolidation of their efforts. The cases suggest that the plans, political skills, and alliances of reform entrepreneurs can make a difference, even in contexts in which the past seems narrowly to constrain the present and future. This chapter summarizes a series of generalizations about agents, projects, and moments that provide insight into room for maneuver in the introduction of institutional change.

Finally, the chapter returns to the question of expectations about the consequences of reform. Lauding career civil service systems for their stability, predictability, and political neutrality, reformers anticipate that new rules will also result in better performance in the public sector. The cases in this book, however, suggest a tradeoff between stability and neutrality in the management of public affairs and the flexibility to encourage initiative and commitment in finding solutions to public problems. Indeed, as we have seen, in developed countries, disillusion with civil service systems has promoted alternative visions of what an effective, efficient, and responsive public sector looks like. In developing countries, on the other hand, reformist initiatives continue to anticipate a clear link between civil service reform and improved performance. The histories of patronage and civil service reform recounted here suggest the need to continue to search for an elusive grail of good governance.

Legacies of the Past in Institutional Change

All reforms take place in historical contexts that shape and constrain possibilities for change, as the increasingly influential literature on historical institutionalism argues. This is certainly true for cases explored in this book. Patronage systems—their purpose, coherence, and structure— shaped what replaced them and significantly influenced the trajectory of how they were replaced. These systems, and the potential to alter them, were in turn products of how they reflected broader institutional and historical contexts and were shaped by them. In particular, the degree to which state leaders were able to dominate decision making, the effects of class and education systems, and the extent to which patronage systems had been captured by political parties emerged as important factors explaining differences and similarities among cases.

Decision-Making Dynamics

Decision-making structures, often long and deeply embedded in a range of political institutions, helped structure the dynamics of change in the country cases. In this regard, the important factor was the extent to which the political systems concentrated decision-making power in state institutions and in state leaders. For example, the introduction of civil service systems in Prussia and Japan was clearly anchored in authoritarian institutions of power. In both, state leaders had used patronage purposively to build strong and centralized states. This then provided them with significant capacity to introduce reform from the top down and to remain in control of the new systems until they became features of normal administration that in turn added to the strength of the state. In introducing change, they had to contend with the beneficiaries of past patronage—powerful elites who claimed privileged access to public positions—but reformers used the introduction of a civil service to co-opt such claims and to replace them with standards of their own. While these standards continued to privilege many of the same elites, authoritarian leaders claimed the right to set them and thus to ensure the subordination of powerful elites to the state.

In the very distinct cases of Mexico and Chile, embedded and centralized decision-making structures also facilitated the introduction of change. In both countries, strong party structures permitted top-level legislators to negotiate policy with leaders in the executive and to reach agreement that would be binding on legislative parties. In the case of Mexico in particular, a previous set of rules had privileged a hegemonic political party and provided the underpinning for a relatively strong state and ensured an unusual degree of political stability across many decades. Chile's political stability was less prolonged, but even across regimes, the coherence of the central state was consistently sought in the institutions of well-managed patronage. In the cases of Brazil and Argentina, in contrast, concentrated power was simply a temporary hiatus in a long history of much greater contention among different levels of government and different institutions of the state. In these cases, the ability to spearhead reform was also temporary, and the potential to ensure the continuity of new institutions was highly constrained when the norm of dispersed power was reestablished.

Power was also dispersed in Britain and the United States, although state structures were more enduring than in the cases of Brazil and Argentina. Although the use of patronage had been widespread in both these early adopters of civil service systems, claims for managing it were dispersed among local, regional, and national levels, between executives and legislatures, and within the bureaucracy. The promotion of reform, therefore, required a coalition drawn from the ranks of executive leadership, the executive bureaucracy, and lawmaking institutions, an uncertain process that took considerable time and effort, even when public pressure was strongly in favor of change. The dispersion of power also resulted in ongoing skirmishes over the scope and control of the civil service once it had been introduced. The process of change was thus protracted and contested for decades.

The transition from patronage to a civil service system in France reflected the fragmentation of power within a centralized state. Indeed, a centralized state was in part a product of the purposeful distribution of patronage; with time, however, control over it became dispersed among executive agencies, captured by elite education systems, and shared between statist and partisan purposes. As a consequence, the dynamics of change were heavily influenced by ministries and their links to educational institutions, a situation that allowed for extensive cohabitation between discretionary and civil service appointments. This in turn helps explain the gradual emergence of a civil service system that did not directly confront the long-existing patronage system.

Spain was a case of even greater fragmentation. Its patronage system had long been undermined by mismanagement and competing claimants at imperial, national, regional, and local levels. As the state lost coherence, the dispersion of power and competition among *caciques, caudillos,* and *corps* severely weakened the capacity of state leaders to manage patronage or to take effective action to reform the system. Thus, the potential usefulness of the patronage system was undermined by the weakness of the state, and this weakness in turn contributed to the inability to replace the patronage system with an effective civil service system.

The cases, therefore, indicate the important role of existing institutions for making decisions in explaining the degree of difficulty of introducing a civil service system as well as the extent to which its institutionalization was protracted and contested. In these cases, and assuming the longevity of an existing political regime, more centralized systems led to greater capacity to introduce change; moreover, more authoritarian systems had the capacity to maintain their commitment to new institutions in ways that moderated conflict over them. In other cases, the ways in which power over decisions was dispersed indicated not only more difficult transitions, but also the range of actors who were involved in promoting and opposing change.

Imprints of Class and Education

Newly introduced civil services were also strongly stamped by existing structures of class and education in each country. Thus, where traditional patronage-based public services had been dominated by class elites with privileged access to superior education, new recruitment systems tended to reify those class systems. This was clearly the case in Prussia, Britain, Japan, and France, where the distribution of patronage strongly reflected class status; new civil service systems were constructed around educational norms and standards that continued to observe the consequences of a class system. In these cases, change in the public sector tended to focus on higher-level appointments and to preserve them for those who had the "right" preparation and education. Lower-level positions in the new system were considered appropriate for those whose class status naturally steered them toward other kinds of education.

In these cases, the task of reformers was to find ways to co-opt or accommodate traditional elites who claimed rights to public appointments so that they could continue to fit newly defined criteria. At the same time, as state services expanded, there was greater room to accommodate middle-class aspirants to public positions, either at lower levels of government or through greater access to elite education systems. In this way, the "mandarin" systems were perpetuated and civil services continued to reflect educational criteria emphasized at their founding—a strong preference for legal or technical training in some cases, for example, and the equally strong priority given to generalists in the case of Britain.

In these countries, then, new services stabilized and institutionalized much that was already in practice in terms of who was selected to take jobs in the public sector. The process of selection changed, but the profiles of those occupying positions changed much less with the introduction of reform. In these cases also, opposition to change tended to focus on issues such as the extent to which the system would continue to be centralized or decentralized and, while acknowledging the permanence of the new rules, who would be in the driver's seat in terms of recruitment and career decision making.

Alternatively, where patronage systems had been less sensitive to class and where educational systems were less segmented and more porous—in the United States, Brazil, Argentina, Mexico, and Chile—newly introduced civil services were crafted with lower barriers to entry and provided jobs on a much less stringent basis. In these cases, a principal task for reformers was first to ensure the survival of the new institutions and then to negotiate, often over long periods of time, the incorporation of jobs for the boys into the new systems. The capacity of opponents of change to continue to undermine the new civil service institutions was enhanced in these cases, and conflict tended to be more protracted and somewhat more public. Yet, in some cases, conflict was moderated by the expansion of state services that allowed for the accommodation of the reform initiative and the politicians and managers who opposed them. These more "plebian" systems stand in considerable contrast to characteristics of the European and Japanese institutions.

Political Parties and their Claims

Related to barriers to entry and the ease or difficulty of transition, the presence of relatively organized and broad-based political parties affected how change occurred in the cases reviewed here. Thus, where political parties had emerged, had gained some coherence, and had captured some control over patronage prior to the introduction of a civil service, the dynamics of change were different from cases in which political parties were not yet consolidated.[5]

In the United States, Brazil, Mexico, and Chile, public positions had long been allocated through systems that rewarded the winners of electoral competitions and in which government and party leaders shared in their ability to distribute public sector jobs to the party faithful. In these cases, the insulation and autonomy of the emergent civil service tended to be insecure and the hold of the embedded system more tenacious. These conditions also contributed to the long and difficult struggles before the consolidation of new institutions was assured. In the cases of Brazil and Chile, transitions were complicated by regime changes that pushed political parties to the margins for prolonged periods of time, only to witness their extensive claims for patronage when they reemerged as politically relevant.

In contrast, the early consolidation of change in Prussia and Japan was less fraught and more definitive, due in part to the absence of modern political parties. Authoritarian leaders struggled against the claims of elites, but their numbers were fewer and they were easier to co-opt into a new system than the parties that depended on patronage to win elections. In the absence of parties, decision makers were freer to establish barriers to entry based on background and education and were far from having to tussle publicly over the spoils of office. In these cases, the line between winners and losers in introducing a new system was more opaque.

France, Britain, and Spain occupy a middle ground in terms of the development of political parties, the extent to which they had been consolidated around the distribution of patronage, and the extent of conflict in the transition from one system to another. In France and Britain, parties emerged during the course of the nineteenth century, but their claims to patronage were tempered by earlier systems that privileged class elites. As a consequence, their capacity to contest the introduction of new systems was moderated and new systems for public service appointments tended to be biased toward elites with requisite educational preparation. Barriers to entry could thus be more segmented than in the cases in which mass-based political parties had fully captured patronage. At the same time, the claims of party could be accommodated, at least in France and Spain, by the continuation of a patronage system based on party identity. In the case of Spain, political instability and a party-based rotation system led elites within the public service to insulate themselves through the development of *corps* that were guildlike in the protection they provided their members.

While the birth of civil service systems in countries with preexisting party systems was protracted and difficult, subsequent conflicts did not invoke major questions about the loyalty of the new services. In part, this can be credited to a process of reform that included some form of negotiation and accommodation with relatively broad political groups as new institutions were being designed, approved, and introduced. For Prussia and Japan, on the other hand, the absence of elections and party jockeying for power and control over appointments to public positions meant that insulating the public service from political influence was initially less challenging. Over time, however, each of these systems had to face claims by parties for influence over appointments to office, and in each case the very insulation of the services brought them under suspicion by regime leaders.

Agents, Projects, Moments, and Ongoing Struggles

However reflective of the past, the introduction of new rules of the game does not just happen. In the cases explored here, well-institutionalized systems of patronage were challenged by strategic actors who devised and negotiated projects of reform and found political moments when it was possible to move their initiatives forward, at times after a series of prior failures. Political challenges to these projects continued after reform had been legitimized in law, decree, or practice and introduced new actors who became significant players in subsequent reform initiatives. In accounting for institutional reform, then, actors and strategic choices have a role in shaping outcomes, just as institutional legacies do.

Agents

In eight of the ten cases, clearly identifiable historical actors shaped the content of reform and made strategic decisions about how to advance their causes. In these cases, the trajectories of institutional transition cannot be easily explained without reference to these reform entrepreneurs.[6] For example, the specific actions of authoritarian leaders were important in three of the cases. In Prussia, monarchs were central in the self-conscious use of patronage to bring zealous reformers into government to institutionalize many rules about the professional structure of the public service. Thus empowered, high-level officials were able to make significant changes in the state bureaucracy and set a platform of expectations for later reformers to continue their project. In Japan, regime leaders made important forays into professionalizing the public service through the skillful use of patronage appointments and then supported the initiatives of the drafters of a new constitution to establish a career civil service in a reform characterized by the absence of public discussion. In Brazil, an initiative was developed through studies and plans produced by a small group of zealous reformers who had long experience in government but who encountered considerable frustration in trying to make change happen. The eventual adoption of a new system occurred when an authoritarian leader set a high priority on their ideas and ensured that they would be reflected in a new constitution.

In more open political systems, reform entrepreneurs also significantly shaped the outcome of conflicts over change. Thus, given the dispersion of power characteristic of political structures in Britain and the United States, reform leaders had to be active in assembling cross-institutional coalitions for change. In the first case, British reformers in government developed a plan and persisted over several decades in pressing their ideas on key decision makers and authorizing institutions. While they were aided by public opinion that was increasingly hostile to incompetence and corruption in government, the coalition they needed for change was almost exclusively found within government. In the United States, a vibrant and politically embedded spoils system was eventually undermined by the activities of politicians in Congress and the executive working in concert with a broad coalition of middle-class professionals. Highly mobilized interest groups and significant media attention were prominent in this case, and the reform adopted combined their pressure with the zealotry of a few officials who made a concerted effort to negotiate agreement within congressional parties.

In other cases also, reform champions undertook responsibility for generating coalitions to promote change. In Mexico, the plan for a career civil service was the combined result of several members of the congress, a group of academic researchers, and staff in a presidential office for the improvement of government. Its path toward legislative acceptance was negotiated in advance at high levels of government, and party leadership and the agency of specific individuals were important in ensuring success in the congress. In Chile, the initiative for reform was devised in a private think tank, and the final product was produced through negotiations at the highest levels of government among three individuals. With agreement among them, legislative success was ensured. In Argentina, the prime mover of reform was the minister of the economy and his team, who devised the new system as part of a series of significant efforts to restructure the economy and the state. In order to secure the acceptance of the new system, they actively engaged the support of public sector unions.

In each of these cases, identifiable agents of reform were critically important in the design and introduction of a new institution; their ongoing initiatives and strategic decisions about how to advance their causes were significant in explaining what was proposed and how and when it was pushed forward. Because the promotion of institutional change occurs over time, they were able to intervene repeatedly to influence the discussion of reform and to determine who needed to be "at the table" when changes were designed, negotiated, and approved.

In two cases, reform entrepreneurs were much less in evidence, largely because of the evolutionary way in which reform occurred or was forestalled. In France, a nineteenth century rife with conflict and instability encouraged extensive decentralization of decision making to ministries, agencies, and *corps*. Over time, these bodies increased their capacity to control recruitment and careers. In this case, advancement of a highly structured civil service was primarily the result of an evolution of professionalization within individual *corps* and ministries. There were, then, reform entrepreneurs, but they were widely dispersed, and the reach of their actions was constrained by organizational autonomy. In Spain, even more bedeviled by political instability and conflict in the nineteenth and twentieth centuries, civil service reform was a periodic experience without a clear trajectory, and often without much impact. Regime leaders, at best reluctant reformers, were largely unable to advance the institutionalization of civil service and did so only as a way to appease insistent public servants or to consolidate their authority. Eventually, radical decentralization was introduced through a new constitution to circumvent the power of a public service characterized by extremely fragmented autonomy.

Projects

In a wide range of countries, initiatives to introduce and consolidate civil service systems can be described as elite projects. That is, they were led by small groups of individuals who designed the reforms, did most of the work in negotiating them, and made most of the decisions about getting reform approved. Only in the United States—and to a much smaller extent in Britain—did reformers combine their crusades with mobilized interests to pursue institutional reform in government. And only in the United States, Britain, and Chile was public opinion an important factor encouraging reform.

In several cases, reform initiatives were worked out well in advance of opportunities for introducing them, and reformers made use of a variety of experiences, ideas, and intellectual trends as they crafted their proposals. In the development of these projects, they worked to develop changes that were to some degree congruent with domestic institutional contexts, but they also consulted the experience of other countries and the ideas of experts in public management of the times.

In Britain, ideas for reform emerged in the 1840s and were fully developed in the Northcote-Trevelyan Report of 1854. An important influence behind the report was the experience of the East India Company, which had developed a civil service for the management of empire. At the same time, in proposing classes of public servants based on types of work to be accomplished and the educations necessary to carry out this work, the report and its legitimating Orders in Council carefully respected deeply embedded traditions and prejudices of class and education. In the United States, reformers explored the experience of other countries and were impressed by the Northcote-Trevelyan Report, which some used to craft an initial proposal for discussion in Congress. There were, in fact, a number of reform projects, and the Pendleton Act reflected several sources, but also bowed to local traditions of low barriers to entry and the gradualist expectations of politicians whose parties were reluctant to cede much ground to the reformers. The Japanese reform project was also informed by foreign experience, particularly that of Bismarck's Germany. The attractiveness of this model, however, can be significantly explained by a clear preference of the Meiji leadership for a system rooted in an imperial state, emphasizing efficiency and supporting a tradition of elite and specialized education.

As indicated in the case of the United States, proposals were often crafted over time and altered significantly as they were discussed and negotiated. In Brazil, for example, a project of reform was first devised by a small group appointed by political leaders, and then significantly revised by another small group. Strongly influenced by academic discussions of public administration in the United States at the time, these reform proposals differed in the extent to which the tradition of patronage would be observed in the new system. In Mexico, reformers in the congress and the president's office relied on ideas that had been emerging among academic experts and institutions for a number of years. Domestic and foreign experiences were scanned for models that could be adapted to the particular conditions of the country's political system. Similarly, in Chile, a project hatched within a private-sector think tank engaged discussions within academic circles. The experience of the Senior Executive Service in the United States, and that of countries that had adopted new public management approaches, played an important role in informing the plan. At the same time, it was adapted to the exigencies of a political system based on party representation in high-level public decision making.

In Argentina, a project was crafted much more quickly to respond to a very clear moment of opportunity, yet it drew on prior experience and was negotiated in order to manage current and future relationships between government and public sector unions. In a somewhat similar moment of crisis in Prussia, a small number of reform entrepreneurs worked quickly to craft a system that drew on the strongest characteristics of a prior system of recruitment and integrated it into a much broader set of changes expected to transform the country in a way that reflected a more glorious past. Only in France and Spain was it difficult to identify significant and clear projects of reform. Rather, numerous, more decentralized initiatives and projects characterized the evolutionary experience of France and the very long-term failure to advance change in Spain. This is congruent with the difficulty of identifying a clear reform entrepreneur in either of these cases.

These reform designs involved creativity and the adaptation of ideas, as well as considerations related to political acceptability. Adjustments often reflected practical political exigencies and calculations. Most frequently, powerful organizations were allowed to opt out of the new systems to minimize the extent of opposition to change. In most cases, the projects called for the gradual incorporation of existing public servants or public services into the proposed new system. In a number of cases, the management of the new systems was left in the hands of ministries and agencies. Thus, the projects developed by reformers indicated a concern to hedge their goals with an eye to the acceptance of the overall principles of a civil service reform, adapting them to long-existing practice and crafting them around contingent political opposition.

Moments

Because changes in the structure of government service are politically contentious, timing was important in the cases of reform explored in this book. Thus, making strategic choices about propitious moments for action was another way in which reformers influenced trajectories of change in the cases considered here. At these windows of opportunity, they were able to move decisively toward the formal acceptance of their initiative in law, decree, or regulation. These windows corresponded to a temporary undermining of the incentives for adhesion to the patronage system by opponents of change. Such moments did not ensure the survival of the new institutions, but did allow for an important step along the way by providing them a stamp of legitimacy within their respective political systems.

In several cases, significant moments were defined by the perception of a major crisis. In Prussia, the disaster of defeat in the Napoleonic Wars created an opening for a number of important changes in the organization and functioning of the state and the class system that sustained it. As part of this restructuring, important reforms in the qualifications for public service were introduced. In the aftermath of these changes, the process of reform proceeded much more incrementally over the course of the next several decades. In the United States, the spoils system had long been decried, and although a toothless civil service commission was created in 1853, even recurrent scandals were unable to move more serious change forward. It took the assassination of a president in 1881 to allow reform proponents to marshal enough congressional support to pass the Pendleton Act. The strong mobilization of public pressure was characteristic of the reform movement in the United States, but even with this, a political moment made the introduction of a new law possible.

Crisis was also important in Argentina, where reformers were able to move forward in the context of a major economic trauma to establish a new system-wide civil service system. This reform was a small part of a much larger government response to an exceptionally deep crisis, and it was this situation that allowed state reformers great leeway in introducing significant change. Crisis took the form of a scandal in Chile, where revelations of corruption and influence peddling rocked the government and provided incentives for politicians, including a very reluctant president, to support a reform initiative that had been hatched elsewhere. Party calculations were central to the discussions, but it was the eruption over the scandal that provided the room to move decisively in the direction of reform.

In other cases, moments for strategic action corresponded to new political realities created by a change of government or regime. In these cases, reformers and opponents made strategic calculations about the political costs and benefits of reform. Thus, in Great Britain, a plan for reform languished until a change of government brought a reform supporter to the prime ministership and a zealot to the exchequer. In Mexico, the early 2000s created a moment in which party balances in the congress encouraged each of the three leading political parties to entertain reform ideas. At this moment, even a reluctant president was encouraged to support the reform initiatives of the parties and the project that had been brewing for some time among academic advocates of civil service reform.

The introduction of an authoritarian regime in Brazil had a similar impact in that it centralized power and decision making in the hands of reform proponents. In Japan, the consolidation of the Meiji Restoration was an important period for a gradual change in expectations about the criteria needed for public sector appointments, yet it was the drafting of a new constitution—called for by the Meiji leadership to consolidate their regime—that provided an opportunity for the designers of the reform to introduce it into law. Similarly, drafting a new Spanish constitution provided a moment in which it was possible to move against the strongly entrenched *corps* that had long resisted reform. In France, the aftermath of war and the establishment of a new regime created an opportunity for the formal institutionalization of ongoing practice.

Thus, reformers took strategic advantage of moments of crisis or political change, when they calculated that opponents of reform were temporarily weakened, thrown into disarray, or reassessing the incentives they had invested in the patronage system. Yet these moments were often fleeting. Typically, they were followed by counteracts by those who continued to resist change. In Britain, for example, the civil service was rarely free of attacks for its elitism and lack of expertise in areas other than administration; conditions of war and economic crisis increased pressures to appoint officials from outside the service. In the United States, attacks on the newly established civil service were numerous, often vicious, and ongoing. Its survival was in the balance in its first twenty years, and after that, politicians found numerous ways to continue to find jobs for the boys. As elsewhere, wars and emergencies provided important opportunities for political leaders to reassert discretion over hiring. A similar situation was evident in Brazil, but further complicated by regime instability.

In Argentina, Mexico, and Chile, public officials resisted change by finding other mechanisms to bring their people into government. In Argentina, the new system eventually became marginalized from much of the public administration. In Mexico, politicians sought to reformulate the scope of the new civil service system, and a president sought to do away with the organization charged with overseeing it. In the meantime, public sector managers found means to work around the laws and regulations to maintain their capacity to bring their people into government. In Chile, the advent of an administration formed by opposition parties brought a renewal of efforts to return to more discretionary hiring practices. Repeatedly, then, the cases demonstrate that conflict over public sector reform was far from resolved when a new law, decree, or administrative order had been approved.

New Actors and the Trajectory of Ongoing Conflicts

Clearly, implementing and consolidating a new career civil service was a long and difficult uphill battle. Conflicts emerged around the survival of the new institution, who would control it, who could join it, and whether it could be trusted. And those who sought to undermine or curtail the new systems had a wide range of ways they could try to do so. Moreover, successful institutional reforms also introduced a new player into discussions and debates over public sector policies—the civil service and the organizations that represented it.

Thus, where civil services were eventually consolidated as legitimate and important institutions of government, and even as issues of control, composition, and loyalty of the new systems remained contentious, the outcome of these and other struggles was influenced by the emergence of a civil service that was able to enter the political fray and represent its interests. Clearly, this new actor was consistently concerned about bread-and-butter issues of salaries, job security, and benefits, but also wider issues of protection and autonomy. In the ongoing conflicts over characteristics of the public service, interests were increasingly defined in terms of the preference of the civil service for the new status quo. Thus, reformers seeking to encourage greater efficiency, effectiveness, or responsiveness in the civil service faced the opposition of this often-powerful interest. Similarly, later generations of reformers, intent on significantly altering the incentive systems in the public service, had to contend with its resistance.

In Britain, for example, civil service associations became powerful interlocutors in discussions of public sector management by the 1920s, and in the United States, such associations were important in resisting the efforts of politicians to reclaim jobs for the boys in that and the subsequent decade. In Argentina, public sector unions gained power in newly structured opportunities to negotiate salaries, benefits, and conditions of work with government. Few such organizations accumulated as much power to halt and curtail subsequent reform initiatives as the multitude of Spanish *corps* that went to great lengths to protect their members, but German bureaucrats were also largely successful in holding new public management initiatives at bay. In Japan, when parties sought to infiltrate and control the public service system set up by the Meiji reformers, they had little success against the increasingly insulated bureaucrats who owed primary loyalty to the state and to their ministries. These same structures reduced the capacity of Japanese reformers to push new public management reforms forward.

The Public Service and Good Governance

Sociologist Peter Evans opened his important 1995 book, *Embedded Autonomy: States and Industrial Transformation,* with the story of a lion who escapes from a zoo in Brazil, takes refuge in a ministry, dines well on a bureaucrat from time to time, and remains unnoticed for months—until he eats the person who serves morning coffee.[7] A decade earlier, Terry Gilliam, of Monty Python fame, wrote and directed a film about a monstrous technocracy of the future in which errors cannot be corrected and efforts to do so inevitably lead to ever more Kafkaesque situations. The title of the film? *Brazil.*

Similarly, a three-part PBS program on Brazil's twenty-first-century economic boom aired in June of 2008 indicated that "bureaucracy in Brazil is so overwhelming, taxes so overbearing that Brazilian entrepreneurs speak of the *custo do Brasil,* the unique costs of doing business here."[8] The subtitle of journalist Seth Kugel's article "Adventures in Brazilian Bureaucracy" made a related point more lightly: "Foreigners in Need of a Bank Account? Just Follow These 70-Plus Steps."[9] In 1995, a Brazilian writer ridiculed the "bureaucrat's paradise" in the country. "By the government's own admission," she complained, "at least 44,000 [public sector workers] could be sent home without harming the administration of the country."[10]

Indeed, in the popular and journalistic imagination, Brazil's bureaucracy at the outset of the twenty-first century was vast, powerful, and voracious, capable of choking off all initiative and stifling any efforts to limit the inconveniences it meted out to citizens and investors alike. It was not unusual to hear that interactions with the state machinery meant entering a special kind of living hell. Local businesspeople, foreign investors, and unlucky tourists chimed in regularly with tales of woeful encounters with the powers of the state.[11] Academics sometimes joined this chorus, referring to the state in Brazil as "an obese, uncoordinated Gulliver, unable to turn its weight into strength and tied down by innumerable bonds to narrow interest groups and clientelist networks."[12]

Could this be the same public sector that others referenced as not only the oldest but also the most professionally focused public service in all of Latin America? According to the authors of the Inter-American Development Bank Report on the region's public sectors, for example, "In the

Latin American context, the bureaucracy of Brazil's central government is highly meritocratic, and, in addition, has a good technical and social reputation."[13] The report singled out for praise the widespread use of examinations for entry into the public service, a process that extended even to the hiring of temporary employees. It further acknowledged that this public service was well qualified, and that almost 40 percent of nonelected officials held university degrees.[14] Others credited the vast parastatal sector with high levels of technocratic expertise and commitment to industrial growth, and referenced its organizations as as important players in the "Brazilian miracle" of earlier decades.[15]

Well into the early twenty-first century, in fact, many ministries and parastatals had strong reputations for excellence, among them several extremely large banks, including the Bank of Brazil and the Central Bank, the state petroleum company, and other employers of note. Many of Brazil's state-owned enterprises and its large network of universities set standards that other countries were not able to achieve through their public organizations. Moreover, ministries such as finance and foreign affairs enjoyed reputations for the good performance and the professionalism of their staffs. Certainly the economic boom of the mid-2000s suggested that the public sector was not entirely detrimental to the development of the country.

In comparative terms, then, the public sector in Brazil garners frequent praise for the autonomy, expertise, and professionalism of its public service, while also producing sharp criticism for its bureaucratic officiousness, complexity, and disregard for the headaches it causes citizens on a daily basis. Its bureaucratic history highlights a series of organizations credited with an important role in national development, while others demonstrated ongoing failures and dysfunctional performance. These characteristics indicate how difficult it is to link public sector performance with the existence of a career public service. Bureaucracies perform in myriad ways, and the implementation of a career civil service is but a part of broader efforts to introduce more efficiency, effectiveness, and responsiveness to government. Indeed, the experience of many now developed countries suggests that civil services create as many pathologies as they do solutions to public sector problems.

The case of Brazil and the history of the construction of its public service, at once scorned and praised, provide insight into a complex conundrum of merit and patronage, good performance and incompetence. This problem is far from unique to Brazil, however. At the same time, the ambiguities and dilemmas of such real-world experiences are not regularly reflected in reform rhetoric or plans. As we have seen, political struggles to introduce civil service reform in well-institutionalized patronage systems consistently show reformers casting their efforts in Manichean language, and contemporary efforts mirror their predecessors in this regard. Within efforts to promote such changes, greatly improved governance is an article of faith in confronting the persistence and stickiness of patronage in the public sector. In rhetoric, the forces of good governance continue to battle the evil consequences of vice, corruption, incompetence, partisanship, and inefficiency endemic to widespread use of patronage.

Systems of spoils in the allocation of public office can clearly contribute to government corruption and incompetence. In such contexts, rhetoric meets reality, and the promotion of good governance must clearly address the dysfunctional nature of a politicized public service. Yet *Jobs for the Boys* suggests that patronage systems are not synonymous with bad governance, and several cases provided ample historical evidence of this disjuncture. In contemporary contexts, because such systems tend to be controlled by political executives and to be pyramidal in operation, ministers and other high-level officials have the capacity to use their appointment power to attract highly qualified staffs to carry out specific policy initiatives. Within organizations, managers with discretion over hiring have significant opportunities to create islands of excellence, even in larger systems pervaded by the least desirable consequences of patronage. Moreover, discretion in hiring can provide means for escaping the rigidity of personnel laws and regulations and the heavy weight of an entrenched bureaucracy, without at the same time directly confronting or contravening the legal fiction of a career system.

Thus, discretion in the allocation of public sector positions cannot be tied to a universal outcome of bad public sector performance, although it can certainly be associated with considerable potential for unwise use and the undermining of the public purposes of government. Inherent in the flexibility that makes patronage systems available for a variety of goals is the problem of its instability and politicization. Little wonder that opponents of such systems seek stability, predictability, and neutrality through the construction of Weberian civil services.

Again, however, it is clear that the rhetoric of reform can be misleading. Just as patronage systems are not synonymous with corruption and incompetence, neither are civil service systems synonymous with good governance, whatever the claims of reformers. Thus, in countries with well-institutionalized public services, attacks on bureaucrats and on the rigidity and unresponsiveness of government are common, and those who admit to being bureaucrats often do so in mock shame, anticipating derisive snickers in response. In the late twentieth century, the language of reform turned decisively against civil services and civil servants. They are now tarred with the language of inefficiency and incompetence, if not with that of corruption.

As we have seen, reform initiatives linked to the new public management have been designed in some countries to address perceptions that entrenched civil services lack responsiveness to citizen needs, focus on rules and procedures more than giving attention to the public purposes of government, do not respond to ongoing needs for change and efficiency, and are costly, arrogant, and aloof from the real problems of governance. Public sector reformers now call for more efficiency and better performance in government, for a decisive break with stable, hierarchical, and often rigid administration, for mechanisms to correct for impermeable boundaries across institutions, and for the inculcation of creativity and innovation in the public service. Such changes are important in order to introduce greater accountability and flexibility.

Thus, new generations of public sector reformers now take the template of the Weberian civil service as problematic for the ability to achieve good governance and have championed approaches to management from the new public management. Yet, in now developed countries, where such approaches have been systematically adopted, such as in New Zealand, Britain, and Australia, a revisionist critique of the new public management suggests that the goal of good governance continues to remain elusive. And in countries that have not moved far down this particular path, reformers continue to search for ways to marry stability, predictability, and neutrality to good performance and accountability.

The search for good governance goes on. But this book suggests that whether the need is to establish the foundations of a civil service system, as is occurring in many developing countries in the early 2000s, to move toward a model more consistent with the new public management, or to invent creative new approaches to public sector management, moving from objectives to reality, from plan to introduction to consolidation, will follow a process of political construction that also provides opportunities for reconstruction and deconstruction. Good governance is elusive; achieving better governance requires the effective deployment of politics over time.

Notes

Introduction

1. Skowronek 1982:78–79.
2. See especially Skowronek 1982 for this argument.
3. See especially Erie 1988 for a discussion of the distribution of patronage by party machines at local and state levels and national policy initiatives.
4. In this book, I focus on a specific form of patronage in political life—the allocation of public sector jobs to achieve personal or political objectives. Thus, I do not deal with issues such as "pork-barrel politics" and other forms of political largesse based on the allocation of other kinds of public resources—public investments, contracts, a variety of kinds of "deals" that represent personal or party influence in decision making, for example. Patrimonialism, in which public positions are regarded as private property, is a form of patronage, but does not exhaust the possibilities. Patronage in public service is based on a model of patron-client relationships that have diverse forms, some more traditional than others. See, for a discussion of definitions, Piattoni 2001:1–8, although the author distinguishes patronage from patrimonialism. I would argue that patrimonialism is founded on the allocation of public positions through patronage.
5. See Pierson 2004.
6. See especially Barzelay 1992 for a discussion.
7. Weber 1946:228–235.
8. See Barzelay 1992; Pollitt and Bouckaert 2000; Ongaro 2009.
9. See, for example, Geddes 1994; Demmers, Fernández Jilberto, and Hogenboom 2004. See Betley and Larb 2004; McCourt 2000; Van de Walle 2007 for a discussion.
10. Evans and Rauch 1999:760. For Peters (1996:8), for example, "The problem for many governments [in developing and transitional] regimes is in creating the Weberian and rule-directed bureaucracies that are now being supplanted in industrialized regimes."

11. World Bank 1997:79, definition in brackets from p. 80.
12. See, for example, http://web.worldbank.org/website/external/topics /extpublicsectorandgovernance/anticorruption.
13. See Eichbaum and Shaw 2010.
14. Patronage, of course, is not practiced solely by governments; for our purposes, however, I focus only on the use of patronage as a means for acquiring positions in government.
15. Anthropology and political science have generated the most extensive discussions of the theoretical foundations for understanding patronage and clientelism. For important early work, see especially Foster 1961; Landé 1977; Mintz and Wolf 1950; Scott 1972; Powell 1970; Bloch 1961; and Lemarchand 1972. For an application to bureaucracy, see Grindle 1977. For more recent discussions in politics, see Kitschelt and Wilkinson 2007; and Piattoni 2001.
16. Historically, patronage systems long predated any conception of a "public" sector. Indeed, patronage systems proved durable across the transformation from the private households of early rulers to the "public realm" of the state and the nation.
17. Weber outlines these characteristics to demonstrate that public officials in a modern bureaucracy pursue a career of administration and work as servants of the state, not of patrons, kings, or other individuals. See Weber 1946:196–204.
18. Weber 1946:199.
19. Competence, in fact, can be identified in various ways. For example, we can distinguish "formal competence," referring to expertise judged or screened on the basis of an examination or competition; "professional competence," referring to educational attainment or training in a recognized profession (holders of which may still be appointed through patronage); and "political/professional competence," referring to expertise based on educational credentialing and screening for political/personal loyalty (such as the "new professionals" who combine fit for a particular job with appointment based on their personal or political relationship to a patron).
20. The work of Kathleen Thelen and Paul Pierson, among others, provides fundamental grounding for this approach. See, in particular, Steinmo, Thelen, and Longstreth 1992; Streek and Thelen 2005a; Pierson and Skocpol 2002; and Pierson 2004 for discussions of history and institutional change.
21. See Krasner 1984 for an original discussion of path dependence.
22. On embeddedness, see Evans 1995.
23. This literature is extremely broad, encompassing work in economics, political science, and management science. See, for examples, Grindle and Thomas 1991; Kingdon 1984; Barzelay and Gallego 2006.
24. See Barzelay and Füchtner 2003 and Baez and Abolafia 2002 for discussions of policy entrepreneurs in public management reform.

25. This is frequently argued in the case of the United States. On Latin
    America, see Geddes 1994.
26. See Geddes 1994.
27. See Schefter 1977 for an exploration of this conundrum.
28. See O'Gorman 2001.
29. See Silberman 1993.
30. Silberman 1993:43.
31. Grindle 1991.
32. See, for example, Hoogenboom 1968.
33. Streek and Thelen 2005b:19.
34. Weber 1946:196–198.
35. Weber 1946:204.
36. Weber 1946:207.
37. Weber 1946:114.
38. Wilson 1887:201.
39. Wilson 1887:10.
40. This argument is made at a general level by Chang 2002, especially chap.
    3. See also Kitschelt and Wilkinson 2007a:3.

1. A System for All Seasons

1. For these examples, see Griffith 1954:7–8.
2. White 1948:278–280.
3. Nathaniel Hawthorne, *Passages from the American Note-Books* (Boston:
   Houghton Mifflin, 1896), 214 (from March 15, 1840), quoted in White 1954:
   174–175; also 358–359.
4. See Carpenter 2001.
5. *Economist*, December 14, 1991:19.
6. Corrales 1997:64–65.
7. Giraldo 1997:256–258.
8. Patronage is often decried for its failure to distinguish private from public
   ends, implying that it is necessarily a form of corruption. This perspective
   is ahistorical (distinguishing public from private interests in government
   is a relatively modern perspective) and deterministic (implying that the
   form of filling positions determines their use). On the issue of loyalty and
   state building, see especially Fischer and Lundgreen 1975. On the issue of
   early modern bureaucratic development and its relationship to various
   forms of allocating positions, see Ertman 1997, who proposes a general
   theory of state building that includes the process of bureaucratization.
   The gradual end of the idea of the "private" or household nature of
   government under patrimonialism and the growth of a concept of the
   "public" purposes of government in the early modern period is an
   extremely important transition historically. This transition laid the basis
   for the emergence of modern state bureaucracies. For my purposes,

however, what is striking is that patronage was a mechanism employed by patrimonial rulers as well as modernizing ones.

9. Wood 1994; Riche 1993.

10. Rosenberg 1958:9–10; Ertman 1997:7–9.

11. See especially Ertman 1997.

12. Fischer and Lundgreen 1975:516.

13. Rosenberg 1958:32.

14. Clark 2006:85.

15. Ritter 1968:8; and chap. 2; Ertman 1977:245–262.

16. Clark 2006:89; Fischer and Lundgreen 1975:524–525.

17. Ertman 1997:244.

18. Ritter 1968: chap. 7.

19. Ritter 1968:158.

20. Behrens 1985: chap. 1.

21. Rosenberg 1958:65–70. See also Clark 2006: chap. 4; Behrens 1985:60–61.

22. Rosenberg 1958:67–68; Ritter 1968:159–160.

23. Shefter 1977:423–425. The emphasis on the army led one of Frederick the Great's ministers to state that Prussia is "not a country with an army. They have an army with a country that serves it as a headquarters and a commissariat." Quoted in Behrens 1985:38; see also Ertman 1997:253–254.

24. Rosenberg 1958:72.

25. Until about 1750, positions were also purchased and officials made contributions to the state from their salaries, but this practice was ended by the king in an effort to ensure that the bureaucracy was staffed by those qualified by capacity and loyalty. Moreover, when offices were sold, they were not made hereditary, as happened in France and elsewhere, so the central power of the monarch over appointments was retained. Rosenberg 1958:78–79. See also Clark 2006: chap. 4; Ritter 1968: chap. 9; Behrens 1985:57; Fischer and Lundgreen 1975:527.

26. Patronage was focused on ensuring loyalty to the state and the monarch, and was dispensed not only by the king but also by his ministers and other top-level officials.

27. Armstrong 1973:81; Gillis 1971:26.

28. Armstrong, 1973:163, 167.

29. Rosenberg 1958:87.

30. Rosenberg 1958:77.

31. Gordon 2009:4.

32. Gordon 2009:5.

33. Gordon 2009:5.

34. The military dominance of the Tokugawa clan was established through a decisive battle in 1600; in 1603, the emperor formally "bestowed" the title of shogun (generalissimo) on the Tokugawa ruler, Ieyasu.

35. Gordon 2009: chap. 1.

36. For more detail, see Inoki 1964:283–287; Silberman 1993:161.
37. Pempel 1992:19.
38. Gordon 2009:43, 53–54.
39. Silberman 1966:171.
40. Inoki 1964:286.
41. Indeed, the samurai lost power quickly in the years after the Meiji Restoration because many had become "salaried employees of their lords." Gordon 2009:62; Silberman 1993:162.
42. Pempel 1992:19–20; Silberman 1966:159–160.
43. Gordon 2009:63.
44. Gordon 2009:62–64.
45. Silberman 1993:179–180.
46. Muramatsu and Pempel 1995:175; Inoki 1964:287–294.
47. Inoki 1964:289.
48. Doyle 1989:42.
49. Armstrong 1973:95.
50. Doyle 1989:42.
51. Doyle 1989:24–25. See also Fischer and Lundgreen 1975:495–497; and Swart 1989.
52. Behrens 1985:50–53. "As soon as the crown creates an office God creates a fool willing to buy it," according to a minister of Louis XIV. Quoted in Behrens 1985:51. See also Church 1981: chap. 2; and Ertman 1997: 100–110.
53. Swart 1989:87.
54. Swart 1989:92.
55. See Church 1981 for an extensive discussion of the development of the French bureaucracy during the Revolution.
56. Silberman 1993:95; Church 1981:9, 72.
57. Church 1981:77, 128; Fischer and Lundgreen 1975:508.
58. Silberman 1993:95–96; Church 1981: chap. 2; Ertman 1997:151–151.
59. Daly 2001:6. The original idea of "emperors" in the departments is credited to Napoléon, who referred to "low level emperors." Daly (2001) and others argue that the metaphor had its limitations, as prefects accommodated to local interests as a means of accomplishing their administrative duties. Nevertheless, the responsibilities and powers of the prefects were impressive. Silberman 1993:95; Church 1981:9, 72, 77, 128; Fischer and Lundgreen 1975:508.
60. Joseph Fiévée, 1810, quoted in Daly 2001:43.
61. Silberman 1993:109–112.
62. Silberman 1993:112–113; Church 1981: chap. 8.
63. Daly 2001:41ff.
64. Church 1981:276.
65. Silberman 1993:144.
66. Tombs 1996:100; Silberman 1993:136–137.

67. See Toombs 1996.
68. Silberman 1993:141–142.
69. According to Silberman (1993:142), ministers "used examinations as a means of reducing the number of eligibles seeking office," thus "rationalizing" patronage.
70. Hennessy 1989:19.
71. Griffith 1954:6.
72. Griffith 1954:7.
73. Griffith 1954:8. Whitehall, a townhouse belonging to Cardinal Thomas Wolsey, was appropriated by Henry VIII. On the role of patronage in state building, see Fischer and Lundgreen 1975. On the early development of British central bureaucracy, see Ertman 1997: chap. 4.
74. Hennessy 1989:21.
75. Hennessy 1989:20–21.
76. Hennessy, 1989:20–21.
77. Fischer and Lundgreen 1975:486–487; Ertman 1997: chap. 4.
78. In the mid-eighteenth century, fourteen thousand of seventeen thousand public officials worked in Treasury to raise revenue. Hennessey 1989:26.
79. Fischer and Lundgreen 1975:482, 486.
80. Silberman 1993:303–309.
81. Silberman 1993:333.
82. O'Gorman 2001:56–59.
83. O'Gorman 2001:59–64.
84. Silberman 1993:333.
84. Silberman 1993:301.
85. Silberman 1993:312.
86. Burke goes on to acknowledge the distinguished status of many incumbents on the board but demurs that "as an academy of belle letters, he should hold them hallowed; as a board of trade he wished to abolish them." (Edmund Burke, "A plan for the better security of the independence of Parliament and the economical reformation of the civil and other establishments," delivered on February 11, 1780, in Parliament. Quoted in Hennessy 1989:29; and Griffith 1954:9.
87. See Hennessy 1989: chap. 1. For an example, see Bayley 1975.
88. Silberman 1993:287–291.
89. The marriage took place in 1469, and both Aragon and Castile continued with separate political institutions. See Elliot 1990: chap. 1.
90. Cunningham 1919:363.
91. See, for Example, Elliot 1990:81–82, 86–87.
92. Elliot 1990:90–92.
93. Rewards for conquering new territories typically included a government position of eminence in the newly acquired land, as well as hefty spoils from such activities. See Elliot, 1990:58–59. See also Phelan 1967:144; Ertman 1997:110–116.

94. Elliot 1990:170–176.
95. Elliot 1990:170.
96. See, in particular, Phelan 1967: chap. 6. As standard practice, the Council of the Indies produced a list of three or four people considered qualified for a particular post—qualifications almost invariably involved training in law, previous experience, and letters of recommendation from important personages—and the king would then select one for the position. Under weak kings, the influence of the councils and of powerful courtiers expanded, and with it, their capacity to select officials for domestic and imperial service.
97. Elliot 1990:177.
98. See especially Elliot 1990.
99. Elliot 1990:178.
100. Phelan 1967:133, 135–139; Ertman 1997:113.
101. Phelan 1967:143. Ertman (1997:119) reports evidence that by 1650, in the province of Castile, the creation and sale of thirty thousand positions meant approximately one "owned" position for every 166 people.
102. Elliot 1990: chaps. 8 and 9.
103. Palmer and Colton 1963:235.
104. Elliot 1990:375.
105. Callahan 2000:49.
106. Because access to office-holding plays a role in much of the history of the wars for independence in the early nineteenth century, this topic has received considerable discussion by historians. See, for examples, Arnold 1982; Socolow 1987; Burkholder and Chandler 1972. Phelan (1967:140) notes that the bias against those born in the Americas limited the extent to which offices could be claimed as inheritance. See also Mabry 2002.
107. For a variety of perspectives on the nineteenth century in Spain, see Alvarez Junco and Shubert 2000.
108. Parado Díez 2000:252.
109. Jacobson and Moreno Luzón 2000:95.
110. Cruz 2000:43. See also Kenny 1977.
111. Jacobson and Moreno Luzón 2000:100.
112. Carr 1980:9, 11.
113. Carr 1980:11.
114. Jacobson and Moreno Luzón 2000:108.
115. Cruz 2000:36
116. Jacobson and Moreno Luzón 2000:99.
117. Cruz 2000:35.
118. Letter of George Washington to Alexander Hamilton, October 29, 1795, quoted in White 1948:265.
119. White 1948:267–268.
120. White 1948:135–136.

121. White 1948:255. White reports that in 1792, there were 780 positions in government, almost 85 percent of which were in the Treasury Department. These numbers exclude deputy postmasters. By 1801, there were just over two thousand federal employees.
122. White 1948:268, 320.
123. As White points out, at the time of the government of gentlemen in the United States, governments in Britain were notoriously corrupt, inefficient, and "patronage-ridden." White 1948:468–469. In a discussion of character and appointment to office in the first years of the republic, Fish (1905:76) observed that "honesty and efficiency are not entirely synonymous."
124. White 1951:356; See also Wilentz 2005:101–102, 138.
125. White 1951:13.
126. Wilentz 2005:102.
127. The partisan use of state-level office was first apparent in New York. Fish 1905:79, 86. White 1951:362–364. Within the armed forces, appointments to the medical corps were the first to require examinations.
128. White 1954:303.
129. White 1954:4.
130. As Jackson began his presidency in 1829, "Terror, meanwhile, reigned in Washington. . . . The great body of officials awaited their fate in silent horror, glad when the office hours expired at having escaped another day. . . . No man deemed it safe and prudent to trust his neighbor, and the interior of the department presented a fearful scene of guarded silence, secret intrigue, espionage, and tale-bearing." James Parton, quoted in White 1954:307.
131. White 1954:308; see also Wilentz 2005:315–316.
132. Wilentz 2005:316.
133. Andrew Jackson, quoted in White 1954:318. "The duties of all public officers are, or at least admit of being made, so plain and simple that men of intelligence may readily qualify themselves for their performance." Jackson quoted in Carpenter 2001:44. In contrast, Jefferson opined that most were "unqualified for the management of affairs requiring intelligence among the common level." Quoted in Wilentz 2005:102.
134. White 1954:319. See also Carpenter 2001:43–44. Fish (1905:80) traces the idea of rotation in office to the "frame of government" established by William Penn in Pennsylvania in 1682, in which a regular change of office was important "that all may be fitted for government and have experience of the care and burden of it."
135. White 1954:312.
136. White 1954:313; see also Silberman 1993:243.
137. U.S. Office of Personnel Management 1993:28.

138. Carpenter 2001:41.
139. White 1954:531; White (1958:2) indicates 250,000 people were on the civilian payroll by 1900, based on U.S. census data.
140. White 1954:105, 395–398.
141. See White 1958:28–34. The failure to observe this act was the central claim against President Andrew Johnson in efforts to impeach him. Fish (1905:174) notes that in midcentury, a *New York Herald* article indicated that the "Congress showed itself willing to relieve the president of all trouble in regard to the patronage, as it had divided up into committees to portion it out." See Fish 1905: chap. 8.
142. Carpenter 2001:43.
143. White 1958:25.
144. White 1954:350–356; Fish 1905:182–183.
145. White 1954:362.
146. Carpenter 2001.
147. Silberman 1993:253.
148. Carpenter 2001:41; Skowronek 1982:72.
149. Skowronek 1982:69.
150. See especially Teaford 1984; Erie 1988.

2. Politics in the Construction of Reform

1. Gillis 1971:5; Armstrong 1973:79. This code gave the bureaucracy specific jurisdiction and exempted officials from some obligations, such as paying local taxes.
2. Rosenberg 1958:191, 81–82.
3. Rosenberg 1958:179–180.
4. Rosenberg 1958:20.
5. Clark 2006: chap. 8; Rosenberg 1958: chap. 9.
6. By midcentury, university enrollments had expanded by 40 percent. Gillis 1971:13.
7. The reforms of Stein and Hardenberg reorganized the military, granted personal freedom to serfs, and undermined the legal divisions that separated the three estates. Ministers of state gained in strength vis-à-vis the monarchy, and towns and cities gained some rights of self-government. See particularly Clark 2006: chap. 10.
8. Quoted in Armstrong 1973:164; Gillis 1971:17
9. Gillis 1971:6.
10. Ritter 1968:158.
11. Rosenberg 1958: chap. 9; Armstrong 1973:164.
12. See, in particular, Gillis 1971.
13. Gillis 1971: chap. 8.
14. See, for example, Behrens 1985: pt. 3, chap. 3.

15. Armstrong 1973:166–168. Legal studies in Prussia and Germany appeared not to have been very rigorous, and those completing studies generally competed successfully to enter the public service. Indeed, Prussian and German students—as aspirants to public sector jobs—had considerably more capacity to shape their careers than was the case in the more rigorously standardized France. The basic qualification was training in law, and career development emphasized more generalist skills on the British model rather than the specialization of the French. See Armstrong 1973:166; Gillis 1971: chap. 3.
16. Shefter 1977:425.
17. Gillis 1971: chap. 9.
18. Gillis 1971:201–207.
19. Behrens 1985:198.
20. Silberman 1993:162.
21. Gordon 2009:63; Silberman 1993: 178–179.
22. Silberman 1993:180.
23. Silberman 1993:180–181.
24. Gordon, 2009:64; Silberman, 1993:197.
25. Pempel 1992:20.
26. Gordon 2009:105.
27. Inoki 1964:290.
28. Inoki 1964:290.
29. Inoki 1964:291.
30. Pempel 1992:19–20.
31. Inoki 1964:291.
32. Inoki 1964:291.
33. Inoki 1964:295–296.
34. Inoki 1964:294–295.
35. Silberman 1993:220.
36. Gordon 2009:65.
37. Silberman 1993:300–301.
38. Silberman 1993:313–316.
39. See, particularly, Silberman 1993:287.
40. Silberman 1993:330.
41. Silberman 1993:331; Pempel 1992:19–20.
42. Hennessey 1989:32–33. "Life for him was a battleground where the forces of enlightened, altruistic moral progress were to triumph over the dead weight of obscurantism and self interest." Chapman and Greenaway, quoted in Hennessey, 32. He described the existing system as one benefitting " 'sickly youths' whose 'parents and friends . . . endeavor to obtain for them employment in the service of the Government.' " Trevelyan, quoted in Hennessey 1989:27.
43. Armstrong 1973:151. Haileybury College was established in 1809. Entrance examinations for the Indian Civil Service were established in

1855, based on a model of wide and general knowledge that was itself based on the curriculum at Oxbridge, ensuring elite dominance of higher-level civil service positions.

44. Quoted in Armstrong 1971:157.
45. Hennessey 1989:33–34.
46. Hennessey 1989:35–36.
47. Hennessey 1989:43–44; Silberman 1993:363.
48. Silberman 1993:332–350.
49. Quoted in Armstrong 1973:153.
50. The association's primary concerns, however, focused on Parliament and ministers of government rather than on the administrative apparatus. Hennessey 1989:46; Silberman 1993:294. The Administrative Reform Society was short-lived, coming to an end in 1857.
51. Silberman 1993:364.
52. White, Bland, Sharp, and Moorstein Marx 1935:1.
53. In 1859, an act of Parliament determined criteria for pension eligibility and created a category of "established" positions, whose holders were eligible for pensions that were controlled by the Treasury, a recognition of a lifetime career in the public service. Silberman 1993:370–371.
54. Hennessey 1989:48.
55. The argument of their ministers was that confidentiality required character more than intellect, and character could not be judged by examination. Hennessey 1989:48.
56. See O'Gorman 2001:66–67.
57. This history is well told by Hennessy 1989.
58. H. G. C. Matthews, quoted in Hennessey 1989:31.
59. Tombs 1996:98.
60. Tombs 1996:99–100.
61. See Church 1981:294, 296–297.
62. Tombs 1996:123, 129.
63. Silberman 1993:133.
64. Silberman 1993:145.
65. White, Bland, Sharp, and Morstein Marx 1935:100–102; see also Church 1981:274.
66. Silberman 1993:137.
67. Tombs 1996:128.
68. Church 1981:301.
69. Silberman 1993:138.
70. Silberman 1993:137.
71. Silberman 1993:138–139; Tombs 1996:100–101.
72. Silberman 1993:149.
73. Tombs 1996:129–130.
74. Silberman 1993:143.
75. Tombs 1996:101.

76. White 1958: especially chap. 13; reform in the United States is chronicled in a variety of important sources, including White 1958 and Mosher 1968.
77. Silberman 1993: chap. 8.
78. White 1958:18.
79. Julius Bing, quoted in Hoogenboom 1968:1.
80. White 1958:7.
81. *Sentinel,* August 24, 1887, quoted in White 1958:18.
82. *Nation* 13, no. 326 (September 28, 1871):201, quoted in Hoogenboom 1968:98.
83. This initial test of competence was a simple "pass" system, qualifying a clerk for employment, but setting no other constraints on patronage as the mode of entry into service. Hoogenboom 1968:9. See also Fish 1905:182–183.
84. Hoogenboom 1968:9–10.
85. Hoogenboom 1968:9–11; White, 1958:280–281.
86. Hoogenboom 1968:16–17.
87. Skowronek 1982:43.
88. White, 1958:283.
89. Hoogenboom 1961:68.
90. White 1958:291.
91. White 1958:292. Many argued that rotation in office maintained the democratic character of government. And many were aware that a civil service system would not only harm local political machines, but would also make it more difficult to respond to the demands of Civil War veterans and to ensure some equitable distribution of federal jobs based on state and locality.
92. Quoted in Freedman 1994:15–16.
93. See Hoogenboom 1968: chap. 9.
94. See White 1958: chap. 12.
95. Hoogenboom 1968:189. See also Fish 1905: chap. 10.
96. White 1958:300–301.
97. From a poster displayed at post offices around the country, quoted in Hoogenboom 1968:213.
98. White 1958: chap. 13; see also Fish 1905: chap. 10.
99. See, in particular, Alvarez Junco and Shubert 2000.
100. Jacobson and Moreno Luzón 2000:98–101.
101. Carr 1980:34–35.
102. Parado Díez 2000:252.
103. Parado Díez 2000:255.
104. Gutierrez Reñon 1969:135.
105. Romero Salvadó 1999:100–101.
106. Romero Salvadó 1999:161–162.
107. Parado Díez 2000:253.

108. Parado Díez 2000:254.
109. Parado Díez 2000:254; Tussell and Queipo de Llano 2000.
110. Parado Díez 2000:270.
111. Martínez Puón 2005:110.
112. Gutierrez Reñon 1969:133.
113. Gutierrez Reñon 1969:133.
114. Some indication of the complexity of the system is revealed by the Remunerations Act of 1965, which set salaries by "multiplying the basic salary of 36,000 pesetas a year by the coefficient allocated to his corps from a scale of 18 coefficients ranging from 1 to 5.5, of which the lowest applied in practice is 1.3. To that are added two annual bonuses of one twelfth of the salary. For each three years of seniority, 7 per cent is added to the salary and the bonuses." In addition, discretional pay could amount to 10 to 500 percent of salaries. Gutierrez Reñon 1969:138.
115. Moyado Estrada 2006:127–128.
116. Martínez Puón 2005:112.

3. *Après* Reform

1. Franz Kafka, in Janouch 1971:120.
2. On "reform mongers," see Hirschman 1981.
3. H. C. Potter, 1899, quoted in White 1958:303.
4. White 1958:325.
5. White 1958:305.
6. White 1958:303.
7. See, in particular, Erie 1988.
8. White 1958:352–356.
9. Skowronek 1982:68–82.
10. Hoogenboom 1961: chap. 14.
11. White 1958:310.
12. See, for example, Eire 1988.
13. White 1958:350.
14. Skowronek 1982:70–71.
15. Skowronek 1982:179–181.
16. Skowronek 1982:177.
17. See, for example, Skowronek 1982:311.
18. A 1907 law made political neutrality an important feature of the civil service.
19. See Figure 3.1. U.S. Office of Personnel Management 2003:63.
20. Fish (1905:75) dates the first significant conflict between Congress and the president over the control of patronage to 1811, when Congress sought to "divide the patronage between the executive and legislative departments."

21. Senator Thomas Carter, 1909(?), quoted in Skowronek 1982:185.
22. See, in particular, Skowronek 1982:200–202, and chaps. 7 and 8 ff.
23. The classification system incorporated a system that made entry possible at most levels, thus opening up multiple opportunities for federal employment at all stages of a person's career. By avoiding a "mandarin" system requiring a particular educational track, the U.S. system remained open to a large number of "fit" applicants, who could move in and out of the system relatively easily. See especially Silberman 1993 on the consequences of this system.
24. See Figure 3.1. Freedman 1994:19.
25. Unidentified "New Dealsman" quoted in Freedman 1994:20.
26. Freedman 1994:21.
27. In 1890, a Second Division Clerks' Association was created, and in the same decade the Association of Tax Clerks, customs federations, and the Assistant Clerks Association in 1903. See Hennessy 1989:80–81.
28. See, for examples, Hennessy 1989: chaps. 2 and 3.
29. Hennessy 1989:69–70.
30. Hennessy 1989:71. Two exceptions to the new imperium of a unified civil service under Treasury control were the Cabinet Office and the Foreign Office. The architect of unification was the permanent secretary of the treasury, Sir Warren Fisher, who remained in that office from 1919 to 1939.
31. Hennessy 1989:74.
32. White, Bland, Sharp, and Morstein Marx 1935:9–10, 11–12.
33. Hennessy 1989:195–197. The three main recommendations of the Fulton Committee were for a new classification system that would supplant the barriers between classes in the service, the establishment of a civil service training college, and the creation of a civil service department.
34. Fry 2000:19.
35. Hennessy 1989:603–604.
36. Morstein Marx 1961:63–64.
37. Muramatsu and Pempel 1995:175–176; Silberman 1993:213–214.
38. Muramatsu and Pempel 1995:176.
39. Muramatsu and Pempel 1995:177.
40. Silberman 1993:216.
41. Muramatsu and Pempel 1995:185; Silberman 1993:167.
42. Muramatsu and Pempel 1995:180–182.
43. Pempel 1992:20.
44. Inoki 1964:299.
45. Pempel 1992:20.
46. Pempel 1986:123.
47. Pempel 1986:129.
48. Pempel 1992:22–23.

49. Evans 1995:49.

50. Hennessy 1989:49.

51. In 1870, there were some 50,000 positions in the national government; by 1900 there were over 115,000 positions; in 1914, at the outbreak of World War I, there were over 280,000 positions. Hennessy 1989:51, 59. See also Fischer and Lundgreen 1975:462–463.

52. Decades later, the popular television and radio series *Yes, Minister,* lampooned the hapless position of the minister for administrative affairs, Jim Hatch (MP), when confronted by his top civil servant, Sir Humphrey Appleby, who has decades of experience in government, an extensive underground network of old boys throughout the administration, and a long and successful history of manipulating his political masters.

53. Hennessy 1989:56.

54. Sir Warren Fisher, 1919(?), quoted in Hennessy, 1989:71.

55. White, Bland, Sharp, and Morstein Marx 1935:9.

56. Hennessy 1989:60.

57. Hennessy 1989:59.

58. Hennessy 1989:73.

59. Hennessy 1989:86.

60. Hennessy 1989:118.

61. Hennessy 1989:107.

62. Hennessy 1989:373.

63. Hennessy 1989:525, quoting Eugene Grebenik.

64. Hennessy 1989:172, quoting Thomas Balough.

65. As indicated in chapter 3, Silberman's analysis correlates these two characteristics causally precisely because uncertain politicians will favor public services that are strong and autonomous and thus able to carry on with public business despite political instability. See Silberman 1993.

66. Gillis 1971:195.

67. Armstrong 1973:173.

68. Gillis 1971:218.

69. Clark 2006:618.

70. White, Bland, Sharp, and Morstein Marx 1935:196n4.

71. Clark: 2006:621.

72. White, Bland, Sharp, and Morstein Marx 1935:256, 208.

73. White, Bland, Sharp, and Morstein Marx 1935:256.

74. Clark 2008:632.

75. White, Bland, Sharp, and Morstein Marx 1935:266 and 266n.17.

76. Quoted in Goetz 2000:71.

77. See, for example, Cole 1952.

78. Goetz 2000:71.

79. Goetz 2000:71.

80. Goetz 2000:81–83.

81. White, Bland, Sharp, and Morstein Marx 1935:84–85; see also Silberman 1993:120–156.
82. See, for example, Church 1981: chap. 9.
83. Fischer and Lundgreen 1975:508–509; White, Bland, Sharp, and Morstein Marx 1935:100–101.
84. A government circular quoted in White, Bland, Sharp, and Morstein Marx 1935:101.
85. White, Bland, Sharp, and Morstein Marx 1935:98–99; Church 1981:309.
86. White, Bland, Sharp, and Morstein Marx 1935:99.
87. See, for examples, Koreman 2000.
88. Quoted in Sulieman 1974:46.
89. It was renamed the Institut d'Études Politiques.
90. Sulieman 1974:42.
91. Quoted in Sulieman 1974:51.
92. For a discussion, see Olsen 2005.
93. See especially Olsen 2005.
94. The term is used in reference to France in Church 1981:315.
95. For a review of the characteristics of civil service systems and how they were questioned, see Peters 1996: chap. 1.
96. Hennessy 1989:195.
97. Hennessy 1989:199–208.
98. Thompson 2000:199–202; Hennessy 1989:628–629.
99. The 1979 Rayner Scrutinies and the 1983 Financial Management Initiative, both introduced under the Thatcher administration, encountered resistance from Treasury. Thompson 2000:199–201. On the Next Steps initiative, see Gualmini 2007:78–79.
100. Gualmini 2007:88. See also Fry 2000:29–31.
101. Gualmini 2007:84.
102. Gualmini 2007:83.
103. See, for examples, Thompson and Ingraham 1996; Osborne and Gaebler 1992.
104. White, Bland, Sharp, and Morstein Marx 1935:154.
105. Meininger 2000:192–193; see also Rouban 1997.
106. Meininger 2000:207–209.
107. Goetz 2000:84.
108. Goetz 2000:64.
109. Among other values, the traditional principles emphasize commitment to the state, educational qualifications for entry and seniority for promotion, life tenure, professionalism, and neutrality. See Goetz 2000:64–65.
110. Goetz 2000:76–77.
111. Goetz 2000:84.
112. Goetz 2000:86–87;see also Jann 1997.
113. Parrado Díez 2000:256;see also Alba 1997; Gallego 2003.

114. Gualmini 2007:79; see also Torres and Pina 2004.
115. Morstein Marx 1957:65; Muramatsu and Pempel 1995:178.
116. Pempel 1992:24; Shumpei 1984.

4. Latin America

1. Hanson 1974:199.
2. See, for examples, Chaudhry, Reid, and Malik 1994; Evans and Rausch 1999; Ramió and Salvador 2008.
3. Echebarría 2006:vii. Author's translation.
4. Iacoviello 2006:571–572. Much of the difference can be accounted for by regional and local governments that assume more responsibilities than those in Uruguay and the Dominican Republic.
5. Iacoviello 2006:571–572.
6. Longo 2006a:582.
7. Iacoviello 2006:571–572; Reid and Scott 1994.
8. See especially Ruffing-Hilliard 2001:593.
9. For example, the first civil service law in Cuba was enacted in 1909, under U.S. occupation, and similar rules were introduced in the Dominican Republic in 1917, under similar circumstances of occupation. See Kearney 1986.
10. Ruffing-Hilliard (2001:596–597) traced the international influences of several of these reforms, arguing that they demonstrate "point-source diffusion" as they involved international agencies and their consultants writing legislation.
11. Iacoviello 2006:543n.5.
12. See Echebarría 2006; Iacoviello 2006; and Longo 2006a and 2006b. For a summary of the findings, see Iacoviello and Zuvanic 2006a. The report focuses on seven "subsystems" of public sector management—human resource planning, the organization of work, employment, performance, compensation, management of development (training), and human and social relations. It presents five indices related to efficiency, merit, structural consistency, functional capacity, and integrative capacity.
13. Information in this paragraph is taken from Iacoviello and Zuvanic 2006a:53, based on a typology developed by Oszlak 2003. Countries in each category were designated based on conditions existing in 2004.
14. Iacoviello and Zuvanic (2006a:54) do not list Mexico in their categories. I have added it, based on my research.
15. Ruffing-Hilliard 2001:600.
16. Longo 2006b:605.
17. Longo 2006b:606.
18. During those five years, there was no law in place to regulate the civil service. Iacoviello 2006:545.

19. Iacoviello 2006:545.

20. Iacoviello 2006:544.

21. Iacoviello 2006:545–546.

22. Iacoviello 2006:542. Author's translation.

23. See, for examples, decentralization reforms in Argentina, Venezuela, and Bolivia in Grindle 2000.

24. See, for examples, Grindle 1996; 2004; Dominguez 1997; Schneider 1991.

25. Gamarra 1994.

5. Roots and Branches

1. See Socolow 1987 for a good history of the colonial period and the Bourbon reforms. See also Burkholder and Chandler 1972; Haring 1947; Hanson 1974.

2. Socolow 1987; Barbier 1980; Burkholder and Chandler 1972; and Phelan 1967 provide useful chronicles of this system and of its efficiencies and inefficiencies.

3. Parry 1953; Burkholder and Chandler 1972.

4. Burkholder and Chandler 1972:187; see also Hanson 1974; Phelan 1967.

5. Swart (1989:94) makes the interesting observation that when elderly public officials were allowed to sell their positions, they were acquiring a pension for old age.

6. Burkholder and Chandler 1972; Hanson 1974.

7. In an auction of public posts in Chile in the mid-eighteenth century, however, there is evidence that even in this process, purchases were allocated to preselected candidates. Barbier 1980:56.

8. Burkholder and Chandler 1972:201.

9. Stein and Stein 1970:74.

10. See Haring 1947: chap. 6. See also Arnold 1988.

11. Socolow 1987. Interestingly, however, concerns about the merit of the individual that were used to justify an initial patronage appointment did not constrain the subsequent inheritance or transfer of the position to a relative.

12. Sokolow 1987.

13. Socolow 1987:52.

14. Lambert 1969:167.

15. See, for example, Uricoechea 1980:13–14.

16. Manchester 1972:82.

17. Lambert 1969:170.

18. See McCreery 2002.

19. Graham 1968:20; see also McCreery 2002.

20. Nabuco 1977:106.

21. See Centeno 2002.
22. Chile's centralized state was consolidated, in part, through presidential appointments of all regional officials from the 1830s. See Mallon 2002:43.
23. See, for examples, Valenzuela 1978; Chalmers 1977:413.
24. See, for example, Pang 1973.
25. See, for examples, Hirschman 1981; Vernon 1963; Chalmers 1977; Schneider 1991; Cleaves 1974.
26. See, for example, Oquist 1980.
27. See, for example, Mallon 2002.
28. This is what Thomas Flory described as mechanisms less related to the central importance of a monarch than to the "prosaic contours of imperial governance and the local integrative capabilities of imperial institutions." Flory 1975:665.
29. For an exploration of the micro-foundations of political patronage in Brazil, and its role in drawing local, regional, and federal state together, see Greenfield 1977. For a detailed analysis of the system as it operated in the nineteenth century, see Graham 1990. For its translation into military and democratic governments in the twentieth century, see Hagopian 1996.
30. See especially Uricoechea 1980:13–16.
31. Uricoechea 1980:18.
32. Uricoechea 1980:22. For the similarities to Japan, see Chapter 1.
33. Prior to the arrival of the monarchy, the viceroy in Rio had a staff of seven; by 1811, there were over one thousand in the royal court and administration. Manchester 1972:79–80. For a brief review of the history of Portuguese public administration and modern efforts to reform it, see Corte-Real 2008.
34. Manchester 1977:82.
35. Lambert 1969:169–170.
36. See especially Graham 1990.
37. Uricoechea 1980:58–59; Siegel 1978:15.
38. Flory 1975:677; Graham 1990:41; Uricoechea 1980: 64–75.
39. See especially Flory 1975.
40. On the issue of federalism in Brazil, see Martin 1938.
41. Graham 1990:55.
42. Graham 1990:180.
43. Graham 1990:181.
44. Lambert 1969:171. The constitution of 1891 was inspired in part by the federal organization of the United States. Martin 1938:156.
45. Graham 1990:232.
46. Maybury-Lewis 1968:161, quoted in Hagopian 1996:14.
47. Hagopian 1996.
48. Siegel 1978:42n.16.

49. Geddes 1994:44; see also Siegel 1978:41–47.
50. See Levine 1998.
51. Oszlak 1997:47. Author's translation. See also Malamud 1995.
52. Oszlak 1997:63–64.
53. Oszlak 1997:124, 126.
54. Oszlak 1997:127. Only in the second half of the nineteenth century, then, did provincial government begin to lose the right to "raise military forces, issue currency, decree states of siege, administer justice in certain jurisdictions or instances, or collect certain taxes." Oszlak 1997:165.
55. Oszlak 1997:126. Author's translation.
56. Oszlak 1997:230.
57. See for a discussion Oszlak 1997: chap. 4.
58. See Walter 1985 for examples of *caudillismo* in the first half of the nineteenth century.
59. For an extensive history of the incorporation of workers and their unions into political relevance in Argentina, see Collier and Collier 1991.
60. Interview, July 8, 2008.
61. Iacoviello and Rodríguez-Gustá 2006b:95.
62. Benton 2002:26, 28. About 5 percent were confidence employees at high levels.
63. The oldest of these systems was the foreign service, which introduced a competitive recruitment process in 1922.
64. Arellano Gault 2006:217. Author's translation.
65. For a good description of the way the traditional system worked, see Smith 1979; Grindle 1977.
66. Arellano Gault 2006:219. Author's translation.
67. Many students of Mexican politics referred to the "pendulum" of alternating presidential policy agendas enabled through the six-year rotation in office—a president slightly to the left of the center of the PRI would be followed by one slightly to the right, and so on.
68. Grimes and Simmons 1969.
69. See Grimes and Simmons 1969; Centeno 1994.
70. Arrelano Gault 2006:220. Author's translation.
71. Rehren 2000:131–132; see also Valenzuela 1977.
72. See Silva 1994;Urzúa Valenzuela and García Barzelatto 1971
73. Silva 1994:283.
74. Silva 1994:284.
75. See Silva 1994, and especially 295:n.8.
76. Silva 1994:292.
77. Rehren 2000:149.
78. Parrish 1973:242.
79. Interview, Alfredo Rehren, July 2, 2008.
80. Parrish 1973:244.

81. Interview, June 3, 2008.
82. Rehren 2000:156. A useful analysis of how bureaucratic departments and ministries worked within the political system prior to the military dictatorship is found in Cleaves 1974.
83. Remmer 1991:132.
84. Remmer 1991:134–135, 142. Pinochet is reported to have said, "Not a leaf moves in this country if I am not moving it!" Quoted in Remmer 1991:138.
85. Giraldo 1997:257. See especially Puryear 1994.
86. Interview, June 30, 2008.

6. Crafting Reform

1. Gaetani and Heredia 2002:7.
2. Siegel 1966:70–72.
3. Siegel 1978:44–45.
4. Siegel 1978:45.
5. Lambert 1969:173.
6. Siegel 1978:49–50.
7. Quoted in Levine 1998:55.
8. A decree law under the *Estado Novo* had the status of a piece of legislation legitimized by congressional vote, but was issued by the executive.
9. Siegel 1966:47.
10. Siegel 1978:61.
11. Siegel 1978:62.
12. Geddes 1994:53.
13. Siegel 1978:68–69.
14. Geddes 1994:61–69.
15. Siegel 1978:64–69. The leadership of the DASP at the time assumed this burden, in part out of loyalty to Vargas and his broader mission.
16. Letter of December 20, 1944, quoted in Levine 1998:155.
17. Siegel 1966:48.
18. Siegel 1978:77.
19. Iacoviello and Tommasi 2002:11.
20. Iacoviello and Zuvanic 2006a:74.
21. Iacoviello and Zuvanic 2006a:74.
22. Established under the first democratic government of Raúl Alfonsín, these high-level civil servants were later offered a retirement package that diminished their ranks. In the late 2000s, about 120 government administrators existed. Interview, July 6, 2009. See also Iacoviello and Tommasi 2002:7.
23. Ferraro 2006:172.
24. Levitsky 2007 presents an account of the transformation of the labor-based Peronist Party into a more multiclass facilitator of Menem's

neoliberal policies in the 1990s. The use of patronage to fill union leadership positions was an important aspect of this change, as was the ability to develop clientelist networks for electoral competitions.

25. Corrales 1997.
26. On the privatization process, see Madrid 2003:98–99.
27. See, for example, Madrid 2003: chap. 4.
28. Corrales 1997:70. The only Latin American country to privatize more companies was Mexico, which began to privatize the banks that had been seized by the government in 1982. Mexico's experience with privatization was largely concluded by 1994 also.
29. Acuña 1994:46.
30. Madrid 2003:122.
31. For a detailed discussion of the adaptability of the Peronist Party to dramatic policy changes, see Levitsky 2007.
32. Interviews, July 7, 2008.
33. Interview, July 8, 2008.
34. Bonifacio 1995:6.
35. Approximately 40 percent of the total number of national government personnel were part of the collective contract. Iacoviello and Tommasi 2002:10.
36. SINAPA was created through degree 993/91.
37. See Grindle 2007: chap. 3.
38. Méndez 2008:10. My account of the process of reform in Mexico closely follows Méndez 2008. José Luis Méndez was an active participant in the reform group as an academic and later as a manager of the new system. An extensive description of the law and its regulations is found in Iacoviello, Rodriguez-Gustá, and Cruz Orozco 2006.
39. During the 1990s, decentralization initiatives decreased the percentage of public sector employees at the national level from 50 percent of the total to 29 percent. Benton 2002:20.
40. Méndez 2008:10.
41. See Martínez Puón 2005 for a discussion of the characteristics of a civil service this group assessed and debated. See also Arellano Gault 2006.
42. Interview, April 18, 2008.
43. The PRI had 208 seats, 43 short of a majority, while the PAN had 207, and the next most important political party, the PRD, had 53.
44. Méndez 2008:11.
45. Herrera Macías 2008:25. Author's translation.See also Cejudo 2003.
46. The embassies of the United States and Canada, the British Council, and U.S. AID were supporters of this initiative. Among the international experts who spoke in favor of the need for a career civil service were David Osborne, representatives of the United Nations, the Inter-American Development Bank, OECD, and the World Bank. Academics from CIDE, UNAM, FLACSO, the Colegio de México, and ITAM—all important

universities in Mexico, were joined by officials representing the civil service in the United States, Canada, Spain, Great Britain, and France. Finally, the congressional representatives of the three main political parties in Mexico—the PRI, the PAN, and the PRD—spoke in favor of the reform. See Aguilar 2003 for the presentations at the conference.

47. Méndez 2008:11; Arellano Gault 2006:226–229.
48. Méndez 2008:11–12.
49. Méndez 2008:12.
50. Interview, April 18, 2008.
51. Subsequent regulations drawn up in the executive branch also provided some loopholes. Each ministry, for example, was allowed to determine which positions should be exempt from the new system. In addition, ministers and deputy ministers would have a reserve of positions for "free designation" that would allow them to put together teams of their people while they were in office.
52. Interview, April 18, 2008.
53. Méndez 2008:19.
54. Méndez 2008:13. Performance reviews, horizontal entry, and advancement through competition were part of the new system. See also Arellano Gault 2006:224–233 and Martínez Puón 2005:317–320 for a discussion of this theme in Mexico. See also Martínez Puón 2005 for a comparative analysis of the underpinnings of the new Mexican system.
55. Parrish 1973:242.
56. See for an example Zaltsman 2009.
57. Rehren 2000:161.
58. http://www1.worldbank.org/publicsector/civilservice/rsChile.pdf.
59. Interview, July 3, 2008.
60. Interview, July 3, 2009.
61. Interview, June 30, 2008.
62. Ramírez Alujas 2008:54.
63. *Sobresueldos* were so named because they were above *(sobre)* regular salaries *(sueldos)* but also because the cash was delivered in envelopes *(sobres)*.
64. Rehren 2008:7–8.
65. Rehren 2008:5–6.
66. Interview, July 1, 2008.
67. Interview, July 4, 2008.
68. Interview, July 3, 2008.
69. Interview, June 30, 2008.

7. Ambiguous Futures

1. The literature on policy implementation in developing countries is extensive. For early discussions of the politics that affect implementation processes, see Grindle 1980; Bardach 1977; Pressman and Wildavsky 1973.

2. In 1997, the number was 70,705. Ministério do Planejamento 2010:97. Moreover, the number of patronage appointments available to governors, senators, deputies, party leaders, mayors, and other influential politicians at state and local levels easily surpassed central government numbers. At these levels, patronage appointments were extremely important to help politicians accumulate the resources needed for election campaigns. See Samuels 2002.

3. Lambert 1969:176.

4. Siegel 1978:79.

5. See, in particular, Siegel 1978: chap. 5.

6. Siegel 1978:99.

7. Lambert 1969:180.

8. Siegel 1966:49; 1978:93–94.

9. Siegel 1978:106–107.

10. Siegel 1966:50.

11. Siegel 1978:147.

12. Siegel 1978:120.

13. Siegel 1978: chap. 6.

14. Geddes 1994:58.

15. Geddes 1994:59–60.

16. Siegel 1966:45.

17. Hagopian 1996:2, chap. 3.

18. O'Donnell 1973; Hagopian 1996:107–108.

19. Hagopian 1996:104.

20. Hagopian 1996:109–110.

21. Lambert 1969:186–187.

22. Hagopian 1996: chap. 4; see also Schneider 1991:238–242.

23. Hagopian 1996:151–152. Cammarck 1982.

24. Cardoso, *Veja*, June 29, 1988, quoted in Hagopian 1996:xxi.

25. Schneider 1991:6.

26. Ministério do Planejamento 2010:29–30.

27. Gaetani and Heredia 2002:6.

28. See, for example, Bresser-Pereira 2003:95.

29. According to one participant in later reform initiatives, "The basic assessment of Brazil's situation was clear to me from the beginning: the 1988 constitutional attempt to restore or, rather, fully establish classical bureaucratic public administration had been a disaster. With the excuse that the biggest enemy was clientelism, public administration was made rigid and inefficient. The country's bureaucracy lacked a system of incentives and punishments and was overly constrained by redundant regulations and strict procedures. Privileges of all sorts were created that benefited bureaucrats who excelled in rent-seeking at this time. In a country like Brazil, which faced a deep crisis of the state but whose bureaucracy had actually been able to adopt a successful managerial

strategy to promote economic growth some years before, this backward movement toward a classical bureaucratic system meant a serious reversal, resulting in unsustainable increases in personnel costs, deterioration of public services, and a demoralized civil service. . . . Bureaucratization and rent-seeking mixed together during the first five years of the new democratic government, and this had terrible consequences for the prestige of a civil service that had contributed very positively so far to the spirit of the country." Bresser-Pereira 2003:95.

30. See especially Bresser-Pereira 2003; Gaetani and Heredia 2002.
31. On the contents of the reform, see Bresser-Pereira 2003.
32. Bresser-Pereira 2003:98.
33. Gaetani and Heredia 2002:2.
34. Bresser-Pereira 2003:94.
35. Gaetani and Heredia 2002:14.
36. Gaetani and Heredia 2002:20.
37. Gaetani and Heredia 2002:16, 18.
38. Bresser-Pereira 2003:95, 96.
39. Bresser-Pereira 2003:102–103.
40. Bresser-Pereira 2003:96.
41. Bresser-Pereira 2003:99.
42. Bresser-Pereira 2003:105.
43. Gaetani and Heredia 2002:3.
44. Iacoviello and Rodríguez-Gustá 2006a:123.
45. Gaetani and Heredia 2002:22.
46. Gaetani and Heredia 2002:23.
47. Gaetani and Heredia 2002:30. In Brazil and several other countries, some scholars concluded that the new public management reforms had had little impact. See Matías-Pereira 2008.
48. Iacoviello and and Rodríguez-Gustá 2006a:132. Schneider summarized the system as it worked at high levels. "Informal exchange relations permeate the Brazilian bureaucracy. Personal favors are necessary to keep the administrative machinery functioning. They are also important in building one's network of contacts (and hence future career opportunities) and in forging new policy alliances. The appointment exchange rests on the offer of the power and prestige of a top appointment in return for loyalty, competence, and results." Schneider 1991:77.
49. See particularly Hagopian, Gerrason, and Moraes 2009.
50. Ferraro 2006:173.
51. Iacoviello and Tommasi 2002:3.
52. Ferraro 2004:6; Iacoviello and Tommasi 2002:3. Elsewhere, Iacoviello and Zuvanic (2006a:86) give 163,096 as the total number of civilian public officials in the central government in 2003. See Table 4.1.
53. Iacoviello and Tommasi 2002:45
54. Ferraro 2006:171.

55. Iacoviello and Tommasi 2002:44.
56. Ferrero 2006:166.
57. See particularly Ferraro 2004:6–7.
58. Ferraro 2006:167.
59. Iacoviello and Zuvanic 2006a:82.
60. Ferraro 2006:171.
61. Iacoviello and Tommasi 2002:75–76.
62. In Iacoviello and Tommasi 2002:76.
63. UPCN is the Unión del Personal Civil de la Nación, the principal public sector union in Argentina. See Chapter 6.
64. Interview, July 8, 2008.
65. Ferraro 2004:9.
66. For electoral payoff to patronage appointments and their decline, see Calvo and Murillo 2004.
67. Interview, July 7, 2008.
68. Interview, July 8, 2008; for a broader argument, see Calvo and Murillo 2004.
69. Iacoviello and Tommasi 2002:3.
70. Iacoviello and Tommasi 2002:4
71. Interview, July 7, 2008.
72. Interview, July 7, 2008.
73. Interview, July 7, 2008.
74. Méndez 2008:15. As indicated in Chapter 7, SPC is the Servicio Profesional de Carerra, the Professional Career Service created through legislation in 2003.
75. CIDE 2007:Annex 2:12.
76. Méndez 2008:17.
77. Martínez Puón 2005:321. Author's translation.
78. Interview, April 18, 2008.
79. CIDE 2007:29.
80. Interview, April 18, 2008.
81. See Merino 2006 for the studies undertaken.
82. See CIDE 2007 for the full report. See Dussauge 2011 for a discussion of the sources of implementation problems.
83. Merino 2006:18–19.
84. CIDE 2007:37.
85. See Dussauge 2011:59.
86. Interview, November 23, 2009.
87. Interview, April 18, 2008.
88. Interview, April 18, 2008.
89. Auditoría Superior de la Federación 2006.
90. Cited in CIDE 2007:29.
91. See Secretariá de la Función Publica.
92. Interview, April 18, 2008.

93. Dussauge 2011:59.
94. Herrera Macías 2003:29.
95. Méndez 2009.
96. Interview, April 18, 2008; Dussauge 2011 puts more emphasis on issues related to the design, resources, and coordination of the new system.
97. Ramírez Alujas 2008:69; Waissbluth 2010.
98. Costa and Waissbluth 2007:3.
99. Ramírez Alujas 2008:53.
100. Costa and Waissbluth 2007:20.
101. Waissbluth 2010. Author's translation.
102. Interview, July 2, 2008.
103. Interview, July 3, 2008.
104. Costa and Waissbluth 2007:13; Waissbluth 2010.
105. Waissbluth 2010.
106. Interview, July 2, 2008.
107. Waissbluth 2010.
108. See, for example, *LitoralPress*, March 10, 2010:18; March 25, 2010:25; April 23, 2010:42; April 29, 2010:3, 11; May 2, 2010:3; May 9, 2010:4.
109. Waissbluth 2010.

Conclusion

1. See introduction for a discussion.
2. See Andrews 2010 for a discussion of this theme.
3. I am grateful to Judith Tendler, who suggested the allusion and drew my attention to disjunctures in the literature on institutional change.
4. See introduction for a discussion.
5. The argument presented by Shefter 1977 is partially relevant here. See introduction for a discussion of his approach.
6. See especially Barzelay 2003 on this point.
7. Evans 1995:3.
8. Quoting Simon Marks, PBS (Public Broadcasting Service) *Newshour*, June 9, 2008, http://www.pbs.org/newshour/bb/latin_america/jan-une08/brazil_06-09.html, accessed May 27, 2010.
9. *Global Post*, March 2, 2009, http://globalpost.com/dispatch/brazil/090302/adventures-brazilian-bureaucracy, accessed May 27, 2010.
10. Elma Lia Nascimento, "Red Tape Addiction," http://www.brazzil.com/pages/cvrnov96.htm, accessed May 27, 2010.
11. See http://www.brazil.com/pages/cvrnov96.htm, accessed May 27, 2010.
12. Weyland 2000:53.
13. Iacoviello and Rodríguez-Gustá 2006a:119.
14. Iacoviello and Rodríguez-Gustá 2006a:123. At the level of managers, three-quarters have university educations.
15. Schneider 1991.

Bibliography

Acuña, Carlos H. 1994. "Politics and Economics in the Argentina of the Nineties (Or, Why the Future No Longer Is What It Used to Be)," in William C. Smith, Carlos H. Acuña, and Eduardo A. Gamarra, eds., *Democracy, Markets, and Structural Reform in Latin America*. New Brunswick, NJ: Transaction Publishers, 31–73.

Aguilar, Luis F. ed. 2003. *Profesionalización del servicio público en México*. Mexico, DF: Gárgola Ediciones.

Alba, Carlos. 1997. "Modernising Spanish Public Administration: Old Inertias and New Challenges," in Walter J. M. Kickert, ed., *Public Management and Administrative Reform in Western Europe*. Cheltenham, UK: Edward Elgar, 177–195.

Alvarez Junco, José, and Adrian Shubert, eds. 2000. *Spanish History since 1808*. London: Hodder Education.

Andrews, Matthew. 2010. "Good Government Means Different Things in Different Countries." *Governance* 23, no. 1 (January): 7–35.

Arellano Gault, David. 2006. "Los desafíos de una gestión pública meritocrática," in Mauricio Merino, ed., *Los desafíos del servicio professional de carrera en México*. Mexico: CIDE and Secretaría de la Función Pública, 217–244.

Armstrong, John A. 1973. *The European Administrative Elite*. Princeton, NJ: Princeton University Press.

Arnold, Linda. 1988. *Bureaucracy and Bureaucrats in Mexico City, 1742–1835*. Tucson: University of Arizona Press.

Auditoría Superior de la Federación. 2006. *Informe sobre la fiscalización de los Servicios Civiles de Carrera en el Estado Federal Mexicano 2000–2006*. Mexico City: Cámara de Diputados.

Baez, Bien, and Michel Y. Abolafia. 2002. "Bureaucratic Entrepreneurship and Institutional Change: A Sense-Making Approach." *Journal of Public Administration Research and Theory* 12, no. 4:525–552.

Barbier, Jacques A. 1980. *Reform and Politics in Bourbon Chile, 1755–1796*. Ottawa: University of Ottawa Press.

Bardach, Eugene. 1977. *The Implementation Game.* Cambridge, MA: MIT Press.

Barzelay, Michael. 1992. *Breaking Through Bureaucracy: A New Vision for Managing in Government.* Berkeley: University of California Press.

———. 2003. "Introduction: The Process Dynamics of Public Management Policymaking." *International Public Management Journal* 6, no. 3:251–281.

Barzelay, Michael, and Natascha Füchtner. 2003. "Explaining Public Management Policy Change: Germany in Comparative Perspective." *Journal of Comparative Policy Analysis: Research and Practice* 5:7–27.

Barzelay, Michael, and Raquel Gallego. 2006. "From 'New Institutionalism' to 'Institutional Processualism': Advancing Knowledge about Public Management Policy Change." *Governance* 19, no. 4:531–557.

Batley, Richard, and George Larbi. 2004. *The Changing Role of Government: The Reform of Public Service in Developing Countries.* New York: Palgrave Macmillan.

Bayley, David H. 1975. "The Police and Political Development in Europe," in Charles Tilly, ed., *The Formation of National States in Western Europe.* Princeton, NJ: Princeton University Press, 328–379.

Behrens, C. B. A. 1985. *Society, Government, and the Enlightenment: The Experiences of Eighteenth-Century France and Prussia.* New York: Harper & Row.

Benton, Allyson Lucinda. 2002. "Diagnóstico institucional del sistema de servicio civil de México." InterAmerican Development Bank, Regional Policy Dialogue. Typescript.

Bloch, Marc. 1961. *Feudal Society,* Vol. 1. Chicago: University of Chicago Press.

Bonifacio, José Alberto. 1995. "La experiencia argentina en materia de profesionalización de la función pública y la capacitación." *Reforma y Democracia* 4 (July): 1–13.

Bresser-Pereira, Luiz Carlos. 2003. "The 1995 Public Management Reform in Brazil: Reflections of a Reformer." In Ben Ross Schneider and Blanca Heredia, eds., *Reinventing Leviathan: The Politics of Administrative Reform in Developing Countries.* Coral Gables, FL: North-South Center Press.

Burkholder, M. A., and D. S. Chandler. 1972. "Creole Appointments and the Sate of Audiencia Positions in the Spanish Empire under the Early Bourbons, 1701–1750. *Journal of Latin American Studies* 4, no. 2 (November): 187–206.

Callahan, William J. 2000. "Church and State, 1808–1874," in José Alvarez Junco and Adrian Shubert, eds., *Spanish History since 1808.* London: Hodder Education, 48–63.

Calvo, Ernesto, and Maria Victoria Murillo. 2004. "Who Delivers? Partisan Clients in the Argentine Electoral Market." *American Journal of Political Science* 48, no. 4 (October): 742–757.

Cammack, Paul. 1982. "Clientelism and Military Government in Brazil," in Christopher Clapham, ed., *Private Patronage and Public Power: Political Clientelism in the Modern State.* Basingstoke, UK: Palgrave Macmillan, 53–75.

Carpenter, Daniel P. 2001. *The Forging of Bureaucratic Autonomy: Reputations, Networks, and Policy Innovation in Executive Agencies, 1862–1928.* Princeton, NJ: Princeton University Press.

Carr, Ramond. *Modern Spain 1875–1980.* Oxford: Oxford University Press.

Cejudo, Guillermo M. 2003. "Public Management Policy Change in Mexico, 1982–2000." *International Public Management Journal* 6, no. 3:309–325.

Centeno, Miguel Angel. 1994. *Democracy within Reason.* University Park: Penn State University Press.

———. 2002. "The Centre Did Not Hold: War in Latin America and the Monopolisation of Violence," in James Dunkerley, ed., *Studies in the Formation of the Nation State in Latin America.* London: Institute of Latin American Studies, 54–76.

Chalmers, Douglas A. 1977. "Parties and Society in Latin America," in Steffen W. Schmidt, James C. Scott, Carl Landé, and Laura Guasti, eds., *Friends, Followers, and Factions: A Reader in Political Clientelism.* Berkeley: University of California Press, 401–421.

Chang, Ha-Joon. 2002. *Kicking Away the Ladder: Development Strategy in Historical Perspective.* London: Anthem Press.

Chaudhry, Shahid Amjad, Gary James Reid, and Waleed Haider Malik, eds., *Civil Service Reform in Latin America and the Caribbean: Proceedings of a Conference.* Washington, DC: World Bank.

Church, Clive H. 1981. *Revolution and Red Tape: The French Ministerial Bureaucracy, 1770–1850.* Oxford: Clarendon Press.

CIDE (Centro de Investigación y Docencia Económicas). 2007. "Asesoría para la reforma del Servicio Profesional de Carrera en la administración pública federal." Typescript.

Clark, Christopher. 2006. *Iron Kingdom: The Rise and Downfall of Prussia, 1600–1947.* Cambridge, MA: Harvard University Press.

Cleaves, Peter S. 1974. *Bureaucratic Politics and Administration in Chile.* Berkeley: University of California Press.

Cole, Taylor. 1952. "The Democratization of the German Civil Service." *Journal of Politics* 14, no. 1 (February): 3–18.

Collier, Ruth Berins, and David Collier. 1991. *Shaping the Political Arena.* Princeton, NJ: Princeton University Press.

Corrales, Javier. 1997. "Why Argentines Followed Cavallo: A Technopol between Democracy and Economic Reform," in Jorge I. Dominguez, ed., *Technopols: Freeing Politics and Markets in Latin America in the 1990s.* University Park: Penn State University Press, 49–93.

Corte-Real, Isabel. 2008. "Public Management Reform in Portugal: Successes and Failures." *International Journal of Public Sector Management* 21, no. 2:205–229.

Costa, Rosanna, and Mario Waissbluth. 2007. "Tres años de Alta Dirección Pública en Chile: Balance y perspectivas." University of Chile: Department of Industrial Engineering, Management Center Working Document No. 94.

Cruz, Jesús. 2000. "The Moderate Ascendancy, 1843–1868," in José Alvarez Junco and Adrian Shubert, eds., *Spanish History since 1808*. London: Hodder Education, 33–47.

Cunningham, Charles Henry. 1919. *The Audiencia in the Spanish Colonies as Illustrated by the Audiencia of Manila (1583–1800)*. Berkeley: University of California Press.

Daly, Gavin. 2001. *Inside Napoleonic France: State and Society in Rouen, 1800–1815*. Aldershot, UK: Ashgate.

Demmers, Jolle, Alex E. Fernández Jilberto, and Barbara Hogenboom, eds. 2004. *Good Governance in the Era of Global Neoliberalism: Conflict and Depolitisation in Latin America, Eastern Europe, Asia and Africa*. London: Routledge.

Domínguez, Jorge I. 1997. *Technopols: Freeing Politics and Markets in the 1980s*. University Park: Penn State University Press.

Dowling, Julian. 2007. "The Merit of Civil Service Reform." *Business Chile* (March), no. 249. http://www.businesschile.cl/portada.php?w=old&id=409&lan=en.

Doyle, William. 1989. The *Oxford History of the French Revolution*. Oxford: Oxford University Press.

Dussauge, Mauricio. 2011. "The Challenges of Implementing Merit-Based Personnel Policies in Latin America: Mexico's Civil Service Reform Experience." *Journal of Comparative Policy Analysis* 13, no. 1 (February): 51–73.

Echebarría, Koldo. 2006. *Informe sobre la situación del servicio civil en América Latina*. Washington, DC: Inter-American Development Bank.

Echebarría, Koldo, and Juan Carlos Cortázar. 2007. "Public Administration and Public Employment Reform in Latin America," in Eduardo Lora, ed., *The State of State Reform in Latin America*. Stanford, CA: Stanford University Press, 123–155.

Eichbaum, Chris, and Richard Shaw, eds. 2010. *Partisan Appointees and Public Servants*. Northampton, MA: Edward Elgar.

Elliot, John H. 1990 (third edition). *Imperial Spain: 1469–1716*. London: Penguin Books.

Erie, Steven. 1988. *Rainbow's End: Irish-Americans and the Dilemmas of Urban Machine Politics, 1840–1985*. Berkeley: University of California Press.

Ertman, Thomas. 1997. *Birth of the Leviathan: Building States and Regimes in Medieval and Early Modern Europe*. Cambridge: Cambridge University Press.

Evans, Peter. 1995. *Embedded Autonomy: States and Industrial Transformation*. Princeton, NJ: Princeton University Press.

Evans, Peter, and James E. Rauch. 1999. "Bureaucracy and Growth: A Cross-National Analysis of the Effects of 'Weberian' State Structures on Economic Growth." *American Sociological Review* 64 (October): 748–765.

Ferraro, Agustín E. 2006. "Una idea muy precaria: El nuevo servicio civil y los viejos designados políticos en Argentina." *Latin American Research Review* 41, no. 2 (June): 165–182.

Fischer, Wolfram, and Peter Lundgreen. 1975. "The Recruitment and Training of Administrative and Technical Personnel," in Charles Tilly, ed., *The Formation of National States in Western Europe.* Princeton, NJ: Princeton University Press, 456–601.

Fish, Carl Russell. 1905. *The Civil Service and the Patronage.* New York: Longmans, Green, and Co.

Flory, Thomas. 1975. "Judicial Politics in Nineteenth-Century Brazil." *Hispanic American Historical Review* 55, no. 4 (November): 664–692.

Foster, George M. 1961. "The Dyadic Contract: A Model for the Social Structure of a Mexican Peasant Village." *American Anthropologist* 63, no. 6 (December): 1173–1192.

Foster, George M. 1967. *Tzintzuntzan: Mexican Peasants in a Changing World.* Boston: Little Brown.

Freedman, Anne. 1994. *Patronage: An American Tradition.* Chicago: Nelson-Hall.

Fry, Geoffrey K. 2000. "The British Civil Service System," in Hans A. G. M. Bekke and Frits M. van der Meer, eds., *Civil Service Systems in Western Europe.* Cheltenham, UK: Edward Elgar, 12–35.

Gaetani, Francisco, and Blanca Heredia. 2002. "The Political Economy of Civil Service Reform in Brazil: The Cardoso Years." Prepared for the Red de Gestión y Transparencia del Diálogo Regional de Política del Banco Interamericano de Desarrollo, typescript.

Gallego, Raquel. 2003. "Public Management Policymaking in Spain, 1982–1996: Policy Entrepreneurship and (In)Opportunity Windows." *International Public Management Journal* 6, no. 3:283–307.

Gamarra, Eduardo. 1994. "Crafting Political Support for Stabilization: Political Pacts and the New Economic Policy in Bolivia," in William C. Smith, Carlos H. Acuña, and Eduardo A. Gamarra, eds., *Democracy, Markets, and Structural Reform in Latin America.* New Brunswick, NJ: Transaction Publishers, 105–127.

Geddes, Barbara. 1994. *Politician's Dilemma: Building State Capacity in Latin America.* Berkeley: University of California Press.

Gillis, John R. 1971. *The Prussian Bureaucracy in Crisis, 1840–1860: Origins of an Administrative Ethos.* Stanford, CA: Stanford University Press.

Giraldo, Jeanne Kinney. 1997. "Development and Democracy in Chile: Finance Minister Alejandro Foxley and the Concertación's Project for the 1990s," in Jorge I. Dominguez, ed., *Technopols: Freeing Politics and Markets in Latin America in the 1990s.* University Park: Penn State University Press, 229–275.

Goetz, Klaus H. 2000. "The Development and Current Features of the German Civil Service System," in Hans A. G. M. Bekke and Frits M. van der Meer, eds., *Civil Service Systems in Western Europe.* Cheltenham, UK: Edward Elgar, 61–91.

Gordon, Andrew. 2009. *A Modern History of Japan: From Tokugawa Times to the Present.* New York: Oxford University Press.

Graham, Lawrence. 1968. *Civil Service Reform in Brazil: Principles versus Practice.* Austin: University of Texas Press.

Graham, Richard. 1990. *Patronage and Politics in Nineteenth-Century Brazil.* Stanford, CA: Stanford University Press.

Greenfield, Sidney M. 1977. "Patronage, Politics, and the Articulation of Local Community and National Society in Pre-1968 Brazil." *Journal of Interamerican Studies and World Affairs* 19, no. 2 (May): 139–172.

Griffith, Wyn. 1954. *The British Civil Service, 1854–1954.* London: Her Majesty's Stationery Office.

Grimes, C. E., and Charles E. P. Simmons. 1969. "Bureaucracy and Political Control in Mexico: Towards an Assessment. *Public Administration Review* 29, no. 1 (January–February): 72–79.

Grindle, Merilee S. 1977. *Bureaucrats, Politicians, and Peasants in Mexico.* Berkeley: University of California Press.

———, ed. 1980. *Politics and Policy Implementation in the Third World.* Princeton, NJ: Princeton University Press.

———. 1996. *Challenging the State: Crisis and Innovation in Latin America and Africa.* Cambridge: Cambridge University Press.

———. 2000. *Audacious Reforms: Institutional Intervention and Democracy in Latin America.* Baltimore: Johns Hopkins University Press

———.2007. Going Local: Decentralization, Democratization, and the Promise of Good Governance. Princeton, NJ: Princeton University Press.

Grindle, Merilee S., and John W. Thomas. 1991. *Public Choices and Policy Change: The Political Economy of Reform in Developing Countries.* Baltimore: The Johns Hopkins University Press.

Gualmini, Elisabetta. 2007. "Restructuring Weberian Bureaucracy: Comparing Managerial Reforms in Europe and the United States." *Public Administration* 86, no. 1:75–94.

Gutierrez Reñon, Alberto. 1969. "The Spanish Public Service." *International Review of Administrative Sciences* 35:133–40.

Hagopian, Frances. 1996. *Traditional Politics and Regime Change in Brazil.* Cambridge: Cambridge University Press.

Hagopian, Frances, Carlos Gervasoni, and Juan Andrés Moraes. 2009. "From Patronage to Program: The Emergence of Party-Oriented Legislatures in Brazil." *Comparative Political Studies* 42, no. 3 (March): 360–391.

Hanson, Mark. 1974. "Organizational Bureaucracy in Latin America and the Legacy of Spanish Colonialism." *Journal of Interamerican Studies and World Affairs* 16, no. 2 (May): 199–219.

Haring, Charles H. 1947. *The Spanish Empire in America.* New York: Harcourt, Brace and World.

Hennessy, Peter. 1989. *Whitehall.* London: Fontana Press.

Herrera Macías, Alejandro. 2003. "Algunas consideraciones en la implementación del servicio profesional de carrera en México para hacer frente a la globalización." VII International Congress of CLAD about the Reform of the State and Public Administration, Panama, October 28–31.

Hirschman, Albert O. 1981. "Policymaking and Policy Analysis in Latin America—a Return Journey," in Albert O. Hirschman, *Essays in Trespassing: Economics to Politics and Beyond.* Cambridge: Cambridge University Press, 142–166.

Hoogenboom, Ari. 1961. *Outlawing the Spoils: A History of the Civil Service Reform Movement, 1865–1883.* Urbana: University of Illinois Press.

Iacoviello, Mercedes. 2006. "Analysis comparativo por subsistemas," in Koldo Echebarría, ed., *Informe sobre la situación del servicio civil en América Latina.* Washington, DC: Inter-American Development Bank, 533–572.

Iacoviello, Mercedes, and Ana L. Rodríguez-Gustá. 2006a. "Síntesis del diagnóstico: Caso Brasil," in Koldo Echebarría, ed., *Informe sobre la situación del servicio civil en América Latina.* Washington, DC: Inter-American Development Bank, 119–145.

———. 2006b. "La burocracia en México desde una perspectiva comparada: Un análisis institucional de la función pública en el gobierno federal." *Servicio Profesional de Carrera* 3, no. 6 (Mexico): 85–123.

Iacoviello, Mercedes, Ana L. Rodríguez-Gustá, and Ivania de la Cruz Orozco. 2006. "Síntesis del diagnóstico: Caso México," in Koldo Echebarría, ed., *Informe sobre la situación del servicio civil en América Latina.* Washington, DC: Inter-American Development Bank, 319–355.

Iacoviello, Mercedes, and Mariano Tommasi. 2002. *Diagnóstico institucional de sistemas de servicio civil: Caso Argentina.* Diálogo Regional de Políticas (Buenos Aires).

Iacoviello, Mercedes, and Laura Zuvanic. 2006a. "Desarrollo e integración de la gestión de recursos humanos en los estados latinoamericanos." *Documentos y aportes en administración pública y gestión estatal* 6, no. 7:45–92 (Santa Fe, Argentina).

———. 2006b. "Sintesis del diagnóstico caso Argentina," in Koldo Echebarría, ed., *Informe sobre la situación del servicio civil en América Latina.* Washington, DC: Inter-American Development Bank, 119–145.

Inoki, Masamichi. 1964. "The Civil Bureaucracy: Japan," in Robert E. Ward and Dankward A. Rustow, eds., *Political Modernization in Japan and Turkey.* Princeton, NJ: Princeton University Press, 283–300.

Jacobson, Stephen, and Javier Moreno Luzón. 2000. "The Political System of the Restoration, 1875–1914: Political and Social Elites," in José Alvarez Junco and Adrian Shubert, eds., *Spanish History since 1808.* London: Hodder Education, 92–109.

Jann, Werner. 1997. "Public Management Reform in Germany: A Revolution without a Theory?" in Walter J. M. Kickert, ed., *Public Management and Administrative Reform in Western Europe.* Cheltenham, UK: Edward Elgar, 81–100.

Janouch, Gustav. 1971. *Conversations with Kafka.* Translated by Goronwy Rees. New York: New Directions Books.

Kearney, Richard C. 1986. "Spoils in the Caribbean: The Struggle for Merit-Based Civil Service in the Dominican Republic." *Public Administration Review,* 46, no. 2 (March-April):144–151.

Kenny, Michael. 1977. "Patterns of Patronage in Spain," in Steffen W. Schmidt, James C. Scott, Carl Landé, and Laura Guasi, eds., *Friends, Followers, and Factions: A Reader in Political Clientelism.* Berkeley: University of California Press, 355–360.

Kingdon, John W. 1984. *Agendas, Alternatives, and Public Policies.* New York: Longman.

Kitschelt, Hebert, and Steven I. Wilkinson, 2007a. "Citizen-Politician Linkages: An Introduction," in Herbert Kitschelt and Steven I. Wilkinson, eds., *Patrons, Clients, and Policies: Patterns of Democratic Accountability and Political Competition.* Cambridge: Cambridge University Press, 50–67.

———, eds. 2007b. *Patrons, Clients, and Policies: Patterns of Democratic Accountability and Political Competition.* Cambridge: Cambridge University Press.

Knill, Christoph. 1999. "Explaining Cross-National Variance in Administrative Reform: Autonomous versus Instrumental Bureaucracies." *Journal of Public Policy* 19, no. 2 (May–August): 113–139.

Koreman, Megan. 2000. "The Red Tape Option: Bureaucratic Collaboration and Resistance in Vichy, France." *Contemporary European History* 9, no. 2 (July): 261–267.

Krasner, Stephen. 1984. "Approaches to the State: Alternative Conceptions and Historical Dynamics." *Comparative Politics* 16:223–246.

Lambert, Francis. 1969. "Trends in Administrative Reform in Brazil." *Journal of Latin American Studies* 21:2 (November): 167–188.

Landé, Carl H. 1977. "Introduction: The Dyadic Basis of Clientelism," in Steffen W. Schmidt, James C. Scott, Carl Landé, and Laura Guasti, eds., *Friends, Followers, and Factions: A Reader in Political Clientelism.* Berkeley: University of California Press, xiii–xxxvii.

Lemarchand, René. 1972. "Political Clientelism and Ethnicity in Tropical Africa: Competing Solidarities in Nation-Building." *American Political Science Review* 46, no. 1 (March): 68–90.

Levine, Robert M. 1998. *Father of the Poor? Vargas and his Era.* Cambridge: Cambridge University Press.

Levitsky, Steven. 2007. "From Populism to Clientelism? The Transformation of Labor-Based Party Linkages in Latin America," in Herbert Kitschelt and Steven I. Wilkinson, eds., *Patrons, Clients, and Policies: Patterns of Democratic Accountability and Political Competition.* Cambridge: Cambridge University Press, 206–226.

Longo, Francisco. 2006a. "Análisis comparativo por indices," in Koldo Echebarría, ed., *Informe sobre la situación del servicio civil en América Latina.* Washington, DC: Inter-American Development Bank, 573–592.

———. 2006b. "Una lectura transversal de los resultados," in Koldo Echebarría, ed., *Informe sobre la situación del servicio civil en América Latina.* Washington, DC: Inter-American Development Bank, 593–610.

Mabry, Donald. 2002. *Colonial Latin America.* Tamarac, FL: Llumina Press.

Madrid, Raúl L. 2003. *Retiring the State: The Politics of Pension Privatization in Latin America and Beyond.* Stanford, CA: Stanford University Press.

Malamud, Carlos. 1995. "Los partidos políticos en la Argentina, 1890–1914: Programas y plataformas. El caso de la Liga del Sur," in Eduardo Posada-Carbó, ed., *Wars, Parties and Nationalism: Essays on the Politics and Society of Nineteenth-Century Latin America.* London: Institute of Latin American Studies, 71–88.

Mallon, Florencia E. 2002. "Decoding the Parchments of the Latin American Nation-State: Peru, Mexico and Chile in Comparative Perspective," in James Dunkerley, ed., *Studies in the Formation of the Nation State in Latin America.* London: Institute of Latin American Studies, 13–53.

Manchester, Alan K. 1972. "The Growth of Bureaucracy in Brazil, 1808–1821." *Journal of Latin American Studies* 4:1 (May): 77–83.

Martin, Percy A. 1938. "Federalism in Brazil." *Hispanic American Historical Review* 18, no. 2 (May): 143–163.

Martínez Puón, Rafael. 2005. *Servicio professional de carrera: ¿Para qué?* Mexico: Miguel Angel Porrúa.

Matías-Pereira, José. 2008. "Administração pública comparada: Uma avaliação das reformas administrativas do Brasil, EUA e União Européia." *Revista de Administração Pública* 42, no. 1:61–82.

Maybury-Lewis, David. 1968. "Growth and Change in Brazil since 1930: An Anthropological View." In Raymond S. Sayers, ed., *Portugal and Brazil in Transition.* Minneapolis: University of Minnesota Press

McCourt, Willy. 2000. "Public Appointments: From Patronage to Merit." University of Manchester, Institute for Development Policy and Management, Human Resources in Development Group, Working Paper No. 9.

McCreery, David. 2002. "State and Society in Nineteenth-Century Goiás," in James Dunkerley, ed., *Studies in the Formation of the Nation State in Latin America.* London: Institute of Latin American Studies, 133–160.

Meininger, Marie-Christine. 2000. "The Development and Current Features of the French Civil Service System," in Hans A. G. M. Bekke and Frits M. van der Meer, eds., *Civil Service Systems in Western Europe.* Cheltenham, UK: Edward Elgar, 188–211.

Méndez, José Luis. 2008. "Deseño, aprobación e implementación del Servicio Profesional en México: Lecciones y retos." *Servicio Profesional de Carrera* 5, no. 9 (Mexico): 9–24.

———. 2009. "El Gobierno de Felipe Calderón: Balance de un trienio." *El Universal.* Mexico, July 25.

Merino, Mauricio. 2006. "Introducción," in Mauricio Merino, ed., *Los desafíos del servicio professional de carrera en México*. Mexico: CIDE and Secretaría de la Función Pública, 15–28.

Ministério do Planejamento (Brazil). 2010. *Boletim estatístico de pessoal, No. 165*. Brasilia.

Mintz, Sydney W., and Eric R. Wolf. 1950. "An Analysis of Ritual Co-Parenthood (Compadrazgo)." *Southwestern Journal of Anthropology* 6, no. 4 (Winter): 341–368.

Morstein Marx, Fritz. 1961. *The Administrative State: An Introduction to Bureaucracy*. Chicago: University of Chicago Press.

Mosher, Frederick. 1968. *Democracy and the Public Service*. New York: Oxford University Press.

Moyado Estrada, Francisco. 2006. "Reforma de la función pública en España: El estatuto que viene. *Servicio Profesional de Carrera* 3, no. 6 (Mexico): 125–138.

Muramatsu, Michio, and T. J. Pempel. 1995. "The Evolution of the Civil Service before World War II," in Hyung-Ki Kim, Michio Muramatsu, T. J. Pempel, and Kozo Yamamura, eds., *The Japanese Civil Service and Economic Development: Catalysts of Change*. New York: Oxford University Press, 174–187.

Nabuco, Joaquin. 1977. *Abolitionism: The Brazilian Antislavery Struggle*. Urbana: University of Illinois Press.

Navarro-García, Luis. 1976. "Los oficios vendibles en Nueva España durante la Guerra de Sucesión." *Anuario de Estudios Americanos* 32:132–154.

O'Donnell, Guillermo. 1973. *Modernization and Bureaucratic-Authoritarianism: Studies in South American Politics*. Berkeley: University of California, Institute of International Studies.

O'Gorman, Frank. 2001. "Patronage and the Reform of the State in England, 1700–1860," in Simona Piattoni, ed., *Clientelism, Interests, and Democratic Representation: The European Experience in Historical and Comparative Perspective*. Cambridge: Cambridge University Press, 54–76.

Olsen, Johan P. 2005. "Maybe It Is Time to Rediscover Bureaucracy." *Journal of Public Administration Research and Theory* 16:1–24.

Ongaro, Edoardo. 2009. *Public Management Reform and Modernization: Trajectories of Administrative Change in Italy, France, Greece, Portugal and Spain*. Cheltenham, UK: Edward Elgar.

Oquist, Paul. 1980. *Violence, Conflict, and Politics in Colombia*. New York: Academic Press.

Osborne, David, and Theodore Gaebler. 1992. *Reinventing Government: How the Entrepreneurial Spirit Is Transforming the Public Sector*. Reading, MA: Addison-Wesley.

Oszlak, Oscar. 1997. *La formación del estado argentino: Orden, progreso y organización nacional*. Buenos Aires: Ariel.

———. 2003. "El servicio civil en América Latina y el Caribe: Situación y retos futuros," in Kaldo Echebarría, *Servicio Civil: Temas para un diálogo*. Red de Gestión y Transparencia de la Políca Pública. Washington, DC: Banco Interamericano de Desarrollo.

Painter, Martin. 2010. "Legacies Remembered, Lessons Forgotten: The Case of Japan," in Martin Painter and B. Guy Peters, eds., *Tradition and Public Administration*. New York: Palgrave Macmillan, 84–99.

Painter, Martin, and B. Guy Peters, eds. 2010. *Tradition and Public Administration*. New York: Palgrave Macmillan.

Palmer, R. R., and Joel Colton. 1963. *A History of the Modern World*. New York: Alfred A. Knopf.

Pang, Eul-Soo. 1973. "Coronelismo in Northeast Brazil," in Robert Kern, ed., *The Caciques: Oligarchical Politics and the System of Caciquismo in the Luso-Hispanic World*. Albuquerque: University of New Mexico Press, 65–88.

Parrado Díez, Salvador. 1998. "Politicisation of the Spanish Civil Service: Continuity in 1982 and in 1996." Madrid: Universidad Nacional de Educación a Distancia, Document 24.

———. 2000. "The Development and Current Features of the Spanish Civil Service System," in Hans A. G. M. Bekke and Frits M. van der Meer, eds., *Civil Service Systems in Western Europe*. Cheltenham, UK: Edward Elgar, 247–274.

Parrish, Charles J. 1973. "Bureaucracy, Democracy, and Development: Some Considerations Based on the Chilean Case," in Clarence E. Thurber and Lawrence S. Graham, eds., *Development Administration in Latin America*. Durham, NC: Duke University Press, 229–259.

Parry, J. H. 1953. *The Sale of Public Office in the Spanish Indies under the Hapsburgs*. Berkeley: University of California Press.

Pempel, T. J. 1986. "Uneasy toward Autonomy: Parliament and Parliamentarians in Japan," in Ezra N. Suleiman, ed., *Parliaments and Parliamentarians in Democratic Politics*. New York: Holmes and Meier, 106–153.

———. 1992. "Bureaucracy in Japan." *PS: Political Science and Politics* 25:1 (March): 19–24.

Peters, B. Guy. 1996. *The Future of Governing: Four Emerging Models*. Lawrence: University Press of Kansas.

Phelan, John L. 1967. *The Kingdom of Quito in the Seventeenth Century: Bureaucratic Politics in the Spanish Empire*. Madison: University of Wisconsin Press.

Piatonni, Simona, ed. 2001. *Clientelism, Interests, and Democratic Representation*. Cambridge: Cambridge University Press.

Pierson, Paul. 2004. *Politics in Time: History, Institutions, and Social Analysis*. Princeton, NJ: Princeton University Press.

Pierson, Paul, and Theda Skocpol. 2002. "Historical Institutionalism in Contemporary Political Science," in H. Milner and Ira Katznelson, eds., *Political Science: State of the Discipline*. Washington, DC: ASPA.

Pollitt, Christopher, and Geert Bouckaert. 2000. *Public Management Reform: A Comparative Analysis*. Oxford: Oxford University Press.

Powell, John Duncan. 1970. "Peasant Society and Clientelist Politics." *American Political Science Review* 44, no. 2 (June): 411–425.

Pressman, Jeffrey, and Aaron Wildavsky. 1973. *Implementation*. Berkeley: University of California Press.

Puryear, Jeffrey M. 1994. *Thinking Politics: Intellectuals and Democracy in Chile, 1973–1988*. Baltimore: Johns Hopkins University Press.

Ramió, Carlos, and Miquel Salvador. 2008. "Civil Service Reform in Latin America: External Referents versus Own Capacities," *Bulletin of Latin American Research* 27, no. 4:554–573.

Ramírez Alujas, Alvaro V. 2008. "Hacia un modelo de excelencia en alta dirección y gestión de personas para el sector público: La experiencia de la Dirección Nacional del Servicio Civil de Chile." *Servicio Profesional de Carrera* 5, no. 9 (Mexico): 53–88.

Rehren, Alfredo. 2000. "Clientelismo político, corrupción y reforma del estado en Chile." Paper prepared for the Centro de Estudios Públicos (Chile), typescript.

———. 2008. "La evolución de la agenda de transparencia en los gobiernos de la concertación." *Temas de la Agenda Pública* 3, no. 18:3–19.

Reid, Gary J., and Graham Scott. 1994. "Public Sector Human Resource Management in Latin America and the Caribbean," in Shahid Amjad Chaudhry, Gary James Reid, and Waleed Haider Malik, eds., *Civil Service Reform in Latin America and the Caribbean: Proceedings of a Conference*. Washington, DC: World Bank.

Remmer, Karen. 1991. *Military Rule in Latin America*. Boulder, CO: Westview Press.

Riche, Pierre. 1993 (1983). *The Carolingians: A Family Who Forged Europe*. Philadelphia: University of Pennsylvania Press.

Ritter, Gerhard. 1968. *Frederick the Great*. Translated with an introduction by Peter Paret. Berkeley: University of California Press. Originally published in German in 1936.

Romero Salvadó, Francisco J. 1999. *Spain 1914–1918: Between War and Revolution*. London: Routledge.

Rosenberg, Hans. 1958. *Bureaucracy, Aristocracy and Autocracy: The Prussian Experience 1660–1815*. Cambridge: MA: Harvard University Press.

Rouban, Luc. 1997. "The Administrative Modernisation Policy in France," in Walter J. M. Kickert, ed., *Public Management and Administrative Reform in Western Europe*. Cheltenham, UK: Edward Elgar, 141–156.

Ruffing-Hilliard, Karen. 2001. "Merit Reform in Latin America: A Comparative Perspective," in Ali Farazmand, ed., *Handbook of Comparative and Development Public Administration*. New York: Marcel Dekker, 593–603.

Samuels, David J. 2002. "Pork Barreling Is Not Credit Claiming or Advertising: Campaign Finance and the Sources of the Personal Vote in Brazil." *Journal of Politics* 64, no. 3 (August): 845–863.

Schneider, Ben Ross. 1991. *Politics within the State: Elite Bureaucrats and Industrial Policy in Authoritarian Brazil.* Pittsburgh: University of Pittsburgh Press.

Scott, James C. 1972. "Patron-Client Politics and Political Change in Southeast Asia." *American Political Science Review* 46, no. 1 (March): 91–113.

Secretaría de la Función Pública (Mexico). 2007. "Recommendaciones operativas para la puesta en marcha de los 29 puntos críticos del SPC." Mexico City: Secretaría de la Función Pública.

Shefter, Martin. 1977. "Party and Patronage: Germany, England, and Italy." *Politics and Society* 7:403–452.

———. 1994. *Political Parties and the State: The American Historical Experience.* Princeton, NJ: Princeton University Press.

Shumpei, Kumon. 1984. "Japan Faces Its Future: The Political-Economics of Administrative Reform." *Journal of Japanese Studies* 10, no. 1 (Winter): 143–165.

Siegel, Gilbert B. 1966. "The Strategy of Public Administration Reform: The Case of Brazil." *Public Administration Review* 26, no. 1 (March): 45–55.

———. 1978. *The Vicissitudes of Governmental Reform in Brazil: A Study of the DASP.* Washington, DC: University Press of America.

Silberman, Bernard S. 1966. "Criteria for Recruitment and Success in the Japanese Bureaucracy, 1868–1900: 'Traditional' and 'Modern' Criteria in Bureaucratic Development." *Economic Development and Cultural Change* 14, no. 2 (January): 158–173.

———. 1993. *Cages of Reason: The Rise of the Rational State in France, Japan, the United States, and Great Britain.* Chicago: University of Chicago Press.

Silva, Patricio. 1994. "State, Public Technocracy and Politics in Chile, 1927–1941." *Bulletin of Latin American Research* 13, no. 3 (September): 281–297.

Skowronek, Stephen. 1982. *Building a New American State: The Expansion of National Administrative Capacities, 1877–1920.* Cambridge: Cambridge University Press.

Smith, Peter. 1979. *Labyrinths of Power: Political Recruitment in Twentieth Century Mexico.* Princeton, NJ: Princeton University Press.

Socolow, Susan Migden. 1987. *The Bureaucrats of Buenos Aires, 1769–1810: Amor al real servicio.* Durham, NC: Duke University Press.

Stein, Stanley J., and Barbara H. Stein. 1970. *The Colonial Heritage of Latin America: Essays on Economic Dependence in Perspective.* Oxford: Oxford University Press.

Steinmo, Sven, Kathleen Thelen, and Frank Longstreth, eds. 1992. *Structuring Politics: Historical Institutionalism in Comparative Analysis.* Cambridge: Cambridge University Press.

Streek, Wolfgang, and Kathleen Thelen, eds. 2005a. *Beyond Continuity: Institutional Change in Advanced Political Economies.* Oxford: Oxford University Press.

———, eds. 2005b. "Introduction: Institutional Change in Advanced Political Economies," in Wolfgang Streek and Kathleen Thelen, eds., *Beyond*

Continuity: Institutional Change in Advanced Political Economies. Oxford: Oxford University Press, 1–39.

Suleiman, Ezra. 1974. *Politics, Power, and Bureaucracy in France: The Administrative Elite.* Princeton, NJ: Princeton University Press.

Swart, Koenraad W. 1989. "The Sale of Public Offices," in Arnold J. Heidenheimer, Michael Johnston, and Victor T. LeVine, eds., *Political Corruption: A Handbook.* New Brunswick, NJ: Transaction Publishers, 87–99.

Teaford, Jon C. 1984. *The Unheralded Triumph: City Government in America, 1780–1900.* Baltimore: Johns Hopkins University Press.

Tendler, Judith. 1997. *Good Government in the Tropics.* Baltimore: Johns Hopkins University Press.

Thompson, James R. 2000. "Quasi Markets and Strategic Change in Public Organizations," in Jeffrey L. Brudney, Laurence J. O'Toole Jr., and Hal G. Rainey, eds., *Advancing Public Management: New Developments in Theory, Methods, and Practice.* Washington, DC: Georgetown University Press, 197–214.

Thompson, James R., and Patricia W. Ingraham. 1996. "Organizational Redesign in the Public Sector," in Donald F. Kettl and H. Brinton Milward, eds., *The State of Public Management.* Baltimore: Johns Hopkins University Press, 286–306.

Tombs, Robert. 1996. *France 1814–1914.* Harlow, UK: Pearson Education Limited.

Topic, Steven. 1980. "State Interventionism in a Liberal Regime: Brazil, 1889–1930." *Hispanic American Historical Review* 60, no. 4 (November): 593–616.

Torres, Lourdes, and Vicente Pina. 2004. "Reshaping Public Administration: The Spanish Experience Compared to the UK." *Public Administration* 82, no. 2:445–464.

Tusell, Javier, and Genoveva Queipo de Llano. 2000. "The Dictatorship of Primo de Rivera, 1923–1931," in José Alvarez Junco and Adrian Shubert, eds., *Spanish History since 1808.* London: Hodder Education, 207–220.

———. 2002. "The Hollow State: The Effect of the World Market on State-Building in Brazil in the Nineteenth Century," in James Dunkerley, ed., *Studies in the Formation of the Nation State in Latin America.* London: Institute of Latin American Studies, 112–132.

United States Civil Service Commission. Various Years, 1883–1950. *Annual Report.*

United States Office of Personnel Management. 2003. *Biography of an Ideal: A History of the Federal Civil Service.* Washington, DC: Government Printing Office.

Uricoechea, Fernando. 1980. *The Patrimonial Foundations of the Brazilian Bureaucratic State.* Berkeley: University of California Press.

Urzúa Valenzuela, Germán, and Anamaria García Barzelatto. 1971. *Diagnóstico de la burocracia chilena, 1818–1969.* Santiago: University of Chile.

Valenzuela, Arturo. 1977. *Political Brokers in Chile: Local Government in a Centralized Polity.* Durham, NC: Duke University Press.

Van de Walle, Nicolas. 2007. "Meet the New Boss, Same as the Old Boss? The Evolution of Political Clientelism in Africa," in Herbert Kitschelt and Steven I. Wilkinson, eds., *Patrons, Clients, and Policies: Patterns of Democratic Accountability and Political Competition*. Cambridge: Cambridge University Press, 1–49.

Vernon, Raymond. 1963. *The Dilemma of Mexico's Development*. Cambridge, MA: Harvard University Press.

Waissbluth, Mario. 2010. "Chile: En buen estado?" *Qué Pasa* (Santiago, Chile), May 28.

Walter, Richard J. 1985. "Politics, Parties, and Elections in Argentina's Province of Buenos Aires, 1912–1942," in John J. Johnson, Peter J. Bakewell, and Meredith D. Dodge, eds., *Readings in Latin American History*, vol. 2, *The Modern Experience*. Durham, NC: Duke University Press, 58–79.

Weber, Max. 1946 (1922). "Wirtschaft and Gesellschaft," in H. H. Gerth and C. Wright Mills, eds., *From Max Weber: Essays in Sociology*. New York: Oxford University Press.

White, Leonard D. 1948. *The Federalists: A Study in Administrative History*. New York: Macmillan.

———. 1951. *The Jeffersonians: A Study in Administrative History, 1801–1829*. New York: Free Press.

———. 1954. *The Jacksonians: A Study in Administrative History, 1829–1861*. New York: Macmillan.

———. 1958. *The Republican Era, 1869–1901: A Study in Administrative History*. New York: Macmillan.

White, Leonard D., Charles Bland, Walter Sharp, and Fritz Morstein Marx. 1935. *Civil Service Abroad: Great Britain, Canada, France, Germany*. New York: McGraw-Hill.

Wilentz, Sean. 2005. *The Rise of American Democracy: Jefferson to Lincoln*. New York: W. W. Norton.

Wilson, Woodrow. 1887. "The Study of Administration." *Political Science Quarterly*, 2, no. 1 (June).

Wood, Ian. 1994. *The Merovingian Kingdoms, 450–751*. Harlow, UK: Pearson Education Limited.

World Bank. 1997. *World Development Report 1997*. New York: Oxford University Press.

Zaltsman, Ariel. 2009. "The Effects of Performance Information on Public Resource Allocations: A Study of Chile's Performance-Based Budgeting System." *International Public Management Journal* 12, no. 4:450–483.

Index

Absolutism. *See* Royal absolutism

Actors in reform, 250–252

Adams, John, 37, 61

Adams, John Quincy, 62

Administrative Department of the Public Service (DASP), 178, 181–184, 205–215, 229, 231

Administrative Reform Association, 85, 275n50

ADP (Sistema de Alta Dirección Pública), 197, 200, 224–226

"Adventures in Brazilian Bureaucracy," 259

Agents of reform, 250–252

Après reform: overview of, 11; introduction to, 104–105; and conflicts surrounding civil service, 105–106; survival of civil service and, 106–111; control in civil service and, 111–118; and recruitment credentials, 118–122; and loyalty in Germany, 122–125; and loyalty in France, 125–128; efficiency improvements and, 128–135; conclusions on, 135–137

Argentina: study of civil service in, 5, 14, 16; history of patronage in, 166–169, 177; patronage in, 175t, 201–202; reform in, 184–189, 201, 245–246; implementation of career civil services in, 215–220; opposition to reform in, 242; agents of reform in,

252; projects of reform in, 254; timing of reform in, 256, 257

Asociación de Trabajadores del Estado (ATE), 217

ATE (Asociación de Trabajadores del Estado), 217

Autonomous University of Mexico, 191

Autonomy, embedded, 118

Baccalauréat, 50, 51, 88

Bank of Japan, 47

Basic Law (1949), 125, 133

Birthplace, and Latin-American patronage, 157, 158–159

Blair, Tony, 116

Bolivia, 154

Bonaparte, Napoleon, 49–50, 74, 269n59

Bourbon kings, 58, 158–159

Brazil (film), 259

Brazil: study of civil service in, 5, 14, 15; history of patronage in, 159–160, 162–166, 177; patronage in, 175t, 201; reform in, 178–184, 201, 245–246; implementation of career civil services in, 205–215; agents of reform in, 251; projects of reform in, 254; bureaucracy in, 259–260, 288–289n29, 289n48

Bresser-Pereira, Luiz Carlos, 211, 212, 213

D0744395